Immigration Controls

MIGRATION AND REFUGEES
Politics and Policies in the United States and Germany
General Editor: Myron Weiner

Volume 1
Migration Past, Migration Future
Germany and the United States
Edited by Klaus J. Bade and Myron Weiner

Volume 2
Migrants, Refugees, and Foreign Policy
U.S. and German Policies Toward Countries of Origin
Edited by Rainer Münz and Myron Weiner

Volume 3
Immigration Admissions
The Search for Workable Policies in Germany and the United States
Edited by Kay Hailbronner, David A. Martin and Hiroshi Motomura

Volume 4
Immigration Controls
The Search for Workable Policies in Germany and the United States
Edited by Kay Hailbronner, David A. Martin and Hiroshi Motomura

Volume 5
Paths to Inclusion
The Integration of Migrants in the United States and Germany
Edited by Peter Schuck and Rainer Münz

Immigration Controls
The Search for Workable Policies in Germany and the United States

Edited by Kay Hailbronner, David Martin,[*]
and Hiroshi Motomura

*Published in association with the
American Academy of Arts and Sciences*

Berghahn Books
NEW YORK · OXFORD

First published in 1998 by

Berghahn Books

© 1998 American Academy of Arts and Sciences

All rights reserved.
No part of this publication may be reproduced in any form or by any means without the written permission of Berghahn Books.

Library of Congress Cataloging-in-Publication Data

Library of Congress Cataloging-in-Publication Data

Immigration controls : the search for workable policies in Germany and the United States / edited by Kay Hailbronner, David A. Martin, and Hiroshi Motomura.
   p. cm. -- (Migration and refugees ; v. 4)
  ISBN 1-57181-089-7 (alk. paper)
  1. United States--Emigration and immigration--Government policy.
2. Germany--Emigration and immigration--Government policy.
I. Hailbronner, Kay. II. Martin, David A., 1948-   .
III. Motomura, Hiroshi, 1953-   . IV. Series.
JV6483.M54 1997 vol. 4
325.43 s--DC21   97-3810
                                                         CIP

British Library Cataloguing in Publication Data

A catalogue record for this book is available from the British Library.

Contents

Introduction
    Kay Hailbronner and *Hiroshi Motomura*   vii

Chapter 1
The Obstacles to Effective Internal Enforcement of the Immigration Laws in the United States
    David A. Martin   1

Chapter 2
Internal Controls and Actual Removals of Deportable Aliens: The Current Legal Situation in the Federal Republic of Germany
    Hans-Joachim Cremer   45

Chapter 3
The New Techniques for Managing High-Volume Asylum Systems
    Stephen Legomsky   117

Chapter 4
New Techniques for Rendering Asylum Manageable
    Kay Hailbronner   159

Chapter 5
Conclusion: Immigration Admissions and Immigration Controls
    Kay Hailbronner, David A. Martin, and *Hiroshi Motomura*   203

List of Contributors   225

Index   227

Introduction
Kay Hailbronner and *Hiroshi Motomura*

In recent years, immigration has emerged as one of the most heavily debated social and political issues in the industrialized West. Much of the concern stems from the seemingly endless stream of migrants, many of them spurred to leave their native countries by economic misery, political instability, and civil war. These migrant flows have put the major receiving countries of the West under growing pressure to revise existing immigration law and policy, as well as to formulate new law and policy where none has existed. As a result, immigration law and policy throughout the industrialized West have undergone substantial changes of late. The United States and Germany are two countries that have felt these immigration-related pressures with particular force. For this reason, their experiences—including their responses in the form of immigration law and policy—are particularly instructive, not just for each other but for other receiving countries as well.

The problems that the United States and Germany face have much in common, in spite of differences in their traditional attitudes to immigration and their approaches to administrative law and government regulation generally. In Germany, the traditional notion governing immigration law and policy has been that Germany is not an immigration country and therefore that non-Germans (unless they are citizens of a member country of the European Union) may not enter Germany to take up permanent residence. In fact, however, these traditional principles have not kept Germany from becoming a country of immigration. Its noncitizen population increased by 2.3 million from 1988 to 1993, a historically unprecedented flow of immigrants. In sheer numbers, this increase is comparable only to that in the United States, which has a population almost four times as large. The presence of this immigrant population in Germany is the result of several external factors. Migrant workers originally recruited for temporary employment ended up staying on as immigrants. Reunification of these workers with their family members, who came to join them in Germany, added to the noncitizen population. A growing number of asylum seekers also swelled the numbers, as did a substantial influx of "ethnic Germans" from Eastern Europe and the former Soviet Union. Taken together, these factors have made for a sizable de facto immigrant influx into Germany.

In contrast, the United States historically has viewed itself as a nation of immigrants. But it has also faced substantial problems of immigration control, which in turn have attracted a variety of government responses. Illegal border crossings—mainly across the border from Mexico—and the public reaction to the perceived impact of undocumented aliens have prompted the adoption of border control measures much more stringent than in the past. Concerns about the number of undocumented aliens—not just illegal border crossers but also those who overstay valid nonimmigrant visas—have led the federal government and some states to restrict undocumented aliens' access to public benefits, including public education. Uneasiness about the growing number of asylum seekers has led to the adoption of measures to deter and detect frivolous applications and to adjudicate all applications more expeditiously. Legal immigration to the United States has also become the target of immigration control efforts. The traditional system of immigration quotas based on family ties and employment-related qualifications has come under criticism, especially by those who believe that it pays insufficient attention to the economic interests of the United States.

In short, admission policies, political asylum, and control measures have become the focus of serious public discussion in both Germany and the United States. In both countries, the view is widespread that the current immigration laws do not perform their basic tasks of regulating immigration and providing a clear framework to determine who shall be admitted as immigrants, who shall be admitted temporarily, and who shall not be admitted at all.

In an effort to study and analyze these problems in the United States and Germany from a comparative standpoint, the American Academy of Arts and Sciences convened the German-American Project on Migration and Refugee Policies, with financial support from the German-American Academic Council Foundation. The two-year project brought together thirty leading immigration law and policy experts from both countries, among them lawyers, political scientists, demographers, historians, political philosophers, sociologists, economists, and government officials. A joint German-American steering committee initially structured the agendas and determined the membership of the working groups. One working group examined policies toward countries of origin. A second working group, some of whose papers appear in this volume, addressed admission policies, political asylum, and the crisis of immigration controls. A third working group looked at the character of migration flows and the absorption and integration of migrants in the two countries.

Each working group sought to synthesize the best available academic studies and practical experience on the relevant issues, to examine critically the traditional—but partly outdated—paradigms and norms in the field, and to suggest new policy approaches. Toward this end, each group began by developing draft research papers, which were initially presented at meetings of the separate working groups in March 1995 at the House of the American Academy in Cambridge, Massachusetts. The findings of the working groups are being pubished in five volumes in a series entitled Migration and Refugees: Politics and Policies in the United States and Germany, of which this is the fourth volume.

This volume includes four of the revised papers of the working group on admission policies, political asylum, and the crisis of controls. Its unifying theme of this volume derives largely from the general agreement that traditional approaches to immigration control in the major receiving countries of the West have serious shortcomings either in concept or in implementation, or at times in both. Volume 3 includes this working group's seven other papers, which generally concern the topic of immigration admissions.

The volume begins with two papers on the enforcement of immigration controls. David Martin's paper,* "The Obstacles to Effective Internal Enforcement of the Immigration Laws in the United States," provides a textured account of the obstacles to effective internal enforcement in the United States. Based on the hypothetical story of an alien ordered to leave the USA, Martin identifies and analyzes the numerous problems that plague effective enforcement of the immigration laws. He begins by discussing border controls and employment-related controls. Martin then turns to issues concerning deportation procedure and analyzes the processes of apprehension, detention, adjudicating deportation, and finally actual removal from the United States. He concludes by considering some ideas for reform, among them streamlining the appeal structure, permitting earlier removal, simplifying the substantive law, and creating better incentives for early cooperation and truth telling from the commencement of proceedings.

In the next paper, "Internal Controls and Actual Removals of Deportable Aliens: The Current Legal Situation in the Federal Republic of Germany," Hans-Joachim Cremer analyzes the current legal situation in Germany. He begins by discussing the regulations governing aliens prior to and upon entry. Cremer then analyzes regulations governing aliens during their stay in Germany, for example, the system of residence permits. He next considers the removal of deportable aliens, including the legal concept of deportability, forms of relief from deportation, the procedures to effect actual deportation, and judicial review of deportation orders. After discussing the German law governing decisions on asylum claims, Cremer concludes with some general observations on the practical efficiency of control and deportation measures.

The new techniques for managing asylum systems strained by high demand are the subject of the next two papers. Stephen Legomsky's paper, "The New Techniques for Managing High-Volume Asylum Systems," begins by identifying two different perspectives on the so-called asylum problem, i.e., existing procedures that are hard-pressed to decide the number of asylum applications with care but without delay. From one perspective, the problem is one of procedural justice, but from another perspective, it relates to case management. Legomsky then proceeds to discuss and analyze various solutions: (1) reducing the number of cases that require adjudication; (2) prioritizing among filed cases so as to dispose of unfounded claims promptly; (3) streamlining the procedures; and (4) enlarging and improving the adjudicative staff.

Kay Hailbronner begins his paper, "New Techniques for Rendering Asylum Manageable," with a discussion of recent developments regarding asylum adjudication systems in Europe and in Germany in particular. He then situates the asylum problem in the context of national migration policies, global refugee policies, and global development policies. Building on this foundation, Hailbronner surveys recent legislative and administrative initiatives that Germany and the United States have adopted to render asylum more manageable. He then analyzes a number of approaches: (1) special procedures for manifestly unfounded or abusive asylum claims; (2) the concept of a safe country of origin; (3) prescreening or summary exclusion procedures; (4) the concept of a safe third country; (5) temporary protection and regional approaches; (6) interdiction, visa requirements, and carrier sanctions; and (7) international refugee flow management.

The concluding chapter of this volume presents the recommendations of the working group with regard to admission policies, political asylum, and immigration controls. To develop these recommendations, the cochairs of the working group drew on the draft papers by the members of the working group and from the working group discussions in March 1995 in Cambridge, Massachusetts. The working group then discussed the resulting draft policy document in July 1995 at a meeting in Ladenburg, Germany. The draft document was further revised in accordance with the suggestions of the working group members. However, none of the working group members was asked to sign the finished document, and it should be understood that not every member agrees with all of the recommendations.

In sum, the purpose of this volume is to review traditional approaches to two key facets of immigration law and policy—enforcement of immigration controls and management of asylum claims—to describe and analyze possibilities for new approaches and solutions, and to provoke discussion of future policy initiatives in these areas. While we do not expect one single approach to emerge as a panacea, we do hope that some of the ideas laid down here will find their way to policymakers and others interested in the search for workable approaches to one of the most significant issues of our time.

We are grateful to the German-American Academic Council Foundation for its financial support for the project and to its director, Dr. Joseph Rembser; the Gottlieb Daimler- and Karl Benz-Foundation for its support for a meeting of the participants in Ladenburg, Germany; our editor Sarah St. Onge; Lois Malone, for the index; and Corinne Schelling of the American Academy of Arts and Sciences, who has had principal responsibility for the management of the project since its inception.

Chapter 1

The Obstacles to Effective Internal Enforcement of the Immigration Laws in the United States

*David A. Martin**

It may be unfair to blame the failures of our current deportation process for the recent backlash against immigrants in the United States. But an effective deportation system and improvements in related internal controls would have taken much wind out of the sails of Proposition 187, the 1994 California ballot measure that epitomizes the angry reaction. Such improvements would have meant fewer undocumented migrants in the country and thus fewer targets for the particular form of immigrant scapegoating that has accompanied the recent economic recession.[1] If this diagnosis is correct, it leads to a paradox. The most progressive strategy for supporters of generous U.S. immigration policy may be, for this historical moment, the most enforcement-minded. Preserving a generous U.S. immigration policy over the long term requires us now to repair the institutions that are meant to impose deliberate governmental controls on entry and sojourn and enforce penalties on those who fail to honor the immigration laws. As a former Deputy UN High Commissioner for Refugees has written: "The public will not allow governments to be generous if it believes they have lost control"

Notes for this chapter begin on page 37.

(Smyser 1987, 119). A visibly effective enforcement capacity would have merit in its own right, to help reinstate respect for the law. It would also help reassure the citizenry and might free us from some of the demons that drive restrictionism.

This paper describes the major weaknesses of the current system of internal immigration control in the United States, analyzes the reasons for those weaknesses, and sketches paths toward improvement. Congress and the executive branch have actually been fairly persistent and at times even creative in responding, if often after some delay, to the problems that have developed. But despite these efforts, a host of loopholes remains; when one is plugged, others become the focus for aliens who, understandably, would prefer to remain. The actual removal of human beings is inevitably complicated and expensive, at least if the system remains at all sensitive to legitimate claims that ostensibly deportable aliens might put forward. Inattentive to these complications, the steps already taken to overcome problems, and the need for patience before reforms are likely to show significant impact, critics have been too ready to blame the system's ills on lazy or corrupt administration, too ready to indulge in demeaning sarcasm that dismisses the Immigration and Naturalization Service (INS) as incompetent. INS may have its share of lazy, mean, or ineffective officers, but the enforcement task it is given is complex in ways not usually appreciated. The sketch that follows is meant to offer the full picture, as an important step toward designing effective reform.

The Setting

The system's current problems can perhaps best be illustrated by postulating an enterprising undocumented migrant who is the immigration equivalent of the "bad man" Justice Oliver Wendell Holmes described in his celebrated essay "The Path of the Law." This man—I'll call him Oliver in honor of his originator—is unmoved by exhortations to live honorably or to follow moral duty. He is interested in his own welfare, and he will continue to pursue that aim up to the point where the coercive hand of the law intervenes. In Holmes's words, he "cares only for the material consequences which ... knowledge [of the law] enables him to predict" (Holmes 1897, 459). For clarity of analysis, I will also stipulate that Oliver meets none of the standard grounds for lawful admission or even for permitted stay after a prima facie unlawful arrival: he has no close family ties in the United States, no job skills that could be the basis for permission to immigrate, and no plausible grounds for fearing persecution in his homeland.[2]

For the purposes here, I will add a few stipulations that Holmes did not. My bad man is not a hardened criminal; he will not commit an act, such as theft or violence, that is malum in se. But he does not mind violating regulatory enactments, even through fraud, if a cost-benefit analysis demonstrates that he is likely to come out ahead, given the predictable reaction from the institutions that are supposed to enforce such laws. Oliver is also relatively impoverished (that is much of his reason for pursuing employment opportunities in a wealthy society like the United States), and he cannot necessarily seek the advice of top lawyers about his case. But I will postulate that he is well informed about the actual workings of the U.S. enforcement system—through the word-of-mouth network that spreads information with remarkable speed throughout immigrant communities, perhaps, or else by means of the various nonlawyer immigration advisers and consultants whose shops usually cluster around the district offices of the INS. His knowledge of the law extends beyond that of which Holmes wrote; it includes knowledge of the practical limitations that politics and resource shortages impose on the institutions charged with carrying out statutory mandates. Beyond this, Oliver has serene confidence in the information he has amassed. If there is a 70 percent chance that he can get away with a certain move, he plays those statistical odds with perfect equanimity. His life is not haunted by an exaggerated concern over the 30 percent eventuality, the downside risk.

This psychological stipulation, giving him solid confidence in his information about immigration law enforcement, sharply differentiates Oliver from most undocumented migrants in the real-world United States, whose information tends to come in hazy, contradictory, and unreliable form. Few can be confidently aware of the limitations on enforcement that seem glaringly apparent to immigration judges, INS officers, and trial attorneys, those who may feel the most frustration over the system's historical incapacities. Known cases of deportation of friends or family may count for much more in the real-world undocumented alien's anxious perception of his or her own vulnerability than the gross statistics, resource shortfalls, or skewed administrative priorities that regularly chagrin enforcement-minded members of Congress. But Oliver is a different sort of player. This point bears emphasis. The picture painted here is not meant to portray a typical or average alien involved in deportation proceedings. It is a composite worst-case scenario, at least so far as noncriminal aliens go, from the vantage point of government officials charged with law enforcement responsibilities. Nevertheless, its various elements are played out with depressing frequency in the operation of our deportation system. Combining these elements in a single bad-man account facilitates the comprehensive understanding necessary if effective remedies are someday to follow.

The Elements of the Problem

Border Controls

To launch the inquiry, assume that Oliver, in his native country in the developing world, learns that compatriots in the United States are making wages far above anything available to him at home. Having no prospect of steady work there, he decides to try his luck by crossing at night across the southwestern U.S. border. Over the last several years, the INS has improved its entry controls significantly at many locations along that line. It has greatly augmented Border Patrol staffing, from 3,200 in 1986 to 5,600 in 1996 (projected to exceed 7,000 in 1998), installed stadium lighting and seismic sensors at hundreds of well-traveled locations, and adopted new control strategies (*Interpreter Releases* 1994, 210; 1996, 102). Further augmenting the Border Patrol is a favorite theme for members of Congress who want to display their concern about immigration control. Without much study of the real needs of enforcement, they sometimes seem to engage in bidding wars over adding battalions of new Border Patrol agents along the line, as if that one step would master the whole problem. But no matter how many additional agents are added, some foreigners will still manage to elude capture.

Equally important is something politicians often overlook: a high percentage, perhaps as much as half, of the undocumented population in the United States consists of people who entered lawfully on nonimmigrant (temporary) visas and then simply overstayed the period of admission (Fix and Passel 1994, 25). In short, improvements in border enforcement can never obviate interior controls and enforcement. A credible deportation capacity, along with other internal enforcement mechanisms, will always be needed to control that form of illegal migration.

To sneak in along the southern border of the United States, then, Oliver will have to be luckier or more enterprising now than was necessary in earlier years. But the task has hardly been rendered impossible. Moreover, particularly if he is Mexican (or can pass himself off as Mexican upon apprehension), he might enjoy multiple tries at little additional expense. Most of the Mexicans apprehended along the southern border are returned by bus only a short distance into Mexico; some can jump the fence again before the sun comes up. Recent proposals would fund "interior repatriation," to cities far distant from the U.S. border, in order to make repeat attempts more difficult or costly. But even if that practice became more routine, it would remain a rather pale deterrent. Oliver is persistent enough to succeed.

The Employment Scene

After entry, Oliver, of course, will want to obtain a job. Acquaintances from his homeland may know of employers who hire completely off the books, but for most employers that kind of plunge into the underground is not necessary. Oliver's friends are more likely to advise him to purchase false documents on the street, such as an alien registration receipt card (the well-known green card), or a social security card and a driver's license—enough to pass the only sort of scrutiny that an employer may lawfully require before hiring.

The United States' scheme for sanctioning employers who hire unauthorized aliens is not well designed. It eases the way for unscrupulous employers seeking to obtain a bulletproof defense against prosecution for illegal hiring, even while it subjects conscientious employers to a serious risk of fines if they demand too much in the way of documents. How did this happen?

From the first proposal for employer sanctions in the 1970s, much of the opposition has stressed the argument that such sanctions would increase discrimination against those of foreign appearance or having foreign-sounding accents. Latino organizations may have been the most prominent exponents of this view. But employer's organizations have also been happy to feature the claim, in the hope that sanctions would be defeated altogether. It sounds so much more high minded than admitting that employers simply like to hire undocumented workers because they can pay them lower wages and thereby make higher profits. The theory of this opposition was that, if employer sanctions were implemented, risk-averse employers would simply refuse to hire anyone who might possibly be the source of liability: namely, people who look or sound foreign.

Of course, employers who outright wanted to engage in invidious discrimination against certain ethnic groups might be able to portray their actions as mere compliance with the immigration laws. Quite logically and appropriately, then, proponents coupled the introduction of fines for employers who knowingly hire unauthorized foreign workers with a system meant to guard against such unintended discriminatory consequences (Fix 1991, 11). The statute therefore required all employers to check the documents of all new hires, U.S. citizens and foreigners alike (INA §274A[b]). Not only would this practice, in principle, deter unauthorized workers, but, perhaps more importantly, it would assure that all employees, whatever their accents, were treated exactly the same, because proof of good-faith verification of documents would provide an affirmative defense to employers whose workers might later be found to be unauthorized (INA §274A[a][3]). There would be no need, in other words, for the risk-averse personnel manager to shy away from foreign-sounding job applicants, provided they passed a simple documentary test that all new hires had to undergo anyway.

Up to this point the institutional design is sound and indeed far superior to certain proposals that would have left it up to the employer whether to check documents (in which case, even well-intended employers might have imposed uneven and discriminatory document-presentation requirements on minority job applicants). But two other weaknesses have gone a long way toward undermining the verification system in practice.

First, the statute and regulations provide that a host of documents (twenty-nine at latest count) can serve to satisfy the employee's burden.[3] Some on the list are relatively easy to counterfeit, particularly because the arrival of employer sanctions unhappily coincided with the appearance of the personal computer and sophisticated desktop publishing programs. So-called breeder documents showing U.S. birth—e.g., one of the easily faked birth certificate forms used by many local jurisdictions—compound the problem. After acquiring such a document, aliens like Oliver can use it as the basis for the issuance of wholly genuine conforming documents, such as driver's licenses and social security cards. The obvious remedy, if one can be found, would be to shorten the list of documents that can be presented and to move toward greater uniformity in the issuance of breeder documents. The INS has made some progress on this front, but the logical overall solution—adoption of a single national employment identifier—appears to be checkmated by an odd political alliance, involving elements of the Left and Right, against what is always dismissively labeled as a "national ID card." Europeans who live with the realities of national identity cards will surely find such a reaction exaggerated. Some thoughtful U.S. observers, including Father Theodore Hesburgh, former chair of both the Civil Rights Commission and the Select Commission on Immigration and Refugee Policy, after looking carefully at what safeguards could be applied, have been willing to endorse a single employment identifier, demandable only at the time of hire and not to be used for other purposes. They believe that an identification system could be crafted that would make the verification procedures far more reliable without undue costs to civil liberties (Eaton 1986, 36).

The second element hampering the effectiveness of employer sanctions is less significant but still important. In the rush to ensure against discrimination, Congress coupled the enactment of employer sanctions in 1986 with a new section imposing fines on employers who engage in "unfair immigration-related employment practices" (INA §274B). This much is unobjectionable, but Congress later went further: almost any departure from the normal, perfunctory, routine examination of documents proffered by a prospective employee can lead to fines under the antidiscrimination provisions. Employers suspicious about the immigration status of individual applicants for employment are thus tightly hemmed in. They are forbidden, for example, to specify the exact document they wish to examine (INA §274B[a][6]; 8 C.F.R. §274a.2[b][1][v][1990]). Hence even if an employer knows that a local counterfeiting ring is selling false social security cards, he or she may not require noncitizen job applicants to present an INS-issued employment authorization card instead. The only exception to passive acceptance of whatever document from the approved lists the employee presents arises if the document itself falls below the undemanding test of the law: that it "reasonably appears on its face to be genuine" (INA §274A[b][1][A]).

Personnel managers are not forensic document experts. Their safest course is usually to note that a social security card was examined and file away the Form I-9 (the one-page form that must be used with each hire to record that the employee went through the document verification ceremony). Indeed, their incentives are magnified to err in favor of complying with the antidiscrimination provisions even at some cost to the objectives of immigration enforcement, because people who believe they have been subjected to discrimination have a private right of action against employers, whereas the basic employer sanctions scheme allows for investigation and charges only by the INS or its governmental delegates (INA §274B[d][2]; INA §274A[e]). The INS's resources are stretched so thin that a great many sanctions cases are compromised with the employers; the agency cannot afford to pursue more of them through the contested proceedings before an administrative law judge that are required by the statute (a more demanding type of proceeding than is required for deportation).

As a result, even employers who genuinely want to help the INS enforce the law against unauthorized workers are deterred from doing anything more than mechanically examining whatever the prospective employee tenders. Worse, the scheme fairly invites active connivance by shady employers, for they have a prima facie defense against any enforcement action by INS: they need simply pull a sheaf of properly completed I-9s from their files (Calavita 1990, 1058). To charge them under the sanctions scheme, the INS would then have to prove their actual knowledge of the employees' unauthorized status or demonstrate that the documents were not even facially valid, a task rendered difficult in many cases because employers are not required to keep photocopies of the documents they have examined. The INS historically has not had the resources to conduct this kind of labor-intensive effort on any significant scale.

Because of these flaws in the design of employer sanctions, the market for fraudulent documents has adapted. Dealers offer various qualities of documents, but ordinarily the cheapest will suffice in the job market, for they are good enough to survive the undemanding scrutiny of employers, the only kind of scrutiny that employers may lawfully undertake. The cheaper documents are known as "fifty-footers" to INS agents, because the agents can supposedly spot their falsity from that distance. But the dealers do not promise that their discount models (selling for perhaps forty dollars) will survive INS scrutiny, or even the scrutiny of the local liquor store. A document good enough for those purposes might cost ten times as much (King 1991; Meyer 1991; Hernandez 1988; McDonnell and Bravin 1988).

The combination of the sanctions schemes adopted in 1986 tell employers that it is more important to avoid even an appearance of discrimination than it is to wind up employing unauthorized workers. Perhaps that is an accurate reflection of the relative political value judgments in 1986, or more so in 1990, when the antidiscrimination provisions were toughened. But it is not clear that the same judgment would be reached in 1996 or indeed that one could not find a happier medium that would enable better achievement of both objectives.

Congress, of course, has not been oblivious to the problems posed by the rather easy availability of false documents to aliens like Oliver. In 1990 it added a new civil fine provision to the INA, allowing for the efficient imposition of monetary penalties (without the complexities of criminal prosecution) on those who knowingly make, use, or accept false documents (INA §274C). This provision holds some promise, but it is still a bit early to know its ultimate impact. It also has generated some submerged and rather unexpected problems, for its most effective sanctions now appear to fall on many people unwittingly and disproportionately. More about this later.

In any event, for all these reasons, Oliver will probably have little difficulty in obtaining documents good enough to pass most employers' examination. He may then readily join the ranks of several hundred thousand undocumented workers in this country, and the odds are good that he can enjoy years of earnings. Minor encounters with the law, such as stops for traffic violations, do not necessarily result in the reporting of his status to the INS. Historically, local officials often paid no attention to immigration status, and their computer systems, meant to check for stolen cars or dangerous wanted criminals, have not connected with databases that might allow them to identify administrative violators such as entrants without inspection—or even those who have already defied a final deportation order. (Some steps have been taken recently to overcome this deficiency, through wider use of the National Crime Information Center and the opening of an INS Law Enforcement Support Center on a pilot project basis.)

This is not to say that the lives of most undocumented aliens are easy or comfortable. The perceived threat of INS worksite raids or other forms of discovery (vividly present for many undocumented aliens, even if the actual risk is statistically low) may cloud their well-being. More importantly, unscrupulous employers may use the de facto knowledge of their workers' undocumented status for the leverage needed to exploit them, shaving their agreed wages, for example, or holding them in unsafe working conditions. Employees who object can be fired, the employer gambling that they will be unwilling to expose their illegal presence by filing formal complaints. And some such employers are apparently quite willing to notify the INS of a suddenly discovered suspicion that such troublemakers are undocumented, apparently without much fearing that the notification will expose the Potemkin Village quality of most of their I-9 files. They can protest that the initial hiring was according to the book and that only a later anonymous tip suggested that these individuals were undocumented. Recent additions to the employer compliance staff of both the INS and the Department of Labor may help curb this kind of raw abuse, for they may enable a closer audit of employers who claim to have such convenient tipsters. Nevertheless, even the expanded staff falls far short, at present, of a comprehensive deterrence and enforcement capacity.

Investigation and the Initiation of Deportation

Apprehension

Suppose that after two years of uneventful work, Oliver encounters extraordinary bad luck and is discovered, essentially by accident, by an INS investigator. This does represent bad luck, because the INS had only some 1,900 employees, including support staff, in its investigations division in 1994, although the number is slated to expand to 2,400 in 1996 (U.S. Department of Justice 1995, 34). Moreover, the INS's conduct of "area control operations" has been hemmed in by orders issued in class-action lawsuits (*Illinois Migrant Council v. Pilliod*, 548 F.2d 715 [7th Cir. 1977]; *LaDuke v. Nelson*, 796 F.2d 309 [9th Cir. 1985]; *Marquez v. Kiley*, 436 F. Supp. 100 [S.D.N.Y. 1977]) and by a congressional decision in 1986 to require a warrant before undertaking investigations in a farmer's open fields, theretofore an oft-used and frequently successful tactic (INA §287[e]). The INS's track record in carrying out such investigations in the nation's interior has been problematic, owing in large part to the profound societal ambivalence that surrounds this activity. While most of the public and Congress see catching people at the border as almost certainly a good and worthwhile activity, checking worksites and removing people who have long been peaceful residents often evokes a strong negative reaction.

It has also seemed possible to generate better statistics and more solid evidence of agency accomplishment by concentrating INS resources elsewhere. Border apprehensions, for example, have always been featured more prominently than statistics involving interior enforcement; the numbers are big, and they result in a technical success—actual departure—over 90 percent of the time (U.S. Department of Justice 1994a, 25). Because of the dynamics of the border operations, most who are apprehended along the southern border voluntarily return to Mexico the same night, after completion of some paperwork. As indicated, many can simply try a clandestine entry again soon, but in the meantime the INS scores an apparently solid statistic.

In recognition of this skewing of priorities, the INS made an effort in the 1980s to reform the system of institutional incentives and give higher priority to interior enforcement through the adoption of an Investigations Case Management System (ICMS). The ICMS was designed to give priority weighting to the various kinds of enforcement activities so that resources would be more strategically targeted rather than simply going to the activities that produced the flashiest statistics. Under this scheme, interior enforcement (locating, apprehending, charging, prosecuting, and ultimately removing a deportable alien) would count for more in assessing unit productivity and accomplishment than the less time-consuming job of catching aliens at the border.

The concept is eminently sensible. But in actual practice, the potentially beneficial effects of the ICMS were watered down. Under the original conception, the investigations division could not take full credit for the interior enforcement until the alien was removed from the country (or his or her case was otherwise definitively resolved); after all, removal is the point of the exercise. But removal is dependent on actions by several other players, including the INS's Detention and Deportation division, the alien's counsel, and the immigration courts, an independent arm of the Justice Department. If the case was not expedited, the individual was likely to be released (for reasons to be examined below), and INS investigators might then, through no fault of their own, have to go back to square one to locate and arrest the alien once again before removal could occur.

By 1993, therefore, the ICMS scale was adjusted to count as a success the original apprehension and charging, even if the alien later had to be released and could then never be found for removal. Such a change in internal scorekeeping made bureaucratic sense—the investigations division should not be blamed if other units of the Department of Justice proved unable to sustain custody or if the immigration court's caseload was badly backlogged—but it obviously lost touch with the ultimate objectives of real enforcement. Investigators are also hardly inspired to zealous pursuit of this function when they know that many of the garden-variety deportable aliens they locate will be put through an empty charging ceremony and then released. The INS is now considering ways to restore the original objectives, reorient the case management system, and perhaps find more systematic ways to avoid having to catch deportable aliens twice.

Detention

But now we return to the perspective of the apprehended deportable alien. His capture may appear a catastrophe. Wrenched from his earlier underground existence, he now knows that his illegal presence has been discovered and that the authorities are in train to remove him. The INS has the authority to detain him throughout the proceedings or to require the posting of a substantial bond if he is released (INA §242[a][1]). Detained cases are expedited, both by immigration judges and, if there is an appeal, by the Board of Immigration Appeals (BIA). And aliens who are detained throughout the proceedings are, of course, the most likely to be subjected to actual removal, perhaps within a few weeks of their discovery.

Oliver, however, with his confident knowledge of the workings of the system, knows that he has little reason for short- or even medium-term concern. The INS has limited detention space and limited detention budgets. Detention costs over seventy dollars per day per alien on average, far more in some locations. A 1992 General Accounting Office study reported that INS facilities were capable of detaining 2,864 people and that through contractual arrangements with state, local, and federal authorities the INS had expanded its overall detention capacity to 6,259 aliens. The INS then had plans under way to expand the capacity to 8,600 beds by FY 1996 (GAO 1992, 12, 37). But average detention time had also expanded from 7.3 days per alien in 1984 to 22.9 days in 1990, owing to a combination of INS and immigration court backlogs and other delays won through legal complications.

The INS obviously has had to make difficult decisions about priorities in using the bed space in its detention facilities. In doing so, it established these six priority categories, in descending order of importance (GAO 1992, 14):

1. Aliens convicted of crimes or identified through the Alien Smuggler Identification and Deportation Project
2. Excludable aliens (those caught at the border or preliminarily judged inadmissible on appearing at a port of entry; this category theoretically includes all excludable aliens but places an internal priority on those who have criminal or terrorist histories or have attempted to enter with fraudulent documents)
3. Deportable aliens who have committed fraud
4. Deportable aliens who have absconded or who have outstanding deportation orders
5. Deportable aliens apprehended while trying to enter illegally
6. Other deportable aliens

This priority system does not necessarily indicate that all aliens in category 1 will be detained. Actual implementation is carried out by district, not nationwide. If a particular district has used up most of its detention budget for the current month, or if locally available detention facilities are full, it may have to release even high-priority detainees. The GAO reported, for example, the release on their own recognizance of 382 convicted criminal aliens in the Western Region and of 201 in the Boston district in late 1990, in both cases because of limited detention space (GAO 1992, 41).

Such releases of criminal aliens have, not surprisingly, drawn vehement congressional criticism, and the Department of Justice has devoted considerable attention over the last five years to improvements in this area.[4] One important corrective has been to try to complete deportation processing while the convicted aliens are still in custody for the criminal offense.[5] They then take up no INS detention space, and all hearings and appeals can be completed, yielding up a final and enforceable deportation order, before the underlying sentence ends. In principle, they should then be removable with only the most minimal stays in INS detention. To accomplish this end, the department has established an Institutional Hearing Program (IHP) whereby immigration judges, INS trial attorneys, and other needed support personnel are assigned to hold hearings in the prisons in which the aliens are held. This program began in federal facilities in 1990, has now been extended into many state facilities, and experienced a major expansion in the prison systems of the five states that now hold over 70 percent of all foreign-born individuals currently incarcerated (U.S. Congress 1994, 18–19; U.S. Congress 1995b, 7). The evolution of the IHP represents major progress and presents obvious advantages to both state authorities and the INS.[6] Still, even with the changes, many criminal aliens still complete their sentences before a hearing on deportability. First-priority cases therefore still make a major claim on INS detention space.[7]

Oliver falls into category six on the detention ladder. With so many dangerous or more devious individuals ahead of him, he has little worry that INS will choose to detain him. In fact, INS agents who discover aliens in his situation often do not even bother to arrest them and take them to the district office. Instead, such individuals can simply be issued an Order to Show Cause (OSC), the charging document that initiates deportation proceedings, without an arrest. And even if the agent decides in his case to initiate proceedings by way of arrest, Oliver is quite likely to be released on his own recognizance or on posting a bond after a brief sojourn at the INS office for completion of the paperwork.

Why doesn't the INS make more use of stiff bond requirements to improve the odds that aliens will show up both for their hearings and later for ultimate departure from the country? The statute provides clear authority for imposing such measures (INA §242[a][1]). And after all, many deportation respondents, particularly single people with few roots in the community, would seem to present high risks of absconding, according to the criteria often used in the criminal justice system to determine who may be released and on what terms. There is a simple and straightforward reason for the limited use of high bonds, however: limited detention capacity. Aliens offered release on relatively stiff monetary terms are unlikely to post bonds, unless they both have the funds and really believe that detention will otherwise ensue. Because the typical deportation respondent is not a good statistical risk to appear for his or her hearing, commercial bonding companies in many districts simply refuse to take on such cases (Gilboy 1988, 551). As a result, aliens typically must post the whole amount without help. If they have little money or choose not to apply what they have to the bond, they are essentially calling the INS's bluff. The INS cannot extract the kinds of high bonds whose forfeiture would be sufficiently painful to assure appearance unless it is capable of imposing long-term detention on those who cannot make bond. If the monthly detention budget is reaching its limit on the fifteenth of the month, the INS may have to reduce bonds on low-priority detainees (or even high-priority individuals) or allow wide-scale releases of aliens on their own recognizance, for reasons having little to do with any assessment of flight risk.[8]

Deportation Proceedings

On discovery, then, the INS agent is most likely simply to serve Oliver with an OSC detailing the grounds on which the investigator believes him to be deportable. And even if arrested, Oliver is likely to secure early release on his own recognizance or on the basis of a bond he could well afford to forfeit, simply treating the payment as a sort of tax for the capacity to live and work here for several more years. Of course, one should note that the INS does still detain many noncriminal aliens and requires significant bonds even in some low-priority cases, depending on local conditions. But Oliver is an odds player. For a category 6 deportable alien, the odds remain decidedly favorable and will continue so until the INS makes significant strides in increasing detention space or reducing average detention time.

In Absentia Deportation Orders

For years, many Olivers simply ignored the service of the OSC, meanwhile moving to new jobs and new homes. This tactic made sure that only through another equivalent accident would they ever be discovered and realistically have to appear to face charges. And the INS's data system was so primitive that there was some chance that the second investigator would not even know that an OSC had once issued.

Why weren't those who absconded after service of the first papers simply ruled deportable, by default? The statute has long contemplated such an outcome. Since 1952, INA §242(b) has provided for the issuance of deportation orders in absentia against those who failed to appear for their hearings. And yet it became apparent in the 1980s that immigration judges used this authority infrequently (GAO 1989, 4). The original OSC rarely contained notice of the time and date of the hearing. A later notice specifying those details therefore had to be sent to nondetained aliens, and a great many of those notices came back undelivered. Properly inspired by the "due process revolution" of the 1970s, immigration judges demanded better proof than the INS could usually muster that the attempted notice was sufficient under the circumstances. Aliens were under a duty to keep the INS apprised of address changes, but INS address files were often deemed too unreliable to provide the needed assurance of constitutionally adequate notice. Unable to issue orders under these circumstances, IJs dismissed the cases. Rediscovery of the alien later would thus require initiation of a brand-new set of deportation procedures.

Congress responded to the desuetude of in absentia orders in 1988, by enacting INA §242B: essentially a demand by the legislators that the INS and the Executive Office of Immigration Review (EOIR, a separate quasi-judicial Justice Department unit that has been the institutional home of the immigration judges and the BIA since 1983) develop a system for the systematic use of in absentia deportation orders when aliens fail to appear for their hearings. The new legislation required the Attorney General to create a reliable address file. It also specified that aliens initially served with OSCs be told of their firm duty to keep the INS informed of address changes and that immigration judges issue deportation orders in absentia if the aliens failed to appear. The law also greatly restricted the grounds on which such an order could be vacated if the alien later showed up, requiring proof of defective notice or an event akin to "serious illness of the alien or death of an immediate relative" (INA §42B[c][3][A], [f][2]).

Concerns about civil liberties, however, championed by effective lobbying from immigrant advocacy organizations, resulted in many compromises before enactment of section 242B. Mere failure to appear is not enough to justify issuance of the order; the INS still has to prove to the immigration judge "by clear, unequivocal, and convincing evidence that the written notice was so provided and that the alien is deportable." (Most deportation charges, however, are quite straightforward, based on entry without inspection (EWI), visa overstay, or criminal conviction; this seemingly heavy burden on the INS is thus not a major problem in practice.) Moreover, the statute mandates that all OSCs be served in both English and Spanish, in addition to the usual notifications and warnings that are always translated into the alien's language during the course of any appearance or hearing before the immigration court. The English and Spanish requirement survives even though by 1993 the EOIR's statistics showed that fewer than half of deportation respondents spoke Spanish. Printing the standard form in the two languages is not a problem, but assuring that the nonstandard portions, especially the detailed charges, are thus translated, can be a burden for smaller INS offices, particularly in regions where Spanish is not widely used. And a later subsection of section 242B, intended to disqualify aliens from many forms of possible immigration relief if they commit various defaults,[9] was amended to impose this punishment only on those who had first received certain kinds of written and oral warnings in their native languages. Even then it further limits the disqualification to five years from the default, meaning that an absconder who stays out of the INS's clutches for five years can revive his or her access to such relief (INA §242B[e]).

Despite these obstacles, INA §242B has had many beneficial effects. Department of Justice address keeping is much improved, the alien's duty to keep the INS apprised of an address where he or she can be reached is clarified, and the use of in absentia orders has risen significantly. Anecdotal evidence does suggest that such orders, once issued, are more easily vacated than the statute's demanding standards would seem to allow, often because of lingering IJ concerns about notice problems and the IJ's natural human desire to let aliens present any defenses they might have once they are actively taking part in the proceedings.[10] But the INS and EOIR are now cooperating in the implementation of a system to minimize still further any plausible claims of defective notice. To be subject to in absentia orders under section 242B, an alien must receive both a valid OSC detailing the charges and a notice of the precise date and time of the hearing. Until recently, because hearing calendars were within the authority of the EOIR and because of extensive backlogs in many immigration courts, the INS lacked the capacity to place such precise information about hearing times on the original charging document. Another mailing thus became necessary, affording grounds for new arguments about adequate INS compliance with the notice provisions. To minimize such contentions, many INS districts and asylum offices are implementing computer links with the EOIR that enable placing an actual hearing date and time on the initial charging document, which is typically served in person, in a manner that leaves little room for argument about actual receipt of statutorily sufficient notice.

Now that section 242B has tightened up the regimen for using in absentia orders, how should Oliver calculate the odds after being served with the OSC? If he simply disappears—moving to another town, taking his false work documents with him, and failing to comply with the statute's requirements for notifying INS of any address change—he is now highly likely to become the subject of a final, enforceable deportation order, without ever being able to present defenses. But if he has no defenses to present (absent an asylum claim, he probably lacks even a prima facie basis until he has managed to live here for seven years),[11] he is giving up nothing of substance. And INS must still locate him once again in order to make any use of that deportation order. Moreover, there is some chance that he might accumulate, while on the run, the seven years that place some form of relief within reach. By then he would face substantial hurdles to get his case reopened, but perhaps he would find a sympathetic IJ once he had a real claim to present.

Still, the well-informed bad man will probably not disappear at the point when he is served with an order to show cause. His later discovery after a final order has been issued would make it far more likely for him to be detained. By then he would have demonstrated his risk of flight, he would occupy a higher priority on the detention ladder, and the INS would calculate that his detention period could be quite brief before execution of the already final in absentia deportation order. If he could not find a sympathetic IJ, his judicial appeals and remedies would be sharply limited. As will become apparent, he therefore has reason to stick around for at least a bit more of the procedure before disappearing.

The Proceedings for a Nondetained Alien

As noted, Oliver is unlikely to be detained. If his district office is not yet equipped to place the time and date of the hearing on his OSC at the time of issuance, he may wait weeks or months before even receiving notice of the scheduled hearing. Whenever he receives that information, on the OSC or later by certified mail, the hearing is still likely to be several weeks away. Detained cases receive priority, and many immigration courts are badly backlogged, even for the scheduling of a nondetained alien's first appearance.

What provision will be made for Oliver's sustenance between apprehension and hearing or indeed between apprehension and eventual removal (or the granting of relief that makes his status lawful)? Until January 1995 the regulations allowed for the issuance of bona fide work authorization papers to nondetained aliens against whom exclusion or deportation proceedings were pending (8 C.F.R. §274a.12[c][13], 1994). Issuance, at the discretion of the INS district directors, was supposed to be based in part on a determination of economic necessity and the plausible availability of some kind of defense or relief in the proceedings. But in fact work authorization became fairly automatic. Economic necessity was usually obvious, given that the proceedings might well last years, and judging the validity of any defenses required a deep plunge into the merits, often before the alien had formally pled to the charges listed in the OSC. Consequently, issuance of work authorization in these circumstances became so routine in some districts that aliens occasionally showed up and demanded to be placed in proceedings (wherein they planned to file asylum applications) so as to receive near-immediate issuance of work authorization papers under this regulation.[12] The regulation was adopted for the most humane of reasons, especially because, in the United States, most forms of public assistance are closed to undocumented aliens, even while proceedings are under way. But in the process it created an odd sort of inducement for people to contest and string out deportation proceedings, because they could thereby gain access to, and retain, bona fide work documents. The INS finally responded to this anomaly in December 1994, when it repealed this paragraph of the work authorization regulations (*Fed. Reg.* 59 [1994]: 62284), but the full implications of that repeal have not yet become clear.

The alien's first appearance in immigration court is typically for what is known as "master calendar"—some thirty or so cases scheduled before an immigration judge for routine business on a stated day.[13] At this appearance aliens are more thoroughly advised of their rights, each in a language he or she can understand, and are asked about their wishes regarding counsel. If an alien express a desire for counsel, the case is typically recalendared for a few weeks later.[14] The INA specifically provides that aliens have a right to counsel "at no expense to the government" (INA §§242[b][2], 292). It also requires (building on a practice pioneered administratively) that unrepresented aliens be given lists, updated quarterly, of attorneys or organizations in the district who provide representation on a pro bono basis (INA §242B [b][2]). (Of course, aliens who are able may obtain hired counsel elsewhere.) This process by no means guarantees representation. Pro bono attorneys typically choose their cases carefully; their resources are stretched thin, and they sensibly try to focus on cases with the strongest possible claims for defense or relief.

At master calendar aliens are required to plead to the charges in the OSC—either at the first appearance (if counsel is waived) or at a second (or third or fourth) master calendar if time has been allowed to obtain counsel. Because most cases are so straightforward (EWI,[15] visa overstay, or criminal conviction), aliens commonly admit deportability and then apply for a form of relief under the statute, such as asylum, adjustment of status (e.g., based on marriage to a U.S. citizen), or one of the two forms of discretionary relief available to aliens who have been present for a minimum of seven years.[16] A prominent immigration attorney has recently suggested that alien's counsel should stop admitting deportability so routinely (Maggio 1993, 940). It is unclear whether such a course would be consistent with an attorney's ethical obligations,[17] but if that suggestion catches on, it will undoubtedly prolong proceedings and make them more costly. If deportability is conceded and none of the more extensive forms of relief is sought, the IJ may go ahead at master calendar and issue a deportation order or, more likely in nondetained cases, permit "voluntary departure with safeguards" by closing the proceedings with an "alternate order of deportation" (U.S. Department of Justice 1994b, 155). Such orders allow individuals a certain period, typically thirty to ninety days, to leave at their own expense and on their own schedule. Those who honor this period are not considered to have departed under a deportation order; hence they escape certain disabilities under the statute (primarily regarding their later eligibility for a valid admission, should they find another basis for entry [INA §212 (a)(6)]). But if they do not leave within the stated period, the alternate order becomes a fully effective and executable deportation order. Of course, by then, a bad-man alien has had thirty to ninety days to move and leave behind a cold trail for any later enforcement action.

The Effect of Ill-founded or Fraudulent Claims

Having been here less than seven years and not having married (or found anyone willing to engage in a sham marriage sufficient to form the basis for an application for immigration benefits),[18] Oliver has no real-world basis for relief. His only honest course at master calendar is to admit deportability and hope for an "alternate order" and a head start. But neither marriage nor prior lengthy stay is required to pursue one recently popular form of relief: political asylum.[19] Unfortunately, ill-founded asylum claims have often been filed (albeit in recent years probably more frequently as "affirmative claims").[20] In the early 1990s, some shady entrepreneurs set up virtual asylum application factories, grinding out, for stiff fees, what have become known as "boilerplate applications." The affidavits accompanying such application forms told a tale that at least prima facie set forth valid claims. Hundreds, however, were filed with virtually the same tale, and they proved, once a hearing or interview was reached, to have nothing to do with the applicant named on the face of the document.

If Oliver expresses concern about committing perjury through the filing of such an application, the entrepreneur might well advise that the risk to him is minimal. Although submitting a false asylum claim is criminally actionable (as would be any false testimony on the stand intended to back it up), neither the INS nor EOIR can pursue a prosecution themselves.[21] Such cases must be referred for prosecution to the U.S. Attorney's Office, an office already busy with drug cases and other higher-priority federal prosecutions. Virtually no simple asylum applicant is prosecuted for such fraud, no matter how blatant the falsehood. Indeed, until recently U.S. Attorneys have often placed even the investigative folders of immigration fraud ringleaders on the bottom of their overcrowded prosecution piles.[22] This setting of priorities by federal prosecutors may have been rational, given the other claims on their resources, but it was deeply debilitating for the deportation process.

Recent developments may have given the INS a tool that puts teeth back in their efforts against those who commit such frauds, but perhaps in ways not fully intended by Congress. Aware of prosecutors' frequent inattention to immigration fraud, Congress added a new section 274C to the INA in 1990 to allow for the imposition of civil penalties on people using fraudulent documents. The government's burden of proof is easier in these civil proceedings than in criminal trials, and the charges can be brought by the INS according to its own priorities, not those of the U.S. Attorney. Civil document fraud cases are tried before administrative law judges (ALJs) in the Department of Justice, who may impose fines from $250 to $5,000 per false document created, used, or accepted.[23] Because the fines are calculated per document, section 274C can appropriately lead to very large fines for major operators.

INS personnel originally used this remedy to concentrate on the major operators but then with growing frequency invoked it against individual aliens, apparently in the hope of applying initially overlooked deportation and exclusion grounds. The statute provides that anyone subject to an order under section 274C is ipso facto deportable and then perpetually excludable (INA §§241[a][3][c], 212[a][6][F]). Such an order therefore greatly simplifies deportation proceedings, but it may have a devastating and perhaps disproportionate impact on aliens who are not document vendors and who may have used a false document only once, to obtain a job. Although the statute is flexible regarding fines, allowing ALJs to take into account the relative seriousness of the fraud, it appears quite inflexible regarding the immigration consequences for aliens who are ruled guilty of any such use of fraudulent documents. Even if such an alien later marries a U.S. citizen in a wholly bona fide ceremony, he or she will probably be unable to overcome the disability imposed by a section 274C order, even if the ALJ regarded the offense as minor and imposed only the minimum fine. The powerful effect of a section 274C ruling is only now becoming evident to INS personnel and the immigration bar. Congress should revisit the statute and consider providing ALJs or IJs some dispensing power for less serious incidents before the current lifetime exclusion bar attaches.

Realistically speaking, however, the worst consequence that Oliver faces if he files a false asylum claim is the issuance of a deportation order, exactly what he would incur if he had never filed for asylum. If the agents also obtain a section 274C order against him, he might then be perpetually banned from reentry. But this fate is unlikely to alter Oliver's calculus greatly (though it might be a more effective deterrent for a fair number of other undocumented aliens); under the stipulations here he has no real prospect of ever obtaining permission to immigrate lawfully in any event. And in the meantime his false asylum claim might still succeed. At the very least it buys time, because the IJ must then calendar the case for a merits hearing, historically as much as a year or more later. In contrast, if he tenders nothing by way of defense or relief, his case is likely to be disposed of at master calendar, within a few weeks of service of the OSC.

IJ Decision and Appeal

Assume then that Oliver requests time to find counsel at his first master calendar. At the second such hearing, weeks later, he admits deportability but requests asylum. He will be allowed a period of weeks, at the discretion of the IJ, to file his asylum application form, and a merits hearing will be calendared, in some districts a year or more later, though recent increases in staffing are considerably improving the scheduling. When the hearing date arrives, if Oliver proves to be an effective dissembler, and especially if he comes from a country with a poor human rights record, he just might obtain asylum, which will put him on the road to permanent resident status after a minimum of one year. But it is more likely that his claim will fail, and he will be issued an order of deportation or perhaps an "alternate order" allowing a period for voluntary departure.

At this point, having lost his case, Oliver poses a greater risk of absconding, and it would be sensible to require him to post a bond, if none was set before, or increase the bond amount. Apparently such increases have been quite infrequent, however, in part because of the attitudes and assumptions of IJs (Gilboy 1988, 556–57) and in part because the INS is subject to the same bluff-calling at this point that has defeated wider use of detention upon issuance of the OSC: if Oliver failed to make bond, INS would have to detain him. But detention might then still be quite lengthy and expensive. He has ten days—soon to increase to thirty—to appeal the IJ's order to the BIA, and he is not removable before then. If he appeals, the order is not final and subject to execution until the administrative appeal is decided (8 C.F.R. §§243.1, 243.2). The BIA expedites detained cases, but such appeals still typically require months, as compared to non-detained cases, which have recently required well over a year.

In light of these backlogs and a greatly expanding caseload (to over 12,000 appeals in 1994 and 17,000 in 1995), the Attorney General promulgated new regulations in June 1995 expanding the board to twelve members from its previous five, an expansion to be accompanied by a significant increase in the board's eighty-lawyer staff (*Fed. Reg.* 60 [1995]: 29,469; *Interpreter*

Releases 1995, 197–98).[24] The backlogs should be significantly reduced once the expansion is fully implemented, but even so, detaining an alien from the time an IJ issues a deportation order remains potentially quite expensive. And BIA appeals are not the full story. Even after the BIA rules, the INS might well have to continue the custody still longer, because a deportable alien's application for judicial review generally leads, by statute, to an automatic stay of deportation (INA §106[a][3]).[25]

Oliver therefore is quite likely to remain free throughout the many months, or more likely years, that may be consumed on administrative appeal and judicial review. At the end of that process, if he was originally granted an "alternate order," his period of voluntary departure will commence running once again (*Contreras-Aragon v. INS*, 852 F.2d 1088, 1096 [9th Cir. 1988]; Matter of Chouliaris, *Immigration and Naturalization Decisions* 16 [BIA1977]: 168–70). A "bad man" with a thirty-day alternate order, in other words, will still have a thirty-day head start, even if he has pursued highly questionable appeals. And even without an alternate order, INS typically does not try to take an alien into custody coincident with notification of the final ruling on any appeals. In short, Oliver will not find it hard to abscond again, perhaps taking on a new identity and a new job in another region of the country.

Final Apprehension and Removal

Whenever the deportation order becomes final, it falls to special agents or deportation officers of the INS district office to locate Oliver and effect his removal. Locating a determined absconder is never easy, but some curiosities of INS practice have sometimes made the task even more difficult. For many years, INS regulations required that deportable aliens be issued a "bag-and-baggage" letter notifying them of their obligation to appear for deportation at a time no sooner than seventy-two hours after service of the notice. Because over 70 percent of the recipients of such letters disappeared after service, the bag-and-baggage letters came to be known to INS agents and immigration lawyers alike as "run letters" (*Fed. Reg.* 51 [1986]: 23041; Gilboy 1988, 533 n). Sensibly, the INS amended the regulations in 1986 to eliminate the bag-and-baggage letter, instead assuring that the

INS would hold the apprehended person for a minimum of seventy-two hours before removal, so as to allow for any last-minute filings to raise possible objections to deportation under the authority of the final order (*Fed. Reg.* 51 [1985]: 23041, amending 8 C.F.R. §243.3). Even after that, however, the bag-and-baggage letter has not disappeared from agency practice. INS agents still sometimes send such letters by certified mail in order to provide a hot trail, in case the certificate comes back with a signature showing receipt. Or perhaps agents use such letters solely to show in low-cost fashion some sort of action in a higher percentage of the mountains of deportation cases piling up in the district office. After all, some aliens do respond by reporting for deportation (Harwood 1986, 45–46).

Aside from these oddities, the continued shortage of sustainable detention space also greatly hampers, and discourages, vigorous pursuit of aliens like Oliver. Why should detention space be a problem at this stage, given that the INS has a final and enforceable deportation order in hand? Because our complicated and labyrinthine system affords several avenues whereby actual removal can still be stalled or delayed even after an alien is taken into custody prior to deportation.

First, a deportable alien probably will not be accepted aboard a commercial airliner for travel back to his or her home country without appropriate travel documents. Oliver will not willingly produce his passport, even if he has one; that is, he will destroy or conceal it. The INS will thus probably have to seek new travel documents from Oliver's country of nationality. Some countries are notoriously slow or unreliable in this process. They may, for example, keep demanding better proof that the individual really is one of their citizens. If the alien is uncooperative, such proof may be hard to come by. Moreover, no matter how important a particular removal may be to the INS, that agency is not in a position to escalate the diplomatic pressure on a balky country of presumed nationality. Instead such dealings are the province of the State Department, and effective pressure therefore depends on that department's assessment of the importance of such cooperation, weighed against other matters of interest to the bilateral relationship. Whenever travel documents are delayed, the alien takes up scarce detention space that may be needed for a higher-priority alien, perhaps one with a serious criminal record. By making it difficult to obtain travel documents, Oliver may still win release and another opportunity to defy apprehension by going underground and moving elsewhere within the United States.

The drafters of the INA made some provision against noncooperation on the part of both aliens and their home countries. For example, the act specifies criminal penalties for aliens who refuse to assist in making these sorts of travel arrangements. But curiously, as adopted in 1952, these penalties applied only to recalcitrant deportees whose orders were based on the more serious grounds of deportation, such as criminal convictions (INA §242[e]). Finally, in section 130001 of the *Violent Crime Control and Law Enforcement Act of 1994*, Congress decided that all uncooperative aliens in these circumstances should be subject to criminal sanctions, no matter what the ground of deportation. Of course, effective use of such sanctions requires the cooperation of the U.S. Attorney's Office, and these cases are not obvious candidates for prosecutorial priority.

In parallel fashion, the INA provides for sanctions on noncooperative countries (who may of course adopt that posture even if individual aliens cooperate). Under INA §243(g), the State Department is to suspend issuance of immigrant visas to the nationals of states that fail to cooperate in accepting back their nationals subject to deportation orders. But this is a somewhat clumsy and inflexible tool, and it has been invoked against only a few countries (8 C.F.R. §243.8 [1995]).

In addition to travel document complications, it is always possible for an individual deportee to launch a new round of legal challenges, even to an ostensibly final and unappealable deportation order, after being taken into custody. He or she may, for example, file a motion to reopen or reconsider the case, with an accompanying request for a stay of deportation. Although the statute and regulations naturally impose strong presumptions against such late filings, the motion still can buy time and consume INS and EOIR resources to respond. Moreover, all stay denials are potentially reviewable in district court on a petition for habeas corpus (*Dhangu v. INS*, 812 F.2d 455, 457–59 [9th Cir. 1987]), and actual denials of motions to reopen are reviewable in the court of appeals, where a petition for review of a motion denial again triggers an automatic stay of deportation

(*Giova v. Rosenberg*, 379 U.S. 18 [1964]; *Cheng Fan Kwok v. INS*, 392 U.S. 206, 217 [1968]). Apparently because of this automatic stay, until recently the BIA was usually very slow to rule on such a motion when the underlying order was otherwise final. Instead, it typically denied the accompanying stay request and then sat on the motion, apparently hoping that the individual would be deported in the meantime. Under the "departure rule" contained in the statute and regulations, the alien's departure from the country, for whatever reason—even under the compulsion of a deportation order—precludes consideration of either the motion or any administrative or judicial review (INA §106[c]; 8 C.F.R. §3.2 [1995]).

Courts are sometimes quite receptive to habeas corpus petitions that seek a stay of deportation in these circumstances, for a couple of crucial reasons. First, denial of a stay, as indicated, will not simply mean that the alien awaits a ruling overseas but instead that he or she will receive no ruling on the merits whatsoever, because of the rule precluding consideration after departure. But second, and more important, courts are often sympathetic to reopening when an alien, now represented by an attorney, seeks to vacate the results of an earlier proceeding where he or she appeared without counsel (*Mayo v. Schiltgen*, 921 F.2d 177, 180–81 [8th Cir. 1990]; *Snajder v. INS*, 29 F.3d 1203, 1207 [7th Cir. 1994]). They are often quite willing to find in the alien's earlier pro se appearance both an excusable reason for the earlier defaults and likely prejudice justifying reopening, particularly if the alien does not even speak English. A great many deportation orders carry this latent vulnerability, precisely because appointed counsel, paid for by the government, is essentially forbidden by INA §§242(b)(2) and 292. In partial response to this difficulty (and also because immigration court hearings simply proceed with greater clarity, dispatch, and fairness when aliens are represented), the current chief immigration judge is launching a new pro bono initiative to obtain representation for a higher percentage of indigent deportation respondents (*Interpreter Releases* 1995, 195). This may help, but as long as representation depends to a large measure on the volunteer services of the private bar, many deportation cases will still go forward without counsel, sowing the seeds of judicially ordered reopening even years later, just at the point when the

INS believes it is finally poised to execute a final order. The only wholly adequate remedy would be to find ways to assure representation at the first stage, for example, by means of a kind of public defender's office specifically for deportation cases. Funding such an office at taxpayer's expense appears politically impossible—unless perhaps a pilot project, carried out in selected districts over a lengthy period, showed both improved removal records and hard-headed financial savings.

The curious structure of certain grounds for relief from deportation further magnifies the chances for later plausible filings of motions to reopen. Two major grounds for relief, as noted, require, at the threshold, seven years of presence or domicile in this country. Under current law, an alien may continue to accrue the seven years even after the service of the order to show cause, indeed even after the IJ issues a deportation order. In such circumstances, there is a ready explanation for the alien's decision, just before deportation, to file a motion to reopen: the issue could not possibly have been presented or resolved earlier, because the seven-year predicate had not yet been satisfied. Congress has considered proposals to require that the seven years accrue before OSC service or some other finite and identifiable point in the proceedings or indeed to impose far more stringent restrictions on these forms of relief.

All these filings, before either administrative authorities or the courts, remain potentially available, even to aliens who absconded earlier and have resolutely failed to cooperate. Such defaults do not disable such filings, because it is always possible that some in the class of noncooperators may yet have a valid claim—for example, for political asylum. For these reasons, Oliver will almost surely wait to see whether, against substantial odds, the INS does discover him after the deportation order has become final and take him into custody before he can move again. At that point, he can then attempt these additional legal maneuvers. Of course, he may well fail; the deck is properly stacked against him at that stage, given that he has already had access to one full round of proceedings to present any claims or defenses. But note that he need not actually prevail on the merits of a motion to reopen or a petition for habeas corpus in order to win the larger battle. If the filings consume several weeks for the initial hearing and ruling or for appeal, the INS incurs substantial detention costs while Oliver occupies a bed that might well be needed for a higher-priority detainee. Every additional day improves the odds that a shortage of INS resources will force his release before the legal battle has run its course. And if he is released, a bad man like Oliver will almost surely abscond again. INS investigators will then face the demoralizing task of starting all over again to locate him, apprehend him, and then secure new travel documents while facing down any new legal challenges.

One final feature should be noted. These later complications (travel document problems and belated legal filings) remain possible stumbling blocks to actual removal whether or not aliens ever pursue their initial rights to administrative and judicial review. The very prospect of such difficulties can discourage the limited cadre of investigators and agents from the moment a final deportation order is first issued. Of course, not all aliens will be as recalcitrant as Oliver. But investigators can never know, when deportation orders reach their desks after the conclusion of IJ proceedings, just how resourceful and persistent the named respondents might be. Every respondent taken into custody but released before removal represents flatly wasted resources: both days of custody expenses that have served no concrete, realized objective and the labor-intensive investigative resources that are necessary whenever an absconder is tracked down. Add to all these complications the adverse publicity sometimes generated when noncriminal aliens who have been long resident are seized by the INS. Leading citizens, even members of Congress (including even some who give voice to general calls for tightening immigration enforcement) may then join in the denunciation of investigators who pick on nonviolent and hard-working residents rather than going after the so-called real criminals.

With all these barriers to successful deportation, it is little wonder that tracking down absconders came over the decades to be seen within the INS as an unrewarding line of work or that the INS progressively dedicated less and less of its resources and talent to such pursuits. It is hardly surprising, then, that deportation orders, once obtained through diligent work by INS trial attorneys and issued with care by immigration judges, have often simply gone to the enforcement staff to sit in boxes and collect dust. It is not worth the time, effort, and hassle to find and round up a long-resident noncriminal alien unless one can be sure that he or she will actually be removed. And because one could scarcely have that kind of assurance about any particular respondent, historically only a few have become the object of the kind of dogged work needed. And so the cycle has compounded, sowing a poisonous form of cynicism throughout the ranks of the INS and EOIR.

Toward Effective Reform

Stopping this vicious circle requires, above all, additional resources, both for detention space and for more personnel. It also demands determined leadership in the Justice Department units responsible for deportation. The recent clamor for more resolute enforcement (perhaps the real message of Proposition 187), coupled with rapidly growing INS budgets, just might enable the massive and determined effort that will be needed on many fronts if a credible deportation capacity is to be created. But the obstacles still loom large.

Detention capacity is crucial. If the INS had greater detention capacity, it could finally present a real and credible deterrent to manipulation by deportation respondents, for their filings or maneuverings would not be able to outwait the INS's restricted detention budgets. Detention should not be used indiscriminately, of course, but the present inability to detain even people who are flight risks—including some who have absconded before—badly demoralizes all phases of the process. In contrast, aliens who are aware that detention will probably persist throughout the proceedings tend to be far more cooperative and less likely to indulge in ill-founded delaying tactics. And greater detention capacity would allow the setting of release bonds at more realistic levels, including possible increases after an IJ issues a deportation order in the case of a previously undetained alien. Such increases would merely take account of the increased likelihood of flight at that stage. They would also provide an enhanced inducement for aliens to depart under orders or during any voluntary departure period so as to reclaim the posted amount on proof of departure.

The White House and the Congress are both aware of this need for detention space and added resources and leadership.

The INS's appropriations and other allotted funds went up 25 percent from FY 1994 to FY 1995 and another 24 percent the following year. The president's budget for FY 1997 proposes another 16 percent or 428 million dollar increase. A sizable portion has been targeted for improvements to the deportation mechanism, including further increments to detention space (Ostrow 1995; *Interpreter Releases* 1995, 232; 1996, 187; U.S. Congress 1996, 8). If detained aliens remain in custody an average of 22.9 days (the 1990 figure), then each new bed allows the INS to detain another 16 aliens annually. The INS's recent 8,600-bed total would then permit the detention of 137,600 aliens in a year.

But these projections may prove deceptive, because the 1990 baseline reflects a period when detention was concentrated on those with final orders or criminal convictions, people with few prospects for possible relief and therefore limited possibilities for delay.[26] Along with added resources, then, considerable thought must be given to how to gain custody at strategic times when aliens are more easily accessible (such as when they show up for proceedings), and how to minimize the time a typical respondent spends in detention. From a large universe of possibilities, four strategies may deserve an early focus. Each needs much additional scrutiny and debate before adoption, however, because some may carry substantial disadvantages or pose disproportionate risks to aliens less manipulative than Oliver.

Streamline the Appeal Structure

Most aliens now have ninety days to petition for judicial review; that period could be reduced to thirty days without major impairment of the opportunity to contest adverse rulings. More ambitiously, appeals from the BIA might be centralized in the Federal Circuit, which is based in Washington, D.C., and they could be discretionary with the court—for example, through use of a required "motion for leave to appeal" somewhat like the procedure in Canada (Hathaway 1988, 707). A significant percentage of such appeals could probably be finally resolved through a cursory order denying the motion, after only a brief delay.

Permit Earlier Removal

In comparison to the United States, few European countries provide for stays of deportation, or "suspensive effect," for such lengthy periods while appeals are pending, at least not on an automatic basis. At the same time, few countries utterly preclude, as we do, appeals or motions filed by aliens who have departed or been deported. The United States could adopt a scheme similar to those more common across the Atlantic, eliminating automatic stays on appeal but allowing aliens to appeal from abroad. In return, the system could then insist that many categories of deportation respondents leave after an initial adverse ruling by the IJ or perhaps by the BIA, subject to permitted return if the ruling is ultimately overturned and resident status awarded.[27] The European experience suggests that most aliens lose interest in further proceedings after removal. Moreover, in this way, custody periods could obviously be greatly reduced, even if the INS detained a higher percentage of respondents from the outset (for example, because of failure to make bail).

With such a change, the INS might even begin taking custody at the close of the IJ hearing—a strategically chosen time when the Olivers of the world may be easiest to locate.[28] The threat of such detention would doubtless increase the number of no-shows at the hearings, with a concomitant rise in the issuance of in absentia deportation orders. Whether that development is good or bad depends on whether the no-shows are predominately those who have no claim of substance to present. That category of respondents would probably have absconded at some point anyway, and their nonappearance would allow the issuance of an enforceable deportation order at master calendar, without the costs and delays entailed in merits hearings. Of course, there is no assurance that only such aliens would be deterred from appearing. A hard call would have to be made about whether the loss by some fearful aliens of an opportunity to present a genuine claim would be outweighed by the likely gains in enforcement against others.

Simplify the Substantive Law

Many of the problems in our deportation system derive from the complexities of the substantive law, which affords a variety of possible forms of relief even to those who admit deportability. Asylum relief, as frustrating and difficult as its administration can sometimes be, should not be changed in substance. Recent procedural reforms hold promise and should be allowed a few years of testing before additional changes affecting asylum are considered.

This leaves principally the two forms of deportation relief available to seven-year residents under INA §§212(c) and 244. Repealing such relief would naturally simplify the deportation process, reducing many proceedings to a mere consideration of baseline deportability (which is often hard to contest and is in any event conceded in the overwhelming majority of current proceedings). Such a step is probably too extreme, however. The system needs some remedy less complex than private bills enacted by Congress to accommodate cases where deportation would impose highly disproportionate hardship. But some tinkering should be possible, for example, to stop the accrual of the necessary residence period after the issuance of an OSC or to clarify the circumstances under which certain kinds of serious criminal convictions will prevent even section 212(c) relief.[29]

Moreover, these forms of relief remain discretionary with the Attorney General, a feature whose implications have probably received too little attention. The exercise of this discretionary power has long been delegated to the immigration judges. Court review, however, is often highly intrusive, even though the Supreme Court has issued several rulings seemingly meant to require the circuit courts to defer to the BIA.[30] Is court review worthwhile, particularly when it seems so often to tend toward highly intrusive nit-picking? Because of the discretionary nature of these remedies and the rather hazy standards that govern their reward, there is no clear right or wrong answer on each individual's application. Do we really need to subject such dispensing of administrative grace to full-scale judicial review? Of course, the answer depends greatly on the degree of confidence we have in the administrators whose judgments will hold complete sway if the courts are dropped from the process. Perhaps the recent reconstituting of the BIA as a twelve-member body provides a fitting occasion for Congress to confine review of the denial of discretionary relief (save asylum) to the BIA, taking that function away from the courts. Such an amendment would give us a system more like Canada's, where a decision by the Minister of Citizenship and Immigration to grant or withhold "humanitarian and compassionate" relief is essentially immune to judicial review (Stobo 1993, 388; Marrocco and Goslett 1995, 66, 74).

Create Better Incentives for Early Cooperation and Truth-telling

The current system, as is evident, provides too few incentives for the Olivers of the undocumented world to cooperate after they are apprehended. In virtually every case, it was to Oliver's advantage to defy the agency, resist cooperation, and call the agency's bluff, because the INS usually has been unable to impose the sanctions appropriate to such manipulation. The problem is endemic: this largely indigent group of undocumented deportation respondents is essentially immune to monetary penalties,[31] while criminal punishment is extremely costly and cumbersome, not usually worthwhile for garden-variety noncooperation on the part of a noncriminal deportable alien. These facts leave little foundation for improving the incentive structure, but a couple of possibilities may be worth pursuing. First, aliens who show early cooperation by departing promptly after apprehension could receive a modest stipend to help them get back on their feet after returning home. Some European countries have used assisted return schemes, with decidedly mixed success.[32] What is contemplated here, however, is more modest, and it would respond to the real needs of someone facing a transition to life in another country after years away. The political moment seems exactly wrong for what could be dismissed as paying lawbreakers to do what all others must do for free: abide by the law. Nevertheless, if such a scheme actually saved the government money in the long run, a hard-headed economic case might be made for its adoption. Well-designed pilot projects could be chartered in certain INS districts, with congressional authorization, in order to test whether assistance would improve overall enforcement while reducing detention expenses.

A second form of incentive is also possible. Aliens who fail without excuse to honor a final order of deportation or a voluntary departure agreement to which they had consented might be permanently barred from any future immigration benefit rather than being subjected to the rather toothless five-year ban now in place (INA §242B [e]). This result would be similar to what some districts now achieve through tough-minded use of INA §274C, the document fraud provision that carries with it lifetime excludability. The version proposed here, however, would be better tailored to achieve results more closely proportioned to the gravity of an alien's misbehavior. The ban of section 274C often falls on those who in desperation or ignorance decided, without any possible contact or warning from the formal immigration system, to make use of a bogus document. In contrast, the sanction sketched here would apply only to those who had at least been served with an OSC bearing such a warning, and in most cases only to those who were present when the deportation order was issued and there received a carefully designed warning to this effect from the IJ. Of course, this sanction has teeth only for those aliens who believe they might someday have the basis for other immigration benefits. Such aliens represent only a fraction of the total class of those who become subject to final orders, but the fraction is nonetheless significant.

Structural reforms like those sketched here can make real contributions toward improved enforcement. But there is no magic bullet that will make effective enforcement cheap. No structural changes will obviate the need for the central ingredient: additional detention and deportation resources on a highly significant scale.

---

*The work on this paper was virtually complete before the author took office as general counsel of the Immigration and Naturalization Service in August 1995. In any case, the opinions expressed herein are solely those of the author and do not necessarily represent the position of the INS, the Department of Justice, or the U.S. government. Moreover, the paper does not reflect the substantial changes to U.S. immigration laws enacted on September 30, 1996 in the *Illegal Immigration Reform and Immigrant Responsibility Act of 1996,* some of which parellel suggestions tendered here.

Notes

1. After several decades of civil rights efforts, in the 1990s it is generally not acceptable to blame economic setbacks on immigrants or to incite animosity toward all foreign-born; this attitude is in sharp contrast to earlier recessionary periods in American history (Higham 1988) and to the situation in some European countries today. The recent versions of scapegoating and blame-mongering focus explicitly on illegal migrants, not all aliens, and thereby tap into a deep wellspring of support from a wider circle of Americans who are not xenophobic but are offended and upset by widespread lawbreaking.
2. If Oliver is not from Mexico or one of about a dozen other high-volume immigrant-sending countries, the diversity admission provisions of the Immigration and Nationality Act (INA), section 203(c), remain a possibility for eventual lawful status, but Oliver is unwilling to wait at home for the dicey results of that annual lottery. In any event, his earlier unlawful presence will not necessarily disqualify him if lightning should strike and he wins the drawing.
3. The INS announced in 1995 a process that would reduce the list of permissible documents to sixteen (U.S. Congress 1995b, 5).
4. In 1988 Congress also began a progressive tightening of the substantive and procedural provisions that apply to those convicted of serious offenses. That year it defined a new category of "aggravated felons" who are denied many forms of release and who are supposed to be detained throughout proceedings, with narrowly limited exceptions (INA §§101[a][43], 242[a][2], 242A). Later laws have greatly expanded the list of felonies considered to be "aggravated." For the latest expansion of that category, see the *Immigration and Nationality Technical Corrections Act of 1994*, amending INA §101 (a) (43). In April 1996 Congress adopted a host of additional restrictions on criminal aliens in the *Antiterrorism and Effective Death Penalty Act (AEDPA)*. Further restrictions (and possible modifications of *AEDPA*) were pending in major immigration reform legislation that had passed each chamber in 1996 but had not been reconciled as of this writing.
5. Serious criminal activity will make virtually any alien deportable, and proof of the criminal conviction does not require elaborate fact-finding by the IJ. Even so, criminal aliens may have some alternative defenses to raise, principally (if they were admitted as lawful permanent residents (LPRs) and have lived here seven years) relief under INA §212(c). (In April 1996 *AEDPA* restricted section 212(c) relief so greatly as to render it virtually unavailable.)
6. Statutory changes in 1994 streamlined the process still further for criminal aliens. The INS now has authority to issue deportation orders against non-LPR aliens convicted of a crime without taking the case before an immigration judge, albeit with certain remaining safeguards (INA §242A[b], as amended by the *Violent Crime Control and Law Enforcement Act of 1994*, §130004, 2026–27). And Congress granted federal judges the authority to issue deportation orders at the time of passing sentence on alien offenders (INA §241[a][2][A], as amended by the *Immigration and Nationality Technical Corrections Act of 1994*).

7. The Justice Department estimated in 1990 that as many as 20 percent of the 600,000 federal and state prisoners were potentially deportable aliens (GAO 1992, 38).
8. IJs have authority to redetermine the bond amount initially set by the INS. Owing to a sharp "value dissensus" between these two Justice Department units, IJs also frequently reduce the amount substantially, for reasons independent of detention shortages (Gilboy 1988, 566).
9. The specified defaults include failure to appear for deportation hearings or asylum hearings and failure to show up for deportation or to depart when granted the privilege of voluntary departure (INA §242B[e]).
10. After apprehension under the authority of a deportation order issued in absentia, an alien can move to reopen the proceedings to present any claim that the notice was defective or that he or she meets the rigorous statutory exception for "exceptional circumstances" (INA §242B[c][3]). The statute allows motions based on an "exceptional circumstances" claim only within 180 days of the order's issuance, but it imposes no time limit on inadequate notice claims.
11. See INA §244, which allows "suspension of deportation" on a discretionary basis for aliens, even those who entered clandestinely, who have been physically present for seven years, possess good moral character, and can show that deportation would work extreme hardship on them or a close family member who is a citizen or LPR. Changes made by section 414 of the *AEDPA*, however, appear likely to foreclose suspension to those who enter without suspension.
12. All such papers are temporary, and the regulation provided that permission under this section was available only until the issuance of a final order of deportation. But INS officers speculate that with a bona fide work authorization (Employment Authorization Document, or EAD, Form I-688A), an alien could go to other state or federal authorities and receive genuine documents listed on the I-9, such as driver's licenses or social security cards, that would not be provisional. From that point on, without committing document fraud, the alien could always satisfy any new employer's demand for work authorization papers, even if the EAD itself (never shown to the employer) had long since expired. In part because of this problem, the Social Security Administration began in 1992 to issue specially designated cards to people with limited work authorization (*Federal Register* 57 [1992]: 28872).
13. These proceedings have sometimes been carried out telephonically, and the INS is now experimenting with systems that would permit video teleconferencing. Such procedures allow for conducting the relatively straightforward master calendar proceedings without having to incur the costs of moving either the alien (especially detained aliens, for whom INS must pick up the transportation tab) or the immigration judges.
14. OSCs must, by statute, advise about counsel rights and be accompanied by lists of pro bono counsel in the district. In theory, this written advisal could possibly justify requiring a plea at the first master calendar appearance, even if an alien is unrepresented, but in practice IJs allow at least one continuance, and sometimes several, for this purpose.
15. If the INS charges entry without inspection, it must still prove by clear and convincing evidence the basic elements of the charge. Proving a negative (the absence of inspection) could be quite difficult, but for the operation of

a helpful and soundly conceived statutory presumption. INA §291 requires the alien to prove the time, place, and manner of entry, but it gives him or her the right to have access to visa and inspection documents to carry this burden of proof, thus protecting a validly inspected alien who has lost the documents memorializing this fact. In order to protect against misuse of this procedure against citizens, practice has long required the INS first to carry the burden of proving that the deportation respondent is in fact an alien (Aleinikoff, Martin, and Motomura 1995, 613–16).

16. For a description of suspension under INA §244(a)(1), see n. 11, above. Waiver of deportation under section 212(c) is available, in essence, only to people admitted for lawful permanent residence more than seven years earlier, and, by the terms of this section, a few deportation grounds are not waivable. Other than this seven-year domicile requirement (far more exacting than the physical presence requirement in section 244[a][1]), section 212(c) imposes no real eligibility criteria, but practice in the exercise of discretion suggests that extreme hardship and moral character remain important factors for those seeking to obtain relief (Yale-Loehr 1995, 8–9).

17. Criminal defendants, of course, may plead "not guilty" no matter what their attorneys' honest assessment of their guilt or innocence. But deportation proceedings are considered civil proceedings, and it is a fair question whether an attorney could be disciplined for filings that lack a good-faith foundation in fact or law.

18. Oliver and others might not care about the prospect of future disabilities if a sham marriage is exposed (INA §§204[a][2], 204[c]), but prospective coconspirators (sham U.S. citizen spouses) may well be deterred by the greatly expanded criminal penalties Congress enacted in 1986: up to five years in prison and $250,000 in fines (INA §275[b]).

19. This description of a bad man's use of asylum is not meant to disparage the efforts of numerous aliens and their counsel to present good-faith asylum claims, even when these are not filed until deportation proceedings are already under way.

20. "Affirmative claims" (roughly 140,000 of which were filed in FY 1993 and a like number again in FY 1994) are those submitted by aliens against whom no proceedings are pending. Until 1995 such claims would first be heard by INS asylum officers in nonadversarial interview settings; the officers would issue full decisions granting or denying such claims. Those denied could refile if they were ever brought into deportation proceedings. The immigration judge would then hear the claim de novo. Bad-man aliens not known to the INS would have incentives to file ill-founded asylum claims because, until the changes in 1995, affirmative asylum applicants routinely obtained work authorization documents upon application, permission that could last for years, owing to enormous backlogs in the asylum system. The 1995 changes are designed to improve productivity through significant streamlining, to lead to swift issuance of OSCs against applicants with weak or bad-faith asylum claims, and to withhold work authorization for a minimum of 180 days. Work authorization is ruled out altogether for applicants whose cases make it to the point of final denial by an immigration judge within 180 days. Major additions of resources to the system, doubling the asylum officer corps and providing a nearly comparable increase in immigration judges, are also helping to work a major change in the incen-

tive structure (Martin 1995). The new system took effect in January 1995. Affirmative claims in calendar year 1995 declined to 53,000 from 123,000 the previous calendar year (not counting claims filed under the special terms of a 1991 class-action settlement).

21. IJs also lack contempt powers and must initiate highly cumbersome disciplinary proceedings (8 C.F.R. §292.3) even against attorneys found in open court to be engaging in dilatory, fraudulent, or other improper practices.

22. There are signs that this practice is ending. Entrepreneurs who make a profit from peddling bogus documents and advice have recently been targeted for more systematic federal investigation and prosecution. Dramatic accounts of the conviction and sentencing of some big-time operators have recently appeared in the press (Miller 1995; O'Connor 1995).

23. The INS has tried to apply the civil fines provision outside the context of false documents presented for exmployment—for example, to sanction people involved in placing false information on INS application forms. But two 1995 decisions by the chief administrative hearing officer of the Department of Justice, reversing earlier ALJ decisions, have greatly limited this use of §274C (*United States v. Remileh*, 5 O.C.A.H.O. 724 (1995); *United States v. Noorealam*, 5 O.C.A.H.O. 797 (1995); *Interpreter Releases* 1995, 319; Levy 1994, 6).

24. The BIA has also tried to dispose of meritless appeals more expeditiously by summary dismissal of those that fail to indicate with some precision, in either the appeal notice or a later brief, exactly what errors are alleged in the IJ's decision (Matter of Valencia, *Immigration and Naturalization Decisions* 19 [1986]: 354–56 [BIA]). The courts have given this new strictness a mixed reception.

25. The stay is theoretically subject to vacation on INS application to the court, but the INS never applies in ordinary deportation cases. Since 1990, however, aliens who have been found guilty of aggravated felonies, as defined in INA §101(a)(43), are not entitled to automatic stays. Few such aliens receive discretionary stays from the reviewing court, with the net result that they are removed from the country before their appeals are heard. Under the curious provisions of INA §106(c), aliens who have left the country, even under INS compulsion, are thereafter disqualified from pursuing judicial review (Aleinikoff, Martin, and Motomura 1995, 953–57).

26. Until 1996, an aggravated felony conviction, for example, wholly precluded asylum and related forms of protection (INA §§208[d], 243 [h][2]). In 1996, however, *AEDPA* §413 added a new INA §243(h)(3) providing that this preclusion may be overridden where necessary to comply with international refugee treaties.

27. Asylum claimants with a credible basis for the claim should, of course, be excepted from such a return requirement until all appeals have been exhausted. I have spelled out a tentative version of this proposal in greater detail elsewhere (Martin 1987, 816–19).

28. This proposal is sometimes known as the "bring your toothbrush option." Respondents appearing for the IJ hearing would know that if their defenses or claims for relief did not succeed, they should be prepared to remain in INS custody from that point on. (IJs usually deliver their opinions orally from the bench at the close of deportation proceedings, perhaps after a short recess.)

29. The immigration reform bills passed by the House and Senate in early 1996 contained these sorts of modest reforms to the relief sections, including a provision ending the accrual of the residence period after issuance of a charging document. But in the meantime the *Antiterrorism and Effective Death Penalty Act*, enacted 24 April 1996, virtually eliminated relief under section 212(c) and also made entrants without inspection ineligible for suspension as of 1 November 1996. Whether these severe restrictions will be undone by the final version of the immigration reform bills is not known at the time of this writing.
30. Compare, e.g., *INS v. Wang* (450 U.S. 139 [1981]), with *Ravancho v. INS* (658 F.2d 169 [3d Cir. 1981]).
31. Undocumented aliens do often earn money at a decent wage. The problem instead is where they keep those assets, often not in the kinds of bank accounts or real property easily subject to levy. Moreover, a great many undocumented migrants remit much of their earnings to their families in their home countries, often through informal channels that are not easily traced. But the fact remains that relatively little is known about these matters. It may be that the new seriousness about immigration enforcement will require enhanced efforts to find ways to collect in these circumstances.
32. The United States used a limited form of such assistance to encourage Haitians to return home from their Guantánamo "safe haven" after President Aristide was restored to power. Most of the Haitians repatriated willingly in fall 1994, shortly after the junta's removal. Later, 670 volunteered to return before 5 January 1995, the cutoff date, in return for the eighty-dollar stipend the U.S. government was then offering. These departures left 3,900 to be repatriated involuntarily. (*Refugee Reports* 1994, 1; ibid. 1995, 5–6).

References

Aleinikoff, Thomas Alexander, David A. Martin, and Hiroshi Motomura. 1995. *Immigration: Process and Policy*. 3d ed. St. Paul: West.

Antiterrorism and Effective Death Penalty Act (AEDPA), Pub. L. No. 104-132, 110 Stat. 1214 (1996).

Calavita, Kitty. 1990. "Employer Sanctions Violations: Towards a Dialectical Model of White-Collar Crime." *Law and Society Review* 24: 1041–69.

Eaton, Joseph W. 1986. *Card-Carrying Americans: Privacy, Security, and the National ID Card Debate*. Totowa, N.J.: Rowman and Littlefield.

Fix, Michael. *The Paper Curtain: Employer Sanctions' Implementation, Impact, and Reform.* Washington, D.C.: Urban Institute, 1991.

Fix, Michael, and Jeffrey S. Passel. 1994. *Immigration and Immigrants: Setting the Record Straight.* Washington, D.C.: Urban Institute.

Gilboy, Janet A. 1988. "Administrative Review in a System of Conflicting Values." *Law and Social Inquiry* 13: 515–79.

Harwood, Erwin. 1986. *In Liberty's Shadow: Illegal Aliens and Immigration Law Enforcement.* Stanford: Hoover Institution.

Hathaway, James C. 1988. "Selective Concern: An Overview of Refugee Law In Canada." *McGill Law Journal* 33: 676–715.

Hernandez, Marita. 1988. "INS Reports 'Dramatic' Rise in Fake Work Papers." *Los Angeles Times*, 17 Nov., sec. 2, 1.

Higham, John. 1988. *Strangers in the Land: Patterns of American Nativism, 1860–1925.* New Brunswick: Rutgers University Press.

Holmes, Oliver Wendell. 1897. "The Path of the Law." *Harvard Law Review* 10: 457–78.

Immigration and Nationality Act of 1952. Pub. L. No. 82-414, ch. 477, 66 Stat. 163 (1952) (codified and amended at 8 U.S.C. §§1101–1524, current to 1 July 1995).

Immigration and Nationality Technical Corrections Act of 1994. Pub. L. No. 103-416, §222, 108 Stat. 4305 (1994).

Interpreter Releases: Report and Analysis of Immigration and Nationality Law. 1996. Vol. 73. Washington, D.C.: Federal Publications.

_____. 1995. Vol. 72. Washington, D.C.: Federal Publications.

_____. 1994. Vol. 71. Washington, D.C.: Federal Publications.

King, Peter H. 1991. "Yet Another Roadside Attraction." *Los Angeles Times*, 26 Nov., A1.

Levy, Daniel. 1994. "A Practitioner's Guide To Section 274C: Parts I and II." *Immigration Briefings* 94, nos. 6 and 7.

McDonnell, Patrick, and Jess Bravin. 1988. "Some Employers OK Illegal Aliens' Fake Work Papers, Study Shows." *Los Angeles Times*, 14 Jan., 2:1.

Maggio, Michael. 1993 "Exclusion and Deportation Practice Advisory: Burden of Proof Basics." *AILA Monthly Mailing*, Dec., 940–41.

Marrocco, Frank N., and Henry M. Goslett. 1995. *The 1996 Immigration Act of Canada.* Ontario: Carswell.

Martin, David A. 1995. "Making Asylum Policy: The 1994 Reforms." *Washington Law Review* 70: 725.

_____. 1987. "Mandel, Cheng Fan Kwok and Other Unappealing Cases: The Next Frontier of Immigration Reform." *Virginia Journal of International Law* 27: 803–19.

Meyer, Josh. 1991. "Fake Green Card Ring was Largest in U.S." *Los Angeles Times*, 28 Sept., B1.

Miller, Bill. 1995. "INS Cracks Down on Immigration Fraud for Profit; Consultants Who Falsify Documents, Arrange Phony Marriages Are Target of Federal Probes." *Washington Post*, 15 Jan., A8.

O'Connor, Matt. 1995. "Bride Left Standing at Altar after INS Spoils Wedding; Something Borrowed Turns Out to Be Agent." *Chicago Tribune*, 5 May, 1.

Ostrow, Ronald J. 1995. "Clinton Seeks Funds to Curb Illegal Hirings." *Los Angeles Times*, 5 Feb., A1.

Refugee Reports. 1994. Vol. 15 (Dec.).

_____. 1995. Vol. 16 (Jan.).

Smyser, W. R. 1987. *Refugees: Extended Exile*. New York: Praeger.

Stobo, Gerald H. 1993. "The Canadian Refugee Determination System." *Texas International Law Journal* 29: 383–425.

U.S. Congress. 1994. House Judiciary Subcommittee on International Law, Immigration and Refugees. Testimony of Doris Meissner, 5 Oct.

_____. 1995a. House Judiciary Subcommittee on Immigration and Claims. Testimony of James A. Puleo, 24 Feb.

_____. 1995b. House Judiciary Subcommittee on Immigration and Claims. Testimony of James A. Puleo, 3 Mar.

_____. 1995c. House Judiciary Subcommittee on Immigration and Claims. Testimony of T. Alexander Aleinikoff, 23 Mar.

U.S. Congress. 1996. Senate Appropriations Subcommittee on Commerce, Justice and State. Testimony of Doris Meissner, 9 May.

U. S. Department of Justice. 1995. *INS Fact Book: Summary of Recent Immigration Data*. Document no. M-338. Washington, D.C.: U.S. Department of Justice, June.

_____. 1994a. *INS Fact Book: Summary of Recent Immigration Data*. Document no. M-338. Washington, D.C.: U.S. Department of Justice, June.

_____. 1994b. *1993 Statistical Yearbook of the Immigration and Naturalization Service*. Document no. M-367. Washington, D.C.: U.S. Department of Justice, Sept.

U. S. General Accounting Office. 1992. *Immigration Control: Immigration Policies Affect INS Detention Efforts*. Document no. 92-85. Washington, D.C.: GAO, June.

_____. 1989. *Immigration Control: Deporting and Excluding Aliens From The United States*. Document no. GGD 90-18. Washington, D.C.: GAO, Oct. 1989.

Violent Crime Control and Law Enforcement Act of 1994, Pub. L. No. 103-322, 108 Stat. 1796 (1994).

Yale-Loehr, Stephen. 1995. "An Overview Of INA §212(c)." *Immigration Briefings* 95, no. 2: 1.

Chapter 2

Internal Controls and Actual Removals of Deportable Aliens
The Current Legal Situation in the Federal Republic of Germany

Hans-Joachim Cremer

The Scope of Application of the German Aliens Act

The current Law on the Entry and Sojourn of Aliens in the Territory of the Federal Republic of Germany (Gesetz über die Einreise und den Aufenthalt von Ausländern im Bundesgebiet: Ausländergesetz; henceforward AuslG)[1] entered into force on 1 January 1991.[2] Its regulations concern aliens *(Ausländer)* as defined by § 1 (2) as every person who is not a German in the sense of Article 116 (1) of the Basic Law.[3] Thus the AuslG largely applies to any person who is niether of German nationality nor has, whether as an ethnic German or as the spouse or descendant of such a German, been admitted to the territory of the German Reich as it existed at the date of 31 December 1937; nor is the descendant of such a person.[4] In short—and with the roughness of all summaries—aliens generally are all non-nationals and stateless persons. Exempted from the scope of the AuslG are certain persons who, according to the general rules of international law or to specific provisions of international treaties, enjoy certain diplomatic or consular privileges

Notes for this chapter begin on page 87.

(see AuslG § 2[1]). Modifications of the general regulations laid down in the AuslG are made by the Law on Entry and Sojourn of Nationals of the Member States of the European Economic Community (Residence Law/EEC)[5], the intention of which is to adapt German national law to the prescriptions of the law of the European Union (cf. AuslG § 2 (2)). Even without national legislation, the law of the European Union may have a direct impact on the German legal order.[6] Further modifications of the regulations of the AuslG are made by the Law on the Procedure in Asylum Cases (Asylverfahrensgesetz; henceforward AsylVfG).[7]

To begin, however, it is advisable to set aside all the possible exemptions and modifications mentioned above and instead to take a look at the rules applying in general to the internationally nonprivileged, non-European Union alien.

Internal Controls of Aliens

Controls Before and on Entry

The Basic Rule: Residence Permit Required for Entry

In principle, every alien needs a residence permit in order to enter the territory of the FRG and to reside therein (AuslG § 3 [1], sentence 1).

Exceptions

The Federal Ministry of the Interior has the power, by ordinance principally requiring the consent of the Bundesrat (Federal Council)[8], to make exemptions from this rule.[9]

The residence of an alien who is not required to possess a residence permit can, however, be subject to a time limit or made dependent on certain conditions or requirements.[10] At the expiration of the time limit or after failing to fulfill the fixed conditions or requirements, the alien loses the privilege of not having to possess a residence permit.

Residence Permits in the Form of Visas

In the normal case of a residence permit being required, the permit, as a rule, must be acquired, in the form of a visa, before the alien enters the country. This provision of AuslG § 3 (3), sentence 1, has no precedent in the Ausländergesetz of 1965, which was replaced by the present Ausländergesetz in 1991. Its intention is to improve the control of foreigners entering the country.

Visas are issued by the diplomatic missions and consular agencies authorized to do so by the Federal Foreign Office (AuslG § 63[3]). This allows external control of aliens wishing to enter the country. But, again, the Federal Ministry of the Interior can release an ordinance permitting aliens to obtain residence permits directly from the national aliens' office[11] before or even after their entry (a visa for entry then not being required) (AuslG § 3[3]). The validity of such an ordinance, however, principally[12] depends on consent by the Bundesrat. The ministry has made use of this power in §§ 9 and 10 of the Ordinance for the Execution of the Aliens Act (Verordnung zur Durchführung des Ausländergesetzes; hereafter DVAuslG).[13] Unsurprisingly, the extent of such exemption from the requirement of visas reduces the tightness of controls before and on entry.

Recently, the Treaty of Maastricht[14] entered into force, establishing a framework of cooperation in various matters of justice and home affairs, including asylum, border control, and immigration policies (Arts. K through K.9) and introducing Article 100c into the Treaty on the European Community (formerly the European Economic Community). This provision empowers the Council of Ministers to define those non-EU states whose nationals are required to possess valid visas for crossing the external borders of the EU/EC member states. The council can act only on a proposal of the commission and after consulting the European Parliament. Before 1 January 1996, the council's decisions required unanimity;[15] since then a qualified majority, as defined by Article 148 (2), is sufficient (Art. 100c[3], sentence 1). But even before that date the council, by a qualified vote to be taken on the proposal of the commission and after consultation with the European Parliament, is to issue the acts necessary for the introduction of a standardized visa form (Art. 100c [3], sentence 2).[16]

Warding Off Attempts of Illegal Entry

Any foreigner who attempts to enter the country illegally will be rejected at the border (AuslG § 60[1]).[17] The AuslG considers this to be a case of nonadmission rather than removal of an alien.[18] The reasoning behind this view is that since the territory of the FRG may in general be entered only at an official border-crossing point (AuslG § 59[1]), a foreigner arriving at such a crossing point, according to the legal definition given in AuslG § 59 (2), has not entered the country until having both crossed the border and passed through the official border-crossing point.

Still, the decision of the border control officers is the first instance at which—apart from the process of issuing visas abroad—actual control over aliens can be exercised. To understand the extent of such control one must have a look at the definition of illegal entry given by the Ausländergesetz.

Illegal Entry

Aliens enter the territory of the FRG illegally if they do not possess a residence permit or a passport required by law or—save for some specific exceptions—they have before been expelled or deported by the German authorities, their entry and sojourn in the country hence being forbidden according to AuslG § 8 (2).[19]

I have already touched on the question of whether a residence permit is needed; I cannot answer this in detail in this context because it depends not only on the nationality of the given foreigner but also on the intent and duration of stay (see DVAuslG § 1–4, 6–8).

The requirement of a valid passport for entry and sojourn is set up as a principle in AuslG § 4 (1). By an ordinance requiring the consent of the Bundesrat, however, the Federal Ministry of the Interior can exempt aliens whose return (to their home countries or their countries of former residence) is secured from the duty of possessing a passport; it may also introduce or accept other official papers of identification as substitutes for passports.[20]

Aliens arriving at a border-crossing point, whose entry into the country is to be allowed, must submit to identification measures if doubts arise as to their identities or nationalities (AuslG § 41[1] and [4]). In the absence of other equally efficient and readily accessible sources of identification, certain methods applied in criminal prosecution may be permissible in the light of constitutional law and expressly allowed by AuslG § 41 (2). These include taking photographs and fingerprints and measuring and physically examining the people concerned, even against their will.[21] These means can be resorted to even more readily when foreigners attempt to pass border checkpoint, or even succeed in doing so, with forged passports or forged substitute passport documents, or when, having been denied admission or having been removed from the territory before, they again try to enter the country illegally (AuslG § 41[3]). The Federal Bureau of Criminal Investigation (Bundeskriminalamt) assists the aliens' offices in evaluating the information gained by such investigations (AuslG § 78[1] and [2]). The information can be used in criminal prosecution and for the protection of public security (§ 78[3]; AuslG § 78[4] makes it compulsory to delete all such files and information after use in certain cases).

Developments under the Second Treaty of Schengen

Certain changes have recently been brought about by the so-called Second Treaty of Schengen,[22] the Treaty of 19 June 1990 on the Execution of the First Treaty of Schengen,[23] which has entered into force for Belgium, Germany, France,[24] Luxembourg, and the Netherlands, as well as for Spain and Portugal,[25] on 26 March 1995 (final communiqué of the session of the Schengen Executive Committee of 22 Dec. 1994, in Bonn, *Bulletin der Bundesregierung*, no. 3 [13 Jan. 1995]: 16). The treaty defines as internal borders the common borders between the parties to the treaty, as well as their air- and seaports as far as direct routes between the states are concerned. All other borders, air-, and seaports are considered to be external borders (Art. 1; but see Art. 4[4]). In principle, internal borders may—with certain exceptions for reasons of public order or national security—be crossed at any point without there being border controls of persons (Art. 2[1] and [2]). Only external borders may be crossed only at specified border-crossing points and at fixed traffic hours (Art. 3[1]). Only people entering the territory of the parties to the treaty via the external borders—i.e., from nonparticipating states—are subject to border controls.[26] Such people are to be dealt with by the contracting state they first enter when crossing the external borders. Any non-EU citizen is allowed to transit to a participating state that has issued him or her a residence permit or a reentry visa, unless she or he is being searched for "denial of admission" (Art. 5[3]). An important feature of the treaty is that it requires participating states to tighten controls at the external borders;[27] this may prove to be one of the most difficult tasks of Schengen since it could lead to a painful slowdown of border traffic with third states.[28]

Participating states strive to harmonize their visa policies vis-à-vis nationals of non-EU states (Art. 9; cf. Art. 1's definition of *Drittausländer*).[29] As a result, they have agreed to introduce a uniform visa that is to be valid for up to three months in the territories of all contracting states (Art. 10 (1)).[30] The competence to issue such a visa is to rest with the diplomatic or consular offices of the contracting state that is to be the main destination of travel, or, if that state is indefinable, the contracting state to be entered first (Art. 12[1] and [2]).

Visas for entry and sojourn of non-EU citizens whose validity exceeds three months are issued by the participating states as national visas according to their respective national laws. The bearer of such a visa who meets the requirements for permission of entry (Art. 5), however, is entitled to travel through any other participating state in order to enter the issuing state (Art. 18). Furthermore, aliens possessing a valid residence permit issued by one of the contracting states are, under certain easily met conditions, permitted to move freely in the territories of all other contracting states for a period of up to three months (Art. 21[1]).[31] Finally, foreigners from third states who are exempt from the duty of possessing a visa can also travel freely in any of the participating states' territories for up to three months within the first half year after their entry into one of the participating states (Art. 20).

The resulting relaxation of border controls is to be balanced by the participating states' cooperation in the field of police and public security (Arts. 39–91).[32] An important foundation on which this cooperation is to rest is an automated international network of information (the Schengen Information System [SIS], Arts. 92–119).[33] Within this system a contracting state has the possibility to put a person's name on a "wanted persons" list if that person is wanted for extradition (Art. 95) or, as a national of a third-party (i.e., non-EU) state, is "wanted for denial of admission" because he or she is a threat to public security and order in the contracting state (Art. 96; see also Art. 5 [3]). Should any contracting state intend to grant a residence permit to a foreigner "wanted for denial of admission" by another contracting state, it must beforehand consult the state denying admission, and it shall allow the person's entry and sojourn only for important reasons, especially of a humanitarian nature or resulting from international obligations (Art. 25[1]). Similarly, when the state on whose "wanted persons" list an alien's name stands finds that another contracting state has issued him or her a residence permit, it contacts the issuing state in order to learn if there are sufficient grounds for the revocation of the permit (Art. 25[2]).

The information system is also to contain data on missing persons or persons who are to be detained for reasons of public or their own personal security (Art. 97), witnesses and defendants in criminal cases who must appear before court, people on whom an order of detention is to be served (Art. 98), and, finally, persons or vehicles wanted for secret registration or for ad hoc controls according to the national law of the controlling state (Art. 99).

It should be mentioned that, within the framework of the EU, the commission—reacting to proceedings brought before the Court of the European Communities under Article 175 of the Treaty on the European Community—has made proposals for EC directives, based on Arts. 49, 54 (2), 63 (2), and 100 of the Treaty on the European Community, aimed at granting foreign nationals of third-party (i.e., non-EU) states legally staying in any EU member state the freedom to travel in the territory of all other EU member states for up to three months and at abolishing controls of persons at the internal borders of the EU member states (proposals of 12 July 1995, COM [95] 346 final—95/0199, COM [95] 347 final—95/0201 [CNS], COM [95] 348 final—95/0202, and COM [95]). The desired result would be a system of personal freedom of movement quite similar to that under the Second Treaty of Schengen but including all EU member states, which the commission seems to regard as one of the final pieces completing the puzzle of the internal market (Art. 7a of the Treaty on the European Community). However, Great Britain does not stand alone within the EU in its reluctance to allow free transborder movement of persons (*Frankfurter Allgemeine Zeitung*, 13 July 1995, 5). As a result, it is likely that the directives will not be adopted by the Council of Ministers in the near future.

Controls During Sojourn

Control through Residence Permits and Notification of Residence to the Aliens' Office

Having entered the territory of the FRG aliens who are exempt from the requirement of a residence permit or who have valid visas generally need not contact the competent aliens' office (as long as their sojourns are legal and, especially, their visas have not expired). However, by federal ordinance,[34] these foreigners can be ordered to give notice of their presence to the aliens' office or any other authority defined by such ordinance (AuslG § 38; see DVAuslG § 2, 13).

Aliens who have merely been dispensed from acquiring residence permits before entry are obliged to apply for such permits immediately after entry or, if so provided in the ordinance exempting them from AuslG § 3 (3), within the deadline fixed (AuslG § 69[1], sentence 1).[35]

The aliens' offices exercise internal control over aliens wherever their residence permits or visas are valid for only a fixed period of time (see AuslG § 12[2], 19[2], 23[2], 28[2], and 34[1]). These people must apply for extensions before their permits expire. Only if they have made such applications are their sojourns considered to be permitted (see cases of AuslG § 69[3]) or tolerated (see cases of AuslG § 69[2]) after the date of expiration has arrived. This legal fiction protects them from having to leave the country or—more narrowly, in the case of mere fictitious toleration—from being deported. It lasts only until the aliens' office has decided on the application.

Identification

Foreigners staying in the territory of the FRG must be able to identify themselves to government authorities. In general, their passports are the means of identification required by law (see AuslG § 40). In case they neither possess nor can acquire passports by means acceptable to them, certificates of their residence permits or grants of toleration are considered sufficient proof of identification if they contain information as to the identity of the bearer and a photograph (AuslG § 39[1]).

DVAuslG § 25[36] lays down certain duties concerning identification documents: in sum, every alien must make sure that he or she possesses the legally required papers of identification that are valid and immediately updated in cases of change. These obligations do not exceed those placed on every German citizen living in the FRG.

Foreigners are under a duty to present or temporarily surrender their papers of identification to the competent government authorities insofar as this is necessary to execute or safeguard measures under the Ausländergesetz (AuslG § 40[1]). They need not constantly carry their identification documents with them, but they must be able to produce them within a reasonable space of time (Kanein and Renner 1993, AuslG § 40, 153 n. 2). Failure to do so constitutes a regulatory (not a criminal) offense (AuslG § 93[2], no. 1), for which the alien can be fined.

When the identity or nationality of an alien is uncertain, she or he can be subjected to identification measures including, as already mentioned, those used in criminal prosecution if a residence permit is intended to be issued, or if the alien is to be tolerated despite the duty to depart, or if acts under the Ausländergesetz call for such investigation (AuslG § 41[1] and [4]).

Control through Data Compilation

General Registration Laws

All *Bundesländer* (singular: *Bundesland*), the constituent states of the FRG, have enacted *Meldegesetze*, laws concerning the registration of residence or domicile,[37] which the Ausländergesetz has not touched (Kanein and Renner 1993, AuslG § 38, 151 n. 2). And because of the "vertical" division of powers, these *Länder* laws cannot be touched: Article 75 (1), no. 5, of the Basic Law gives the federal legislature only the power to pass so-called framework laws (*Rahmenvorschriften* or *Rahmengesetze*). As such a law, the Melderechtsrahmengesetz (MRRG)[38] establishes binding guidelines that the *Länder* must follow in their legislation on this subject.[39] The rules of the *Länder*'s registration laws apply to every resident in their territories, irrespective of nationality.

An overview of the *Länder*'s registration laws is best given by sketching the Federal Framework Law on Registration. The aim of this law is to have every "resident" registered in order to be able to establish and prove the person's identity and residence or domicile (MRRG § 1[1]). To this end, certain data are to be collected by the registration offices, including, inter alia, the resident's name, date and place of birth, sex, marital and family status, nationality, other present and former (main or secondary) residences, and dates of taking up residence and moving (MRRG § 2).

Every person taking up a new residence must register with the competent registration office, and the registration office must be notified if the person moves (MRRG § 11[1] and [2]). The landlord or whoever allows a person to take up residence in his or her house or home must assist in registration (MRRG § 11[3], with duties being more closely defined in the *Länder*'s registration laws).[40]

The MRRG makes certain exceptions from the duty of registration.[41] The *Länder* can add other exceptions under the condition that the compilation of data on the people concerned is otherwise secured or that the duration of residence in these cases does not exceed two months (MRRG § 16[1]). If the *Länder* registration laws exempt residents staying at hotels and lodgings from registration duties, guests are required to fill in by hand and then sign registration forms; aliens have to identify themselves further vis-à-vis the manager or his or her representative by presenting a valid document of identification.[42] The registration forms must be collected and preserved for a certain space of time or transferred to the registration office (MRRG § 16[2]). The information thus gathered may be evaluated and used only for purposes of public security or of criminal prosecution and investigation into the fate of missing persons or casualties of accidents, unless federal law[43] or *Länder* law specifies otherwise (MRRG § 16[4]).[44]

A limited exchange of data among registration offices is possible (MRRG § 17; this exchange is known as *Rückmeldung*, "backup control"). More importantly, certain information can be given to other government authorities within the FRG as far as this is necessary for the fulfillment of the recipient's duties (MRRG § 18[1]). This allows the transfer of data to the aliens' offices, on their application, in order to assist their activities under the Ausländergesetz.[45]

The information thus transferable comprises, inter alia, the person's name(s), doctoral degree (if any), adopted name (as of a nun or a monk), pseudonym or pen name, addresses, date of taking up residence and moving, date and place of birth, sex, nationality, family status, and date and place of death. Furthermore, periodical data transfers can be instituted by federal or *Länder* statute (MRRG § 18[4]).

Special Tasks of the Registration Offices and Other Authorities

The Federal Ordinance on the Transfer of Data to the Aliens' Offices[46] puts the registration offices under further special obligations to pass data on to the aliens' offices without the latter's prior request. This information includes the information listed above but also goes beyond this, in that the registration office must give notice of, inter alia, every alien's registration and notification of changing residence, divorce or annulment of marriage, change of name, change of nationality or rectification of its registration, and the birth of an alien (AuslDÜV § 2).

Other public offices obliged to submit information to the aliens' offices ex officio are those dealing with nationality matters (especially concerning naturalization of aliens or loss of German nationality), the judicial authorities for the execution of criminal penalties, the offices of the public employment agencies (concerning matters of work permits, which, as a rule, every foreigner needs in order to be allowed to earn wages in Germany),[47] and the trade supervision offices (concerning trade licenses issued to aliens) (AuslDÜV §§ 3–6).

Additionally, in general, every government authority must immediately inform the competent aliens' office if it learns of an alien's staying in the country without the legally required residence permit or a grant of toleration, of any breach of a territorial restriction on legal sojourn, or any other reason for expulsion of an alien (AuslG § 76[2]).

Furthermore, the competent aliens' office is, as a rule, to be informed of every initiation or final disposal of proceedings against an alien conducted by the public prosecutor's offices, the criminal courts, and government authorities prosecuting regulatory offenses *(Ordnungswidrigkeiten);* it must also be informed of every introduction of extradition proceedings (AuslG § 76[4]). The material thus gathered is especially important for decisions on the expulsion of an alien (see AuslG §§ 45–48).

Collection of Information and Requests for Information by the Aliens' Offices

The Ausländergesetz also allows the aliens' offices themselves to collect and compile information as far as this is necessary for the execution of the Ausländergesetz, the rule being to acquire the information from the person concerned.[48] However, in the absence of this person's overriding personal interests to the contrary, AuslG § 75[2], sentence 2, allows information to be gained without his or her participation from basically every other German[49] or foreign government authority or any private source.

The Central Aliens Register

An important tool enabling internal controls is the Central Aliens Register, an information system operated by the Federal Office of Administration (Bundesverwaltungsamt) that contains data on around ten million aliens (Heyder 1994, 153 n. 1). Under the Gesetz über das Ausländerzentralregister (AZR-Gesetz)[50], this information system has been put on a new legal foundation. Its function is to support the work of public authorities dealing with the execution of the law on aliens or asylum seekers and asylees by collecting and transmitting data (AZR-Gesetz § 1).[51] However, the Bundesverwaltungsamt is not authorized to request or gather information directly from private individuals (Heyder 1994, 155). Instead, its Central Aliens Register serves as a central information pool.

The register consists of two files: The VISA File contains specific information on aliens applying for visas for Germany.[52] On request, the data is transmitted to the border police authorities, the Federal Office for the Recognition of Foreign Refugees (hereinafter mostly referred to as the Federal Office),[53] the federal and *Länder* Bureaus of Criminal Investigation (Bundes- und Landeskriminalämter), the federal and *Länder* Offices for the Protection of the Constitution (Verfassungsschutzbehörden), the Office for Military Counterintelligence (Militärischer Abschirmdienst), the Federal Intelligence Service (Bundesnachrichtendienst), and the courts and public prosecutor's offices (see AZR-Gesetz § 32).[54]

An alien can be registered in the second file, called the General File, when he or she has not merely taken up residence temporarily in the territory of the FRG or in any one of the cases listed in AZR-Gesetz § 2 (2), these being, inter alia, that the alien has applied for asylum; that he or she has received, or applied for, a residence permit; that any administrative decision (whether positive or negative) on his or her sojourn has been taken; that the alien is not to be allowed to enter the country; that his or her name has been put on a "wanted persons" list for rejection at the border[55] or for arrest[56] or establishment of his or her whereabouts;[57] that he or she is suspected of having committed certain severe crimes; and that he or she has been extradited or that his or her transit deportation has taken place (AZR-Gesetz § 2). The General File contains information concerning any of these, as well as on the name(s), pseudonyms, date and place of birth, sex, nationality, and family status of the alien; on his or her document(s) of identification, last residence in the state of departure, and the nationalities of his or her spouse; and on his or her arrival and departure, legal status of residence, and international or national refugee status (AZR-Gesetz § 3).

Public authorities dealing with matters of the laws on aliens, asylum seekers, and asylees are not only entitled to request information from the Central Aliens Register (AZR-Gesetz § 15)[58] but under certain conditions will also be allowed to extract this information via on-line connections for data transmission.[59] Apart from this electronic communication, when collected data concern an act of expulsion, deportation, or limitation or prohibition of political activities or contain arguments for denial of entry, the Bundesverwaltungsamt is to receive and keep in a separate file the written statement of reasons in each case (AZR-Gesetz § 6 [5]). On request, the Bundesverwaltungsamt will transmit these statements of reasons, under the condition that such information is indispensable to the requesting authority and cannot be gained in time from the authority from which it originates and that the relevant data to which the statements refer could themselves be transmitted to the requesting authority (AZR-Gesetz § 10[6]).[60]

In the context of internal controls and actual removals of aliens, search notices in the Central Aliens Register appear to be a useful tool (see Heyder 1994, 156). Any public authority can, when this is necessary to investigate the whereabouts of an alien, request such a search notice to be entered into the General File when the alien concerned is not in the territory of the FRG or his or her abode is unknown (AZR-Gesetz § 5[1]).[61]

Questions of Constitutionality

All these rules add up to quite a tight network of control over aliens.[62] In the light of Article 2 (1) in connection with Article 1 (1) of the Basic Law, such far-reaching competences to "scan" a person might well be criticized as unconstitutional, as the limits of compiling data do not always appear to be clearly defined.[63] In its jurisdiction, the Federal Constitutional Court has derived from the right to free development of one's personality and the inviolability of human dignity the right to "informational self-determination" (*Recht auf informationelle Selbstbestimmung*), thereby protecting individuals from having to disclose personal information to organs of the state and having to endure such information being evaluated and used by them (*BVerfGE* 65: 41–43). Limits to this right can be set by parliamentary statute, but such statute must clearly define the depth and range of the encroachment on informational self-determination to be suffered and must conform with the principle of proportionality (*BVerfGE* 65: 43–44; see Schmitt Glaeser 1989, 84–106). On the other hand, a state's right to internal self-determination, as part of its sovereignty under public international law, speaks in favor of a system of—moderate—control over aliens residing in its territory. It does not seem unfounded to argue that the Basic Law tacitly acknowledges this sovereign right of the state, with which the individual rights of the alien affected by the information system described above must be brought into a balance. Thus, while there is some justification for the network of data compilation, the informational self-determination of the individual, as part of constitutional law, demands equal respect and therefore "radiates" into the interpretation of the rules of the Ausländergesetz, which consequently must be read and handled in the light of this right.[64]

Control of Deportable Aliens

Special controls over aliens who are under the duty to leave the country or who have become deportable are covered in the next section.

Actual Removal of Deportable Aliens

The Duty to Leave the Territory of the FRG

Principle

According to AuslG § 42 (1) an alien is obliged to leave the territory of the FRG if he or she does not hold or no longer holds a "necessary"—i.e., legally required—residence permit. This obligation principally goes into effect at the very moment either an alien enters the territory of the FRG without possessing the necessary permission (cases of illegal entry and subsequent sojourn) or the residence permit of an alien legally residing in the territory expires or otherwise becomes invalid (cases of termination of legal status). In both groups of cases, the alien is, by law (but see AuslG § 69[3]), ipso facto under the duty to leave the country, with no administrative act being called for.

The Relevance of Administrative Acts

Administrative acts do, however, play an important role in connection with AuslG § 42 (1), for an administrative act may well activate the up-to-then dormant duty to leave the country by bringing AuslG § 42 (1) into effect.

One possibility is that the administrative act terminates the validity of a residence permit, whereby under AuslG § 42 (1) the alien becomes obliged to depart.[65] This is the case whenever the alien's right to stay depends on his or her possession of a residence permit, and this, as noted above, is the rule. However, as I have also noted, ordinances of the Ministry of the Interior can specify exemptions from this rule.

The residence of an alien who is not required to possess a residence permit can be subject to a time limit or made dependent on certain conditions or requirements (AuslG § 3[5]). At the expiration of the time limit or after failing to fulfill the fixed conditions or requirements, the alien loses the privilege of not having to possess a residence permit; therefore, if at this instance his or her sojourn is not backed up by a residence permit, AuslG § 42 (1) takes effect, obliging him or her to leave the country.

When a visa or a residence permit expires, AuslG § 42 (1) automatically orders the alien to leave unless he or she has some other right of sojourn. However, a special rule applies to aliens who have entered the country with visas issued with the consent of the national aliens' office or legally stayed in the territory of the FRG for more than six months. When such aliens apply for the issuance or prolongation of a residence permit, they ipso facto enjoy the (temporary) fiction of their sojourn being legal—despite any subsequent expiration of their visas or residence permits—until the aliens' office has decided on their applications.[66]

When this administrative decision denies a residence permit, it terminates the fiction of the legality of the respective alien's stay and activates the duty to depart.

The expulsion (*Ausweisung*)—in the narrow meaning given this term by the Ausländergesetz—is an administrative act that individually orders a single alien to leave the territory. It has the effect of eliminating any residence permit or right of sojourn granted without the requirement of a residence permit (AuslG § 44[1], no. 1, and [5], sentence 1).

The Enforceability of the Obligation to Depart

In order for the obligation to leave the territory of the FRG to come into existence, AuslG § 42 (1) only requires that the alien not or no longer hold a legally required residence permit. The Ausländergesetz, however, discerns between the existence of the obligation and its enforceability, for it more closely defines the content of the legal duty to leave the country only at the stage when it has become enforceable. Then the alien must depart without delay or, if a deadline has been fixed, by that deadline (AuslG § 42[3], sentence 1).[67]

The duty to depart is enforceable in three kinds of cases expressly listed in AuslG § 42 (2): (1) the alien has entered the territory of the FRG illegally; (2) the alien, after the expiration of his or her residence permit, has not yet applied for its prolongation or for the issuance of some other residence permit; and (3) the alien has failed to apply for the first grant of a necessary residence permit and the legally fixed time limit for such application has elapsed. In all other cases the duty to depart is enforceable if the refusal of a residence permit (again, see AuslG § 69, especially [3]) or any other administrative act through which the alien becomes obliged to leave the country—thus especially an act of expulsion—becomes enforceable.[68]

The enforceability of the obligation to depart is thus in most cases linked with the enforceability of the administrative act activating AuslG § 42 (1) in a single specific case. When speaking of the enforceability of an administrative act one must be aware of the procedural context: In general, an administrative act can be enforced after it has become noncontestable. Before court action can be taken, the person affected by an administrative act must—again as a rule—within one month file an objection at the administrative office having issued the act (§§ 68 and 70 of the Verwaltungsgerichtsordnung, or VwGO).[69] By this, a preliminary procedure of administrative control (*Widerspruchsverfahren*) is initiated suspending the enforceability of the administrative act concerned (VwGO § 80[1]). This suspensive effect (*aufschiebende Wirkung*) generally lasts throughout both the ensuing administrative and court procedures.

The result is that by resorting to these remedies an alien can prevent the enforceability of administrative acts terminating the legality of his or her residence and simultaneously suspend the enforceability of the duty to depart emanating from AuslG § 42 (1), under the condition that neither the authority issuing the act nor the authority competent to decide on the objection against the act has, for the public benefit, ordered the immediate execution of the act (VwGO § 80[2], no. 4). All this holds true especially for the act of expulsion (AuslG § 72 [2], sentence 1).

AuslG § 72 (1) makes an important exception to this rule, however: neither the filing of the objection nor the commencement of a court action has such suspensive effect on an administrative act denying the first grant or the prolongation of a residence permit.[70] In these cases only a court order can establish the suspensive effect of the objection or the filing of a suit before the administrative courts (VwGO § 80[5]).

Deportation

Principle

The enforcement of an alien's duty to depart is established by the means of deportation. The foreigner is removed from the territory of the FRG.[71]

Compulsory Deportation

AuslG § 49 (1) demands deportation of an alien who is under the obligation to leave the country if this obligation has become enforceable in the manner described above and if it does not appear certain that the duty to depart will be voluntarily fulfilled in compliance with AuslG § 42 (3) and (4) or if for reasons of public security or order the surveillance of the alien's departure appears necessary.

Voluntary departure is doubtful only if there are substantial grounds for believing that the alien will not leave the territory of the FRG and move on either to a non-EC state or—with the permission of such state—to an EC member state.[72] It is inadmissible for the authorities to presume generally that all aliens are unwilling to depart voluntarily. What is more, a deportation requires a well-founded prognosis that with a probability short of certainty *(mit an Sicherheit grenzender Wahrscheinlichkeit)* the alien concerned will not leave in time. Be that as it may, the alien is nonetheless obliged to forward proof of his or her intention to depart to the competent aliens' office (AuslG § 70[1]; see Kanein and Renner 1993, AuslG § 49, 201 n. 3).

AuslG § 49 (2) lists the cases in which the surveillance of an alien's departure is considered necessary by law, the first of these being that the alien, by judicial order, has been imprisoned or otherwise taken into public custody (Kanein and Renner 1993, AuslG § 49, 201 n. 5).[73] Six further grounds for the supervision of departure are expressly enumerated in AuslG § 49 (2), sentence 2; these comprise instances where the alien

- has failed to observe the time limit for departure;
- has been expelled according to AuslG § 47 (because of his or her criminal dangerousness);
- is impecunious;
- does not possess a passport;
- has, for the purpose of deception, made false declarations or refused to make statements to the aliens' office;[74] or
- has given cause to believe that he or she will not fulfill the obligation to leave.

In each of these instances the Ausländergesetz calls for a foreigner's deportation (Kanein and Renner 1993, AuslG § 49, 202 n. 8; Hailbronner 1995a, AuslG § 49, 7 n. 13). AuslG § 49 (2) does not, however, draw up a closed list of cases in which the supervision of an alien's departure is deemed necessary. Rather, the competent aliens' office may on its own conclude that it should supervise the alien's departure (which makes deportation compulsory) if, for example, the alien needs assistance to arrange for his or her departure, or if he or she poses a threat to others, be this due to insanity, or a contagious disease, or an inclination to violent behavior (Kanein and Renner 1993, AuslG § 49, 201 n. 4).

Making deportation compulsory is of special relevance in Germany as a federal state. The Ausländergesetz is a federal law. As a rule, the execution of federal laws rests with the *Länder*, the constituent states (Basic Law, Art. 83).[75] The Ausländergesetz, like the majority of federal laws, is executed by the *Länder* as a matter of their own concern (*Ausführung als eigene Angelegenheit*; Basic Law, Art. 84[1]). This means that the federal government's (*Bundesregierung*) control of the execution of these laws is restricted to supervision on points of law (*Rechtsaufsicht*; Basic Law, Art. 84[3], sentence 1).

By making the deportation of an alien a matter of legal obligation the Ausländergesetz, as a federal law, tries to ensure that the administrative authorities of the *Länder* do not differ in their executive practices. Differences could arise if deportation of illegal aliens were a matter of discretion that allowed the *Länder* to develop their own deportation policies.[76]

Stay of Deportation: Toleration

The Ausländergesetz acknowledges certain reasons for staying deportation and tolerating an alien despite his or her duty to depart. Toleration is obligatory as long as the alien's deportation is impossible for legal or factual reasons (AuslG § 55[2], alternative 1).[77]

Factual Impossibility of Deportation

Deportation can be considered impossible de facto when—as may especially be the case with stateless persons—public international law does not oblige any state to admit the alien and no state can be found that—although under no duty to do so—is willing to admit him or her. It hardly needs mentioning in this context that the general rules of public international law basically require a state only to admit its own nationals to its territory.[78]

Factual impossibility of deportation can also result when a means of transportation to the state of the alien's nationality, or to any other state willing to admit him, is unavailable because of war damage. Furthermore, the alien's true home state may be disinclined to receive him or her and may therefore challenge the alien's nationality, if only on a pretext. Or the alien may try to conceal his or her nationality (the press, for example, has reported cases of burned passports).

The FRG has entered into several agreements with its neighboring states to facilitate the return of aliens who either are nationals of neighboring states or have illegally entered the territory. These agreements set up a simplified procedure for returning such aliens (it need not occur at the diplomatic level). In addition, each participating state agrees to accept, when requested to receive a returnable alien, a reduced degree of proof either of the alien's being a national or of a foreign national or stateless person having entered the other party's territory across its borders.[79]

Legal Impossibility of Deportation

Cases of legal impossibility of deportation are first and foremost those listed in AuslG §§ 51 and 53 (see Kanein and Renner 1993, AuslG § 55, 223 n. 6).

AuslG § 51 (1) forbids the deportation of an alien into a country in which his/her life or freedom is threatened for reasons of race, religion, nationality,[80] membership of a particular social group or political opinion. AuslG § 51 (2), sentence 1, gives a legal definition of persons fulfilling these conditions that includes two categories of aliens: those who have been recognized as having the right of asylum according to Article 16a of the Basic Law and those who enjoy the status of (foreign) refugee within the territory of the FRG or who have, outside the territory of the FRG, been recognized as refugees under the Geneva Convention Relating to the Status of Refugees.[81] In all other cases, the Federal Office is the single administrative authority competent to decide whether an alien claiming to be persecuted for political reasons meets the requirements of AuslG § 51 (1) (AuslG § 51[2], sentence 2).[82]

AuslG § 53 acknowledges certain legal boundaries to deportation stemming from the situation the deportee would face in the state he or she would be forced to enter. These boundaries are of a largely relative nature; deportation is not banned on the whole. Instead, more narrowly, the specific state is excluded as the destination of a deportation. In other words, the alien can be legally deported to a state that is not banned by AuslG § 53 (or § 51).

Paragraphs 1 through 3 of AuslG § 53 enumerate absolute bans on states as states of deportation. According to these an alien must not be deported into a state

- in which there exists for this specific alien the concrete danger of being submitted to torture;
- in which the alien is wanted for a criminal offense that may be punished with death penalty;[83] or
- which has submitted a formal request for the extradition of the alien or has—in announcing that a formal request for extradition will follow—requested his or her detention pending extradition; in these cases, the law of extradition is given priority, in order to prevent an extradition in disguise that might circumvent existing legal barriers against the granting of extradition.

AuslG § 53 (4) also forbids deportation when it would violate the European Convention for Human Rights and Fundamental Freedoms of 4 November 1950.[84] It thus, according to its wording, at least potentially goes beyond a mere ban on certain "target" states.[85] Regularly, however, implications of the convention are most likely to amount to such a ban as a result of the recent jurisdiction of the European Court of Human Rights. The leading case in this respect is that of Jens Soering.

Soering, a German national, was arrested and detained in England pending extradition. A request for his extradition had been submitted by the USA. Soering was to face charges of murder in the commonwealth of Virginia. The government of the United States—for reasons of the rule of the (vertical and horizontal) division of powers—was unable to assure that the death penalty would not be imposed or, if imposed, would not be carried out. Soering alleged that in the case of a death sentence he would be placed on death row and therefore suffer inhumane treatment during the period between sentencing and execution. The European Court of Human Rights ruled that

> It would hardly be compatible with the underlying values of the Convention, that "common heritage of political traditions, ideals, freedom and the rule of law" to which the Preamble refers, were a Contracting State knowingly to surrender a fugitive to another State where there were substantial grounds for believing that he would be in danger of

being subjected to torture, however heinous the crime allegedly committed. Extradition in such circumstances, while not explicitly referred to in the brief and general wording of Article 3, would plainly be contrary to the spirit and intendment of the Article, and in the Court's view this inherent obligation not to extradite also extends to cases in which the fugitive would be faced in the receiving State by a real risk of exposure to inhuman or degrading treatment or punishment proscribed by that Article. (ECHR, judgment of 7 July 1989; emphasis added)

Although under certain conditions Article 2, § 1, of the convention permits capital punishment, the court would not exclude the possibility that circumstances relating to a death sentence could give rise to an issue under Article 3 of the convention: "The manner in which it is imposed or executed, the personal circumstances of the condemned person and a disproportionality to the gravity of the crime committed, as well as the conditions of detention awaiting execution, are examples of factors capable of bringing the treatment or punishment received by the condemned person within the proscription under Article 3" (ECHR, judgment of 7 July 1989).

In view of the potentially very long duration of the stay on death row, in extreme conditions and with the ever-present and mounting anguish of awaiting execution, and because of the personal circumstances of the applicant, especially his age and mental state at the time of the offense, the court reached the conclusion that

> the applicant's extradition to the United States would expose him to a real risk of treatment going beyond the threshold set by Article 3... .
> Accordingly, the [British] Secretary of State's decision to extradite the applicant to the United States would, if implemented, give rise to a breach of Article 3. (ECHR, judgment of 7 July 1989)

In the case of Cruz Varas and others (ECHR, judgment of 20 March 1991, 28, ¶ 69–70; confirmed in the court's judgment of 30 Oct. 1991, 34 ¶ 103), the court applied these same principles to decisions under which people were expelled from a state party to the convention and a fortiori to cases of actual deportation. It expressed its awareness of the fact that such judgment on the responsibility of the expelling or deporting state necessarily involved an assessment of conditions in the country of destination (which was not necessarily a member to the Convention!). The court emphasized, however, that such judgment nevertheless did not amount to an adjudication on the responsibility of the state of destination under the general rules of public international law, under the Convention, or otherwise.

AuslG § 53 (4) clearly shows that the German aliens law embraces and accepts these—judge-made—rules derived from the convention. Furthermore, it proves the AuslG to be able and willing to adapt to any future developments under the convention induced by the court's jurisdiction.

Finally, within the list of obstacles to deportation, AuslG § 53 (6) allows the competent aliens' office to abstain from deporting an alien into a state where there is a severe and concrete danger to the alien's limb, life, or freedom. This is a matter of administrative discretion, within the limits set by constitutional law.

As I have tried to show, deportation is also legally impossible where it would, outside the jurisdiction of the FRG, result in a violation of one of the constitutional rights or freedoms guaranteed by the Basic Law to every human being regardless of nationality. For an act of deportation to qualify as being in violation of constitutional rights or freedoms, even outside German territory, those consequences must be attributable to the governmental powers of the FRG. This is the case where (1) an alien, if deported, would foreseeably be physically exposed to suffering, loss, or damage in the "target" state; (2) such exposure—were it to occur within the jurisdiction of the FRG—would amount to an unjustifiable infringement upon a basic right (*Grundrecht*); and (3) the FRG cannot on the basis of public international law trust that the "target" state's organs will refrain or, as the case may afford, prevent others (especially private persons) from inflicting such harm.[86] However, not all the basic rights of the constitution can be interpreted as protecting against the adverse effects of state acts beyond the boundaries of German jurisdiction. Furthermore, the adverse consequences of deportation can be justified by the necessity and urgency of an alien's removal if these outweigh, or at least are not out of proportion with, the hardship to be suffered by the deportee abroad (Cremer 1994, 309–411).

Toleration of an Alien Resulting from Decisions Stemming from AuslG § 53 (6) and § 54

The toleration of an alien is the imperative consequence of the competent aliens' office using its discretion to refrain from deporting an alien to a state where his or her limb, life, or freedom would face a substantial and concrete danger (AuslG § 55 [2], alternative 2, in connection with § 53[6], sentence 1).[87]

AuslG § 54 empowers the supreme aliens' offices (i.e., the ministries of the interior of the *Länder*), for reasons of public international law, for humanitarian reasons, or in pursuit of the political interest of the FRG, to issue orders that halt the deportation of aliens from certain states or otherwise classified groups of aliens or suspend their deportation to specified states. The validity of such orders continues for six months at the longest. If a general stay of deportation is to exceed six months, the order, for reasons of the uniformity of federal practice, requires the consent of the Federal Ministry of the Interior. Under such a general order suspending deportation, all aliens concerned must receive a grant of toleration (according to AuslG § 55[2]).[88]

Toleration as a Discretionary Decision

An alien can, by a decision at the discretion of the aliens' office, be tolerated as long as his or her duty to depart has not become noncontestable or where urgent humanitarian or personal reasons or a substantial public interest demand the temporary continuation of his or her sojourn (AuslG § 55[3]).

Limits on Grants of Toleration (AuslG § 56)

The grant of toleration, which does not remove the duty to leave the country, must be limited in time and can never extend beyond one year. After the limit has expired, the grant is renewable. A grant of toleration is valid only in the *Bundesland* of the aliens' office that issued it. Other restrictions—especially as to practicing a trade or otherwise working—can be made. The grant becomes invalid as soon as the deportee leaves the country. It is withdrawn when the (legal or factual) obstacles to deportation no longer exist. Immediately after the grant loses effect, the alien is deported without any further warning or deadline for departure. When the deportee has been tolerated for more than one year, however, deportation must be announced three months in advance, unless the state of destination is only willing to admit the alien earlier.

Three Steps in the Procedure of Deportation

Warning

AuslG § 50 (1) requires the aliens' office to warn an alien of deportation and to fix a deadline for voluntary departure.[89] Both must be issued in writing. This is a rule allowing only well-founded, and therefore rare, exceptions. Setting the deadline specifies the alien's duty to depart according to AuslG § 42 (1), (3): he or she must leave within the time limit.

According to the rule established by AuslG § 50 (1), sentence 2, the warning must be attached to the administrative act that activates the alien's obligation to leave the country. Although the wording again allows exceptions, the principle of combining the act terminating the legality of sojourn with the warning of deportation is meant to be respected quite strictly and is closely followed by administrative practice (see Kanein and Renner 1993, AuslG § 50, 204 n. 2). Thus nearly every administrative act activating AuslG § 42 (1) is accompanied by the warning of deportation.

As a rule, the warning must specify the state to which the alien is to be deported and must inform the alien of the possibility of being deported to any other state that he or she is allowed to enter or that is under an obligation to admit him or her (AuslG § 50[2]).

Bans and restrictions on deportation stemming from AuslG §§ 51 and 53 through 55 do not hinder such warning. However, the warning must list the state or states to which the alien must not be deported according to AuslG §§ 51 and 53 (1)–(4) (AuslG § 50[3]).

Order of Deportation

An explicit or even a written order of deportation is not required by law. Nevertheless, given the practice of attaching a standardized warning of deportation to nearly every administrative act activating the duty to depart, every execution of deportation can be understood to imply the declaration that deportation of the specific alien is compulsory according to AuslG § 49 as long as there are no legal obstacles to deportation (see Legal Impossibility of Deportation, above). This implication, it can be argued, amounts to a tacit order of deportation. On the other hand, there are good reasons for considering the warning of deportation to be an administrative act already arranging for and ordering deportation sufficiently but subject to the condition that the alien does not comply with the duty to depart (Hailbronner 1995a, AuslG § 49, 2–3 n. 3). There can be circumstances, however, that call for an express order of deportation. For example, if, despite AuslG § 50 (2), the warning does not specify the state of destination, a need for further clarification arises. Similarly, when there is more than one target state to which the alien can be deported, one of these states must be selected; in this case, selection can be qualified as an administrative act legally specifying deportation. Furthermore, a separate administrative act ordering deportation is undisputedly necessary when an alien is to be deported without prior warning.

Actual Removal of an Alien

Deportation is executed by actually removing the alien from German territory—by force, if need be. The deportee can be taken to the border and handed over to the authorities of a neighboring state by border patrol police *(Bundesgrenzschutz)* or by the police of one of the *Länder*, depending on specific—general or ad hoc—agreements between the FRG and the neighbor state concerned. Or the deportee can be removed by air (or, seldom, sea) transport to the receiving state and surrendered by an accompanying officer.

To this end, deportees are regularly arrested and forced to travel to the border or to an airport (or seaport) and, not improbably, to wait in custody either until their delivery to the authorities of the relevant receiving state or until the departure of the plane or ship. Such acts, it is understood, restrict personal liberty. However, in the Federal Administrative Court's view (judgment of 23 June 1981, 327–28), it does not amount to an incarceration or deprivation of liberty (on whose admissibility a court would have to decide, according to Art. 104[2] of the Basic Law). Rather, it is judged to be a mere restriction of liberty, which under Article 104 (1) of the Basic Law is admissible by virtue of a formal statute, with no court decision required. The reasoning behind this is that the main purpose of the restriction is to enforce the obligation to leave the country, not to lock up the deportee in a tight room. Only secondarily and very temporarily does deportation, according to the court, impede the deportee's freedom to move. However, the court has left unanswered the question of whether deportation must be regarded as a deprivation of liberty when its execution takes longer (especially beyond the end of the day after the day of apprehension; see Basic Law, Art. 104[2], sentence 3) or when changing the means of transportation demands a substantial interruption of travel during which the deportee is taken into custody (Federal Administrative Court, judgment of 23 June 1981, 329).

Detention Prior to Deportation

AuslG § 57 distinguishes between two groups of cases in which an alien can be taken into custody pending deportation. Always, and thus in conformity with Article 104 (2) of the Basic Law, a court order is required. The alien's office can do no more than to apply for such an order.

Preparatory Detention

In the first group of cases, aliens are detained prior to expulsion (AuslG § 57[1]). An expulsion must actually be intended by the aliens' office without having been ordered yet. Furthermore, it must be impossible for the aliens' office immediately to decide on whether to expel the alien; this is true, for example, when fact-finding has not been completed or when a hearing of the alien is still necessary and will take more than a few hours (Kanein and Renner 1993, AuslG § 57, 228 n. 6). Finally, this so-called preparatory detention (*Vorbereitungshaft*) is only admissible when, in its absence, the alien's deportation would be severely impeded or completely frustrated. There must be substantial grounds for assuming such necessity of detention. The duration of detention is as a rule not to exceed six weeks.[90]

It is the court's task to decide whether in a single specific case there are sufficient reasons to believe that the success of deportation executing an order of expulsion actually depends on the alien's detention. When it reaches a positive conclusion, it must order the alien to be taken into custody. At the same time, it must determine the time of detention.

These competences concerning orders of detention rest with the respective local district court (*Amtsgericht*) (AuslG § 103[2]; § 3 of the Gesetz über das gerichtliche Verfahren bei Freiheitsentziehungen, or FEVG),[91] the *Amtsgericht* being a so-called court of ordinary jurisdiction (*ordentliches Gericht*). In contrast, the decision to expel and deport an alien is an administrative act of the aliens' office. As such, it can only be challenged before the administrative courts, rather than before a court of ordinary jurisdiction in proceedings pertaining to preparatory detention; the *Amtsgericht*'s ordering an alien to be detained pending a decision on his or her expulsion and deportation is of a mere ancillary character. Thus the local district court can question the legality of neither the expulsion nor the deportation intended by the aliens' office.

When the aliens' office actually orders the expulsion of the detainee, a renewal of the court order is not required until the end of the fixed period of preparatory detention. In this way preparatory detention can blend into detention securing deportation, admissible in the second category of cases.

Detention Securing Deportation

AuslG § 57 (2) specifies the conditions under which an alien can be taken into custody in order to secure his or her deportation. Its first sentence lists the cases in which detention is compulsory, allowing the court no margin of discretion (Hailbronner 1995a, AuslG § 57, 6 n. 14). Although only the first of these cases expressly refers to the alien's being under the obligation to leave the territory of the FRG, this is implied in all the other cases; the common final aim is deportation, which is, as shown above, the means of enforcing the duty to depart (see see Kanein and Renner 1993, AuslG § 57, 229 n. 11).[92]

The listing comprises the following cases:

1. Because of illegal entry, the alien is under the enforceable obligation to leave the country.[93]
2. The time limit set for departure has expired, and the alien has changed his or her abode (not necessarily his or her permanent residence) without informing the aliens' office of an address where he or she can be contacted.
3. The alien, for reasons attributable to him or her, was not present at the place specified by the aliens' office at the date announced as the date of deportation.
4. The alien has otherwise evaded deportation.
5. There are substantial grounds for believing that the alien will evade deportation.

In other cases, as a matter of discretion, an alien can be detained for no longer than one week if the deadline for his or her departure has passed and it is clear that he or she will be able to be deported (AuslG § 57[2], sentence 2).

In any event, detention securing deportation is inadmissible when it is certain that, for reasons for which the alien is not responsible, deportation cannot be executed within the next three months (AuslG § 57[2], sentence 4). As the competent court, the *Amtsgericht* otherwise has the power to order the alien to be continuously detained for up to six months (AuslG § 57[3], sentence 1). Only in those cases in which an alien has prevented his or her deportation can the duration of detention be extended, by twelve months at the most (AuslG § 57[3], sentence 2), thus totaling a maximum of eighteen months. In all cases, time spent in preparatory detention is to be subtracted from the maximum legal duration of detention securing deportation (AuslG § 57[3], sentence 3). Consequently, on the basis of AuslG § 57, an alien can never be kept in custody for more than one and a half years. However, both a prison sentence served by the alien and his or her pretrial custody during criminal investigation interrupt the time of detention under § 57 and are therefore irrelevant with regard to the time limits for detention securing deportation.[94]

The *Amtsgericht* must judge whether the alien is under the obligation to leave the country, must decide whether there is a case of compulsory or permissive detention prior to deportation, and must determine the duration of detention. An oral hearing of the person who is to be detained quite obviously appears to be obligatory (AuslG § 103[2], sentence 1, with FEVG § 5[1], sentence 1; see also FEVG § 5[2]–[3] and AsylVfG § 89[2]). As the constitution calls for strict adherence to the rules of procedure in cases of deprivation of liberty (Basic Law, Art. 104[1], sentence 1), it would seem to follow that the court can issue no (final) order of detention when the abode of the person concerned is unknown. Even so, the Bayerisches Oberstes Landesgericht, for example, has held such an order to be admissible, finding it sufficient that an oral hearing follow as soon as possible and judging the court to be under the duty to decide anew on the basis of said hearing (Bayerisches Oberstes Landesgericht, 301; R. Marschner, in Saage and Göppinger 1994, ch. 2 (FEVG), § 5, 74 n. 2). In its order of 1 July 1993 (3069–70), the Bundesgerichtshof (the Federal Court [of Ordinary Jurisdiction]) has gone even further, holding that AuslG § 57 (2), no. 2—as lex specialis in relation to FEVG § 5—does not require the alien to be heard, as it compels the court to order his or her detention only if the time limit set for departure has expired and the alien has changed abode without informing the aliens' office of an address where he or she can be contacted.

It is open to doubt whether these decisions are correct given that there is a way of both strictly abiding by the procedural law of the FEVG and effectively executing AuslG § 57. FEVG § 11 (in connection with AuslG § 103[2], sentence 1) allows an interim order of detention for up to six weeks to be issued when there are urgent reasons to assume that a person's detention can legally be ordered and a final decision cannot be made in time.[95] This can be the case especially when the alien's office has applied for an order of detention and the alien concerned is considered to be a flight risk (R. Marschner, in Saage and Göppinger 1994, ch. 2 (FEVG), § 11, 83 n. 2).

All the *Amtsgericht*'s decisions are appealable (AuslG § 103 [2], sentence 1, with FEVG § 7; for details, see Hailbronner 1995a, AuslG § 57, 25 n. 69).

Legal Boundaries

Article 2 (2), sentence 2, of the Basic Law guarantees every individual's liberty to be inviolable. Any deprivation of liberty cannot be justified by only the existence of an applicable formal statute declaring a restriction of liberty admissible (Basic Law, Art. 104[1]) and the formality of a court order (Basic Law, Art. 104[2], sentence 1). Constitutional law also requires the court to respect the principle of proportionality. This holds true not only when, according to the wording of AuslG § 57, the court has discretion but also when it is under a strict duty to order the alien's detention. A restriction of liberty as grave as detention is justifiable only where it is clearly the ultima ratio—here, in order to prepare for expulsion or to execute deportation. Both the fact of detention itself and its duration must therefore, in the light of all the circumstances of the case, be in a fair balance with the intention of preparing for expulsion (AuslG § 57[1]) or securing deportation (AuslG § 57[2]).[96]

At first sight, one might consider whether the rule of proportionality demands that there be a possibility for the administrative authorities to release a deportee on bond in order to reduce the cases in which detention prior to deportation is actually enforced: when a financial deposit is apt to induce an alien to fulfill the duty to depart, there is, under the principle of proportionality, no room for his or her detention. However, there seems to be no real and practical advantage to introducing such a stay of detention, because most deportees lack the monetary means to furnish such security.[97]

Problems of Detention Prior to Deportation

The situation of deportees detained under AuslG § 57 has been brought to public awareness by cases of attempted or successful suicides and prison revolts.[98] There seem to be substantial differences in the treatment of deportees among the *Bundesländer*. The roots of problems branch out into various fields.[99]

The *Länder* are free to organize the execution of orders of detention. Therefore, a *Land* (e.g., North-Rhine Westfalia) can have special institutions for detention before deportation under the supervision of the aliens' offices. However, in most *Länder*, deportees are put into penal institutions,[100] where it is almost impossible to separate them strictly from convicts. This is most critically regarded because detention under AuslG § 57 is merely a measure ancillary to deportation and can in no way be qualified as the execution of a criminal penalty.[101]

Prison personnel are often not trained to deal with aliens. Communication is stymied, and in some instances rendered nearly impossible, when a deportee speaks no German and the prison officers cannot speak his or her mother tongue. Communication can even be hindered among aliens from various parts of the world detained in the same institution. Furthermore, language difficulties often seem to prevent aliens from understanding their legal situation. Aggressiveness, a possible result of communication problems, is reported to culminate in fights among inmates or guards beating deportees.

From the start, the psychological burden naturally seems to be heavy, as deportees worry about the fates of relatives from whom they are separated and about their own futures after deportation. The situation appears most critical when cells are crowded,[102] visiting hours are few, sufficient possibilities to work, read, or physically exercise are not offered, time spent outdoors, in the fresh air, is reduced to one hour a day, and psychological care is left mainly to private groups and organizations and churches. Ironically, were deportees not separated from convicts, they could enjoy the regular social activities, programs, and services of the prisons.

These problems are aggravated the longer the duration of detention prior to deportation. While the average time spent in detention is several weeks, rising numbers of deportees detained appear to have led to increases that in some cases may reach from several months to more than a year.[103]

Deplorable as this situation may be, one should keep in mind that the detained deportee not rarely has the possibility to shorten the duration of detention by complying with deportation measures (however, detention must not be implemented as a means of compulsion to such compliance) (see Hailbronner 1995a, AuslG § 57, 13–14 n. 37).

How to Find a Deportable Alien

As shown above, the internal controls of aliens are manifold, with the wires of a network of information, especially from public authorities, meeting at the aliens' offices. This should allow sufficient control over aliens in general. Even so, the Ausländergesetz tightens such control not only through the possibility of detaining an alien, as described above (see especially Detention Prior to Deportation) but also through the provisions of its § 42 (5) and (6). According to these, an alien who is under the obligation to leave the country must, when he or she intends to change his or her domicile or to leave the district of the presently competent aliens' office for more than three days, inform the aliens' office of such intention. Furthermore, as a rule allowing only well-founded exceptions,[104] he or she is ordered to deposit his or her passport at the aliens' office.[105]

Especially, when an alien tries to evade deportation by disappearing, the competent aliens' office can, as shown above, have a search notice entered into the General File of the Central Aliens Register. Similarly, when an alien is put on a "wanted persons" list for arrest or for establishing his or her whereabouts, this fact is also registered. In this fashion the regular police or the border police are quickly able to ascertain the alien's legal status whenever they check his or her identity.

Finally, any alien who has been expelled or deported or who has been declared deportable is registered in the Federal Central Register (*Bundeszentralregister*), which essentially serves as a criminal register. The aliens' offices and border police have access to this register, which allows them to see if an alien has been expelled and deported and therefore is not allowed to enter or stay in the territory of the FRG under AuslG § 8 (2), sentence 1, such entry or sojourn being a criminal offense under AuslG § 92 (2), no. 1.[106]

Thus there is no need to place further duties on private employers, school systems, public welfare workers, and other government employees to report the presence of deportable aliens in order to locate potential deportees.

Judicial Remedies against Deportation

As discussed above, aliens are deportable when they are under the duty to leave the country and this duty is enforceable. Bans on certain target states can generally be understood not to bar deportability as such but only to make deportation into these specific states legally (and, it is to be presumed, temporarily) impossible. Nondeportation only results if no other state can be found willing to admit the deportable aliens, which merely leads to their toleration.[107]

Thinking of judicial remedies tactically, a deportee's lawyer will have to aim either at overturning the obligation to leave the country or at least its enforceability or at forcing the competent aliens' office to grant toleration.

Remedies against the Duty to Depart and Its Enforceability

The General Rule

As shown above,[108] an alien's obligation to leave the country is basically enforceable when the administrative act activating AuslG § 42 (1) becomes enforceable.[109]

In general the alien can (and must first) lodge an administrative objection against such an act under VwGO § 68 (1). If that is unsuccessful, he or she must file a legal suit aimed at the cassation of the act before the administrative courts (see VwGO §§ 42, 113[1], *Anfechtungsklage*). Both legal remedies generally[110] suspend the act (VwGO § 80[1]), ridding it of its enforceability.

Important Modifications

However, as has been discussed above, because of AuslG §§ 72 (1) and 69 (3), a special situation arises when an administrative act denies the first grant or the prolongation of a residence permit. In these cases, neither the filing of an (administrative) objection (VwGO § 68[2]) nor the commencement of court action in pursuit of a reversal of the administrative decision (VwGO §§ 42, 113[5], *Verpflichtungsklage*) exerts a suspensive effect. Only a court order under VwGO § 80 (5) can establish the suspensive effect of the objection or the filing of a suit before the administrative courts. Thus only the success of this means of interim judicial relief will prevent the duty to depart from becoming enforceable by such an administrative act. It is worth noting that under VwGO § 80 (5) the court can declare the order to be dependent on the applicant's furnishing security or on other conditions (see Kopp 1994, § 80, 1010 n. 77; and Finkelnburg and Jank 1986, 263 n. 667).

When the objection or lawsuit is successful as to the principal claim, the decision of the (higher) administrative board or the court will order a residence permit to be issued, and the alien's sojourn is to be considered legal ex tunc and without interruption (see AuslG § 72[2], sentence 2).

Remedies against Denial of a Grant of Toleration

A deportable alien claiming that there are legal obstacles to deportation according to AuslG § 53 can apply for a grant of toleration at the aliens' office. If this application is rejected, there is no possibility of an administrative objection under VwGO § 68 (AuslG § 71[3]). Instead, he or she must directly file an action for the issue of such a grant under VwGO §§ 42, 113 (5). Even beforehand, the claimant can apply to the competent administrative court for interim judicial relief. VwGO § 123 empowers the court to order the applicant's deportation to be stayed temporarily if his or her interests prevail over the public interest of the execution of deportation. The grounds on which the applicant bases this right to a grant of toleration and his or her prevailing interests must be substantiated by prima facie evidence (VwGO § 123[5], in connection with § 920[2] of the Code on Civil Procedure; see n. 129, above).

Where the alien alleges there to be persecution in the sense of AuslG § 51 in the state to which he or she is to be deported, AsylVfG § 13 defines such allegation to be an application for asylum. The exclusive competence to decide on such an application rests with the Federal Office (AuslG § 51[2], sentence 2).[111]

The Approach in the Law on the Procedure in Asylum Cases

Although the Ausländergesetz in principle applies to cases of asylum seekers, specific rules for their control and deportation that alter or supplement the general rules of the Ausländergesetz are set up in the Law on the Procedure in Asylum Cases (Asylverfahrensgesetz, or AsylVfG).[112]

Introduction

The Asylverfahrensgesetz sometimes uses the term *Asylbegehrender* (asylum seeker), but primarily speaks of aliens applying for asylum (*Ausländer, die um Asyl nachsuchen*). Applications for asylum are made whenever aliens, by any means whatsoever, express a will to seek, in the territory of the FRG, protection from political persecution (Basic Law, Art. 16a[1]) or from being deported or otherwise returned to a state in which there exist the dangers described in AuslG § 51 (1) (AsylVfG § 13[1]).

The exclusive competence to decide on applications for asylum rests with the Federal Office. The *Bundesländer*, however, are placed under the duty to provide admission centers for asylum seekers (Zentrale Aufnahmeeinrichtungen für Asylbewerber [Aufnahmeeinrichtungen], per AsylVfG § 44). Attached to these there are to be branch offices of the Federal Office (see AsylVfG §§ 5[4], 14[1]).

Internal Controls of Asylum Seekers

Basically all asylum seekers are subject to the same controls as all other aliens within the country. But the Asylverfahrensgesetz puts them under tighter surveillance.

An alien who does not possess the documents required for legal entry into the FRG must seek asylum at the border (AsylVfG

§ 13[3], sentence 1).[113] The border-control office must take certain measures of investigation into the alien's identity and record the results (AsylVfG § 18[5]).[114] This is done in order to prevent both illegal reentries (e.g., with forged passports) and double or multiple applications by single asylum seekers under various identities.

Principally, entry will be refused or an illegally entering asylum seeker directly returned when

- he has departed from a third state considered to be safe under AsylVfG § 26a (i.e., one of the states listed in annex 1 to the AsylVfG or in the Basic Law, Art. 16a[2], sentence 1);
- it is obvious that in any other third state he or she has been safe from political persecution, in the sense of AsylVfG § 27 (1) or (2); or
- the alien is a threat to the public because he or she has been convicted of an especially severe crime and sentenced to a prison term of no less than three years, with the judgment having become nonappealable and his or her having left Germany within the past three years (see AsylVfG § 18 [2] and [3]; but see also the exceptions in AsylVfG § 18[4]).

AsylVfG § 29a sets up a special rule for dealing with applications for asylum by aliens whose home countries are prima facie considered safe (i.e., free of political persecution), having thus been defined by federal statute requiring the consent of the Bundesrat (See AsylVfG § 29a and annex 2 to the AsylVfG).[115] Such applications are generally to be dismissed as obviously unfounded if the alien cannot bring forward grounds for assuming that, contrary to the general situation in his or her home country, he or she is threatened by political persecution there. When an asylum seeker from a safe country of origin applies for asylum at the border, attempting to enter the territory of the FRG via an airport, the asylum procedure is, if possible, to be conducted at the airport before a decision is made to allow the applicant to enter the country (AsylVfG § 18a). This is only possible when a case can be decided within two days after the application for asylum (cf. AsylVfG § 18a[6], nos. 1 and 2). When the Federal Office rejects such an application as obviously unfounded, it will—if the applicant has no other right of entry—warn the alien that he or she will be deported if he or she enters the territory of the FRG, fixing a one-week deadline for departure (AsylVfG §§ 18a[2], 34, 36[1]). Furthermore, the asylum seeker is forbidden to enter the country (AsylVfG § 18a[3]).

Interim judicial relief against such a decision is restricted by a three-day deadline and certain tightened rules of fact-finding.[116] AsylVfG § 18 a (5) sets up the legal fiction that any application for such relief both contains a request for admission and challenges the validity of the (conditional) warning of deportation (issued for the case of entry). Interim judicial relief will only be granted if there are serious doubts as to the legality of the Federal Office's decision forbidding the asylum seeker's entry. This is the case when legal basis for the denial of admission—i.e., the declaration that the application for asylum is obviously unfounded—is questionable (Federal Constitutional Court, order of 2 Dec. 1993, 12; order of 28 Apr. 1994, 52).

When the asylum seeker is not rejected at the border, the border-control office will immediately send him or her to the competent or nearest admission center in order for the alien to report there (AsylVfG § 18[1]).[117]

Aliens illegally entering the territory of the FRG must without delay report to an admission center,[118] an aliens' office, or the police (AsylVfG § 13[3], sentence 2).[119] As a rule (AsylVfG § 14[1]),[120] all asylum seekers must make their applications at the branch office of the Federal Office attached to the competent admission center of a *Bundesland*. It is to this center that they are finally to be directed.[121] Consequently, even aliens legally staying in the country who decide to apply for asylum but do not approach the appropriate admission centers[122] are generally to be sent to such centers (but see AsylVfg § 14[2]). Their identities will be recorded (AsylVfG §§ 16[1] and[2], 19[2]; see also AsylVfG § 22[1], sentence 2).

The competent admission center is to take into custody the passport or substitute passport document and all documents and all other papers relevant to the asylum procedure[123] that the asylum seeker possesses. When any one of the public authorities mentioned has directed an asylum seeker to the competent admission center, it is its duty to have the alien hand over these documents and to transfer them to the admission center, which in turn eventually is to transmit them to the branch office of the

Federal Office attached to the center (AsylVfG §§ 21[1]–[3], 15 [2], nos. 4 and 5).[124]

AsylVfG § 55 allows an asylum seeker to stay in the territory of the FRG in order to conduct the asylum procedure (*Aufenthaltsgestattung*; AsylVfG § 55[1], sentence 1);[125] however, he or she has no right of sojourn in a specific *Bundesland* or in a place of his or her choosing. Rather, the *Aufenthaltsgestattung*, as the permission of sojourn, is restricted to the district of the aliens' office in which the competent admission center lies[126] or in which the asylum seeker is otherwise obliged to stay (AsylVfG § 56[1], sentence 1, and [2]). Some general exceptions from this restriction exist;[127] others can be granted in specific cases.[128] Freedom of movement is thus reduced, both to guarantee the speediness of the asylum procedure and to deter aliens from using an application for asylum as a golden key to entry and sojourn in the territory of the FRG (see Kanein and Renner 1993, AsylVfG § 56, 578 n. 2). AuslG § 36 puts an alien under the duty immediately to leave any district in which he or she is not allowed to stay. Compliance can be—if need be, physically—enforced by the police, the border police, and the admission centers, without prior warning (see AsylVfG § 59).

Burdens can be imposed on aliens enjoying the permission to stay in the form of an *Aufenthaltsgestattung*; in particular, an asylum seeker no longer required to live in an admission center can be made to take residence in a certain district or even in a certain place (AsylVfG § 60). As long as asylum seekers are required to live in an admission center, they must not take up any gainful employment (AsylVfG § 61[1]).[129]

As soon as the application for asylum is made, any exemption from the requirement of a residence permit and any granted residence permit with a total validity of no more than six months become null and void. Furthermore, the fiction of toleration or of legality of sojourn resulting from application for a residence permit in the cases of AuslG § 69 (2) and (3) loses effect. The fiction of legality of sojourn is left untouched when the alien has been in possession of a residence permit with a total validity of more than six months and has applied for its prolongation (AsylVfG § 55[2]).

A (declaratory) certificate of the *Aufenthaltsgestattung*, whose validity is to be restricted to between three and six months, is issued to the asylum seeker by the Federal Office or, when he or she is not required to live in an admission center, by the aliens' office. During the asylum procedure, the alien fulfills his or her duty to present papers of identification by showing this certificate, which contains his or her photograph and specifications as to his or her person (AsylVfG §§ 63, 64).

The *Aufenthaltsgestattung* loses effect at the latest when the Federal Office's decision on the acknowledgement of the alien as an asylee, whether positive or negative, becomes noncontestable (AsylVfG § 67[1], no. 6).[130]

An alien can be put on a "wanted persons" list in the Central Aliens Register (see The Central Aliens Register, above) or on similar search lists of the police when his or her whereabouts are unknown and he or she has in specific ways failed to contact certain authorities within specified time limits.[131] Such a search for an alien can be initiated by the competent admission center, by the aliens' office in whose district the alien is obliged to stay, or by the Federal Office.

In addition, the authorities entrusted with the execution of the Law on the Procedure in Asylum Cases can compile relevant data on an asylum seeker (AsylVfG § 7). Other public offices are, within certain limits, under a duty to transmit relevant information on the request of such authorities (AsylVfG § 8[1]). If the alien has applied for asylum, notice must be given to the Federal Office ex officio of any foreign state's formal request for extradition, of any request for the alien's arrest attached to a state's announcement of a future request for extradition, and of the conclusion of extradition proceedings (AsylVfG § 8[2]).

Deportation of Unsuccessful Asylum Seekers

Divided Competences

The competences for decisions in the course of the asylum procedure are largely concentrated in the hands of the Federal Office; however, measures taken to deport an alien are divided between the Federal Office and the aliens' offices.

The Federal Office issues the administrative act warning the alien whose application for asylum is unsuccessful and who does not possess a residence permit[132] of being deported. This warning (*Abschiebungsandrohung*) is to be attached to the (negative) decision on the application for asylum; simultaneously, a deadline[133] for the alien's departure is to be fixed (AsylVfG § 34, in connection with AuslG §§ 50 and 51[4]).[134] Generally, every decision on an application for asylum must also declare whether there are legal obstacles to the applicant's deportation under AuslG §§ 51 (1) and 53.[135]

The Federal Office will immediately inform the aliens' office in whose district the alien is to stay of any enforceable warning of deportation and will transfer all documents necessary for deportation to the aliens' office (AsylVfG § 40[1], sentence 1).[136] From then on, the deportation procedure is conducted by the aliens' office, which is, however, bound by any decision on legal obstacles to deportation under AuslG § 53 (AsylVfG § 42, sentence 1).[137]

Judicial Remedies

As mentioned before, VwGO § 68 principally requires anyone who challenges the legality of an administrative act to lodge an objection against the act with the competent (higher) administrative office before court proceedings can (when the administrative objection is unsuccessful) be initiated. AsylVfG § 11 makes an important exception to this rule by excluding such administrative objection when acts and decisions under the Law on the Procedure in Asylum Cases are concerned. The asylum seeker must immediately address the administrative courts in these cases.

When the Federal Office has, on an alien's (first) application for asylum, denied recognition of asylee status, filing a claim for recognition suspends the (usually simultaneously contested) Federal Office's warning of deportation if this warning is not connected to a decision declaring the application for asylum irrelevant or obviously founded (see AsylVfG § 75, in connection with AsylVfG § 38[1]).[138] When the Federal Office's decision is suspended, the *Aufenthaltsgestattung* remains valid,[139] rendering deportation inadmissible. In all other cases, the suspensive effect can only be established by a court order under VwGO § 80 (5),[140] the court's decision, whether granting or denying interim judicial relief, being non-contestable (AsylVfG § 80).

In the case of an irrelevant or obviously unfounded application, a motion under VwGO § 80 (5) must be presented to the court within one week of the decision's being made known to the applicant (AsylVfG § 36[3], sentence 1; see also AsylVfG § 10). When such a motion has been made in time, the alien must not be deported before the administrative court's decision (AsylVfG § 36[3], sentence 8). The court is generally under the duty, however, to decide within one week whether to grant interim judicial relief.[141] It can order a stay of deportation only when serious doubts as to the legality of the decision exist. There are also certain restrictions on fact-finding (for details, see AsylVfG § 36 (4)). When the Federal Office's decision declaring an application for asylum irrelevant is suspended by the court, this decision and the warning of deportation become null and void, and the Federal Office must continue the asylum procedure (AsylVfG § 37[1]). When the Federal Office has dismissed an application as obviously unfounded, a court order staying deportation has the effect of placing the alien under the duty to leave the country within one month after either the Federal Office's or the court's decision denying a claim for recognition has become noncontestable (AsylVfG § 37[2]).

Practical Efficiency of Legal Rules of Control and Deportation

The network of internal controls of aliens appears to be conceived and legally laid out to function efficiently. From a technical perspective, however, certain aspects of the information system could be improved, for example, by installing an active on-line correspondence between the aliens' offices and the automated Central Aliens Register,[142] finding ways to ensure periodical and efficient updates, and training the operating personnel adequately. But it must be kept in mind that the constitution demands respect of the freedom of informational self-determination. There should be no doubt that in a democratic state based on the principle of every individual's personal freedom state controls can never be complete and perfect. Only an omnipotent Orwellian Big Brother could guarantee that no illegal alien disappeared evading deportation.

Still, evasion of deportation is a severe problem, especially in cases of unsuccessful asylum seekers.[143] Some have termed deportation in Germany a police state method because the exact date and hour of arrest and forced departure are not announced in advance. Yet, aside from the fact that the laws expressly put the aliens concerned under the duty to leave the country and they are individually warned of the possibility of deportation sufficiently ahead of time, practical experience seems to show that prior announcement of the exact date of deportation tends to induce deportees to disappear, despite the availability of both legal remedies against having to depart and deportation itself. Deportable aliens can furthermore prevent deportation by declining to cooperate with authorities, whether they burn or "lose" their passports and do not reveal their true nationalities or refuse to sign any application forms that their home states demand before issuing or renewing passports.[144]

Home states themselves may be disinclined to take back nationals who have fled the country, although such attitudes are contrary to public international law.[145] One can only speculate on the motivation for such behavior. Fear of letting in terrorists or mere political opponents of the ruling government; disastrous internal economic situations in states with high unemployment rates, to whose increase returning citizens would only contribute; or even the tactical intention of putting political pressure on the FRG by not readmitting nationals cannot be dismissed as completely unthinkable reasons. Promising solutions to these problems will only be found in foreign policies supporting the democratic and economic development of home states, especially those of unsuccessful asylum seekers.

Finally, recent phenomena reveal a third obstacle to the practicability of deportation law: Parishes grant deportable aliens so-called church asylum (*Kirchenasyl*).[146] *Länder* parliaments dealing with aliens' petitions[147] almost act as if they had the power to pardon aliens from deportation and were not bound by federal law—as they truly are (see Art. 31 of the Basic Law)—but could dispose of AuslG § 49 even when it strictly calls for deportation. Political and public pressure may rise so high as to cause government authorities to repeal their decisions on deportation even though these decisions have been held to be legal by the administrative courts. Indeed, there is no guarantee that courts will not make mistakes, and, apart from that, actions against deportation may, in specific cases, appear to be morally justifiable. There seems to be no consensus as to the moral standards to be applied, however; indeed, the all too frequent struggles over the deportation of individual aliens prove that our society on the whole[148] is deeply divided over the questions of fugitives, asylum seekers, and deportees.[149] This may be the reason why, although the rules and regulations of the law on aliens as such are devised to be efficient,[150] the suspicion remains that there may be a lack of political willingness to apply and enforce that law.

Notes

The following abbreviations are used in the text:

AsylVfG	Asylverfahrensgesetz (Law on the Procedure in Asylum Cases; see n. 7, below)
AuslDÜV	Verordnung über Datenübermittlungen an die Ausländerbehörden (Ausländerdatenübermittlungsverordnung: Federal Ordinance on the Transfer of Data to the Aliens' Offices; see n. 46, below)
AuslG	Ausländergesetz (Gesetz über die Einreise und den Aufenthalt von Ausländern im Bundesgebiet: Law on the Entry and Sojourn of Aliens in the Territory of the Federal Republic of Germany, or Aliens Act; see n. 1, below)
AZR-Gesetz	Gesetz über das Ausländerzentralregister (Federal Statute on the Central Aliens Register; see n. 50, below)
BGBl.	*Bundesgesetzblatt* (Journal of publication of Federal Statutes. *BGBl.* 1 contains internal laws; *BGBl.* 2 legislation related to international law. The year of publication is only given if not identical with the date of the legislation or publication cited)
BGHZ	*Entscheidungen des Bundesgerichtshofs in Zivilsachen* (Decisions of the Federal Court of Justice in civil law cases)
BVerfGE	*Entscheidungen des Bundesverfassungsgerichts* (Decisions of the Federal Constitutional Court)
BVerwGE	*Entscheidungen des Bundesverwaltungsgerichts* (Decisions of the Federal Administrative Court)

DVAuslG	Verordnung zur Durchführung des Ausländergesetzes (Ordinance for the Execution of the Aliens Act; see n. 13, below)
EC	European Community
ECHR	European Court of Human Rights
EEC	European Economic Community
EU	European Union
Federal Office	Bundesamt für die Anerkennung ausländischer Flüchtlinge (Federal Office for the Recognition of Foreign Refugees; see n. 53, below)
FEVG	Gesetz über das gerichtliche Verfahren bei Freiheitsentziehungen (Law on Court Procedure in Cases of Deprivation of Liberty; see n. 91, below)
FRG	Federal Republic of Germany
GG	Grundgesetz für die Bundesrepublik Deutschland (Basic Law of the FRG; see n. 3, below)
MRRG	Melderechtsrahmengesetz (Federal Framework Law on the Registration of Residence and Domicile; see n. 38, below)
OJ	Official Journal of the European Communities
StVollzG	Gesetz über den Vollzug der Freiheitsstrafe und der freiheitsentziehenden Maßregeln der Besserung und Sicherung (Strafvollzugsgesetz) (Federal Statute on the Execution of Prison Sentences and Measures for the Prevention of Crime and the Reformation of Offenders; see n. 100, below)
VwGO	Verwaltungsgerichtsordnung (Federal Law on the Procedure of the Administrative Courts; see n. 69, below)

1. Proclaimed as Art. 1 of the Gesetz zur Neuregelung des Ausländerrechts (Law Reforming the Aliens Act) of 9 July 1990 (*BGBl.* 1: 1354), most recently amended by Art. 3 of the Law on the Treaty of Schengen of 15 July 1993 (*BGBl.* 2: 1010, *BGBl.* 2 [1994]: 631) and federal statutes of 26 July 1994 (*BGBl.* 1: 1792); of 28 Oct. 1994 (*BGBl.* 1: 3186), and of 24 Feb. 1997 (*BGBl.* 1: 310).
2. Art. 15 of the Gesetz zur Neuregelung des Ausländerrechts (see n. 1, above).
3. Grundgesetz für die Bundesrepublik Deutschland of 23 May 1949 (*BGBl.*, 1), as most recently amended by the law of 3 Nov. 1995 (*BGBl.* 1: 1492. See also Art. 87 of the Basic Law listing matters of direct federal administration and Art. 86 of the Basic Law.
4. On Art. 116 (1) of the Basic Law, see Renner, in Hailbronner and Renner 1991, part 3 a, GG Art. 116, 328–52 nn. 5–35; and Makarov and von Mangoldt 1993, part 1 2, GG Art. 116, 2–39 nn. 1–66.
5. Gesetz über Einreise und Aufenthalt von Staatsangehörigen der Mitgliedstaaten der Europäischen Wirtschaftsgemeinschaft (Aufenthaltsgesetz/

EWG), revision proclaimed on 31 Jan. 1980 (*BGBl.* 1: 116, most recently altered by Gesetz zur Neuregelung des Ausländerrechts [see n. 1. above] and federal statute of 27 Apr. 1993, *BGBl.* 1: 512, 2436).
6. Without going into details, it should be mentioned that EC law, which has priority over the national law of the EU member states, very widely bestows on nationals of these states, as well as on their spouses and families, regardless of their nationalities, substantial freedom of movement within the Common Market. See, in the EC treaty, Arts. 48–51 (free movement of workers); 52–58 (freedom of establishment for entrepreneurs); and 59–66 (freedom of services transactions). See also, in secondary EC law, regulation (EEC) 1612/68 (*OJ* 1968 L 295/12, most recently amended by regulation [EEC] 2434/92, *OJ* 1992 L 245/1); regulation (EEC) 1251/70 (*OJ* 1970 L 142/24, corrected *OJ* 1975 L 324/31); and directives 73/148/EEC (*OJ* 1973 L 172/14), 68/360/EEC (*OJ* 1968 L 257/13), 75/34/EEC (*OJ* 1974 L 14/10), 90/364/EEC (*OJ* 1990 L 180/26), 90/365/EEC (*OJ* 1990 L 180/28), and 93/96/EEC (*OJ* 1993 L 317/59). Residence permits issued to these people are of a merely declaratory nature. The removal of such aliens is by far more tightly restricted than is the removal of aliens not privileged by EC law (see directive 64/221 [*OJ* 1964 L 850]).

Within the Christian Democratic Union of Germany (CDU), guidelines for the future European policy of the nation are being discussed. One of the proposed guidelines concerns the law on aliens: As Europe gradually becomes a political union, coordination of matters of justice and home affairs should be intensified. To this end, competences in matters of border law (controls), asylum, visas, fugitives, and immigration are recommended to be transferred to the European level. This transfer is labeled with the interesting German word *Vergemeinschaften*, which refers to bringing these matters under EU jurisdiction, whether by an alteration of the EU Treaty or by a supplement treaty. Should this be impossible, a minimum goal is the harmonization of the national legal orders and competences of the EU member states in these areas. See *Frankfurter Allgemeine Zeitung*, 3 July 1995, 4.
7. New publication of 27 July 1993 (*BGBl.* 1: 1361), amended by federal statutes of 2 Aug. 1993 (*BGBl.* 1: 1442), 28 Oct. 1994 (*BGBl.* 1: 3186) and 31 Mar. 1995 (*BGBl.* 1: 430), 28 Mar. 1996 (*BGBl.* 1: 1626).
8. An exception to the requirement of the Bundesrat's consent is made by AuslG § 3 (4) insofar as an ordinance is required to comply with an international agreement or to uphold public interests. Such ordinances, however, lose their binding power three months after entering into force, at the latest.
9. AuslG § 3 (1), sentence 2. The wording there implies that the ministry should make use of this competence in order to facilitate the residence of aliens.
10. AuslG § 3 (5). This provision is untouched by any decisions based on Art. 100c of the EC Treaty.
11. The Ministry of the Interior can, through administrative regulations requiring the consent of the Bundesrat, determine which national aliens' office is competent in cases where the alien does not reside within the territory of the FRG (AuslG § 63[2] no. 1). According to § 10 of the DVAuslG (see n. 134, below), if an alien's regular residence is in a state in which the FRG has no diplomatic mission or consular agency or in which the diplomatic mission or consular agency is temporarily unable to issue visas, he or

she can obtain a residence permit from the aliens' office locally competent at the seat of the Federal Ministry of Foreign Affairs as long as the ministry has not authorized another aliens' office to issue such visas.
12. See AuslG § 3 (4) for exceptions. See also n. 8, above.
13. Of 18 Dec. 1990 (*BGBl.* 1: 2983), as most recently amended by Art. 1 of the Amending Ordinance of 11 Jan. 1997 (*BGBl.* 1: 4).
14. Treaty on the European Union of 7 Feb. 1992, *BGBl.* 2: 1253, which entered into force on 1 Nov. 1993 (publication of 19 Oct. 1993, *BGBl.* 2: 1947).
15. By Regulation (EC) 2317/95 of 25 Sept. 1995 (*OJ* L 234, p. 1), the Council of Ministers has for the first time made use of its competences under Art. 100c (1) of the Treaty on the European Community.
16. It is interesting that the competence of the council to decide according to the procedures of Art. 100c (possibly modified by a different mode of voting) can be extended to matters of justice and home affairs other than the requirement of visas for entry into the territory of the European Union. Such an extension requires a unanimous decision of the council, taken on the initiative of the commission or of one of the EU member states. Furthermore, the member states must consent to this alteration of the treaty according to the provisions of their respective constitutions. See Art. 100c (6) of the EC Treaty and Art. K.9 of the Treaty of Maastricht.
17. When an alien intending to enter the FRG on an aircraft or seagoing vessel or in a land vehicle is rejected at the border, the carrier is obliged to take the alien out of the country immediately (AuslG § 73[1]; as to possible destinations, see AuslG § 73[3]; in addition, the carrier is liable for both the costs of transportation and any administrative costs incurred in the period between the alien's arrival and the execution of the (negative) decision as to entry (AuslG § 82[3], sentence 1). On restrictions of this principle in light of constitutional law, see Kanein and Renner 1993, AuslG § 73, 274–75 nn. 7–8.
18. This view seems to be in compliance with public international law, which as yet continues to discern between nonadmission, on the one hand, and expulsion and deportation, on the other (see Hailbronner 1994, 86).
19. The carrier of an aircraft or seagoing vessel may only bring into the territory of the FRG aliens who possess the necessary documents in the form of passports and visas legally required of nationals from the aliens' respective home states (AuslG § 74[1], sentence 1). On the enforcement of both this rule and specific single-case regulations concerning carriers using other means of transportation (AuslG § 74[1], sentence 2), see AuslG § 74[2]–[3]. In either case of entry, illegal because of AuslG § 8 (2), an exception can be made in the form of special permission to enter the territory of the FRG for a short-term stay if there is an urgent need for the alien to be personally present in the country or if the denial of such permission would cause an unjust hardship (AuslG § 9[3]).

According to the rule set up in AuslG § 8 (2) the prohibition of entry and sojourn resulting from expulsion or deportation is, on application, to be limited in time. Exceptions from this rule are possible. The time span fixed begins to elapse as soon as the alien actually leaves the country. Note, too, that in order to fulfill obligations under public international law, the Federal Ministry of the Interior can, through an ordinance issued with the con-

sent of the Bundesrat, allow aliens to enter and stay in the territory despite their having before been expelled or deported (AuslG § 9[4]).
20. See DVAuslG § 5–8, 14. As AuslG § 4 (2), no. 2, indicates, a passport is an official document of identification; this function requires it to contain information on the name, date, place of birth, and nationality of the alien and on the time and range of its validity; it must also include a photograph of its rightful bearer and identify the issuing authority and the date of issue. Furthermore, as the intention behind the requirement of valid passports is to guarantee that their holders have the right to leave and return to their home countries, a passport is only a document that gives proof of such right. See Kanein and Renner 1993, AuslG § 4, 22–23 n. 5. See also DVAuslG § 14 (3)–(5).
21. According to Kanein and Renner 1993, AuslG § 41, 155 n. 5, using force (*unmittelbarer Zwang*) to ensure compliance with identification procedures is not supposed to be possible.
22. Federal Statute Consenting to the Treaty of 15 July 1993 (*BGBl.* 2: 1010). Treaties of accession have been concluded with Italy (27 Nov. 1990), Spain and Portugal (25 June 1991; federal statute consenting to these treaties of 6 Oct. 1993, *BGBl.* 2: 1902), and Greece (6 Nov. 1992; Federal statute, consenting to the treaty 21 Oct. 1996; *BGBl.* 2: 2542). Austria is also soon to accede to the treaty.
23. Treaty of 14 June 1985 among the governments of the states of the Benelux Economic Union, the Federal Republic of Germany, and the French Republic, concerning the gradual reduction of controls on their common borders, *Gemeinsames Ministerialblatt*, no. 5 (1986): 79–81. For Italy and Greece, the Schengen II Treaty will enter into force at a later date.
24. France, however, unilaterally claimed the right to consider the first three months as a "testing period," during which border controls (of persons) were abolished only at the country's sea- and airports (*Frankfurter Allgemeine Zeitung*, 21 June 1995, 4). At the end of these three months, Prime Minister Juppé declared that France would unilaterally uphold the controls at its internal borders with the other contracting states and demanded the extension of the testing phase by another six months. Among his reasons he included the view that, especially with regard to the Netherlands, the suppression of illegal drug traffic was as yet imperfect.

The seven other contracting states have expressed their regret at this decision of the French government (*Frankfurter Allgemeine Zeitung*, 30 June 1995, 1). Even before that, Manfred Kanther, Germany's federal minister of the interior, had responded to earlier indications of such a decision by pointing out that the treaty left no room for such a prolongation of the "testing phase." The Schengen Information System was working smoothly and had successfully supported searches for wanted persons (*Frankfurter Allgemeine Zeitung*, 21 June 1995, 4). Indeed, in the final communiqué of its session in Bonn of 22 December 1994, the Schengen Executive Committee had emphasized the importance of the "initial phase" of the implementation of the Second Treaty of Schengen "in all its parts." This phase was defined as the first three months following 26 March 1995. The committee underlined every contracting state's responsibility both to execute the treaty and especially to abolish the controls at the internal borders "within the initial phase of implementation." A so-called follow-up structure was to be established to analyze and solve technical problems (*Bulletin der Bundesregierung*, no. 3 (13 Jan. 1995): 16, ¶¶ 5 and 6). Meanwhile, Luxembourg has reacted to France's decision by resuming controls at the French border (*Frankfurter Allgemeine Zeitung*, 13 July 1995, 5).

It might well be that France will gradually change its position and fulfill more and more of its obligations the longer the newly elected French president, Jacques Chirac, is in office.

25. On the relation of the treaties of Schengen to the law of the European Union, especially the European Community, see Art. 134 (establishing the priority of European Community Law) and Art. 142 of the Second Treaty of Schengen; and Bieber 1994, 296–97. See also n. 117, below.
26. As defined by Art. 6 in connection with the requirements for entry permission of Art. 5.
27. For example, Art. 6 (2) (b) demands that all persons must be subjected to such controls as will allow their identification by examination of travel documents presented; (c) calls for an intensified control of aliens from third-party (i.e., non-EU) states according to (a), which, in the practice of the German border police, includes the checking of identification and other documents required for entry, a computer screening (via either the Schengen Information System or the national Central Aliens' Register), personally asking each traveler both for information as to destination and purpose of travel and for proof of sufficient means of financial support during the sojourn; (e) specifies that controls are to be concentrated on certain points when exceptional circumstances forbid strict adherence to the rules of (a) through (d). Art. 6 (3) puts the participating states under the duty of having border patrols observe the external borders in order to oppress any incentive for circumvention of the controls at the official border-crossing points.
28. However, according to a May 1995 report by the Federal Border Police (Grenzschutzpräsidium Ost), border controls during the first two months after the Second Treaty of Schengen entered into force led only to minor delays in border traffic. During this time, the officers of the German border police were—and, it is to be assumed, still are (see Art. 6[2] e of the Second Treaty of Schengen)—under orders not to allow the individual waiting time to exceed one half hour and to loosen controls when necessary to meet this requirement.

Under the Treaty between the FRG and the Republic of Poland on the Promotion and Facilitation of Customs Clearance and Immigration Controls of 29 July 1992 (Abkommen zwischen der Bundesrepublik Deutschland und der Republik Polen über Erleichterungen der Grenzabfertigung, *BGBl.* 2 (1994): 265), both sides are under the general obligation to facilitate and accelerate border traffic. But this imposes no duty on Poland to support the differentiations of the Second Treaty of Schengen. Nor does the readmission agreement among Belgium, the FRG, France, Italy, Luxembourg, the Netherlands, and Poland of 29 March 1991 (*BGBl.* 2 (1993): 1099, which entered into force for the FRG on 1 May 1991; see announcement of 16 Sept. 1994, *BGBl.* 2: 3527) appear to have any relevance in this context. Both Poland and the Czech Republic are said to be largely uninterested in reserving so-called Schengen lanes for speedier transits of EU nationals as long as their nationals do not enjoy the same privileges as EU citizens when entering the FRG. The German Ministry of Foreign Affairs was reported to have criticized the delays at the Polish-German border as "intolerable" (*Frankfurter Allgemeine Zeitung*, 13 June 1995, 7).

Tensions have further arisen over special border agreements between the FRG and both Poland and the Czech Republic concerning the privileges of local frontier zone traffic (*Kleiner Grenzverkehr*). These agreements include provisions according to which people crossing the border are subject to border-police controls and customs inspections (Art. 6 deutsch-tschechisches Abkommen über den Kleinen Grenzverkehr auf Wanderwegen und in Touristenzonen sowie über den Grenzübertritt in besonderen Fällen vom 2 Dec. 1994 [*BGBl.* 2 (1994): 3844]; Art. 5[1] deutsch-polnisches Abkommen über den Kleinen Grenzverkehr of 19 Nov. 1992 [*BGBl.* 2 (1993): 8]). Poland and the Czech Republic feel the spirit of these agreements to be incompatible with Germany's obligations under the Second Treaty of Schengen. Polish and Czech nationals, though privileged under the bilateral Abkommen über den Kleinen Grenzverkehr, are submitted to the tighter controls of nationals of third states as these are prescribed by the Second Treaty of Schengen, with no exceptions being allowed (see *Frankfurter Allgemeine Zeitung*, 31 May 1995, 5).

29. To third states that are not EU members, the "freeze clause" of Art. 9 (2), sentence 1, must appear most dramatic. It restricts any change of visa regulations regarding third states that at the time of signing the treaty were the same for all participating states or that the participating states agreed on afterward. Such regulations can only be altered with the consent of all participating parties.

30. See also Arts. 19–20. Until the introduction of a uniform visa, the participating states will under certain conditions acknowledge each other's national visas (Art. 10[2]). Art. 10 (3) allows certain territorial restrictions of the validity of such visas. Art. 11 describes two forms of the uniform visa: (1) a multiple entry visa, under which the total duration of sojourn may not exceed three months within the half year after the alien's first entry; and (2) a (single or multiple) transfer visa that permits a transfer of no more than five days.

31. With even a preliminary permit being sufficient if the alien possesses a travel document issued by the same contracting state (Art. 21[2]; see also [3]).

32. Matters addressed cover cooperation and transborder communication among the police in general (Arts. 39, 44), the continuation of police observations and pursuits across internal borders (Arts. 40–43), registration of guests in hotels and lodgings (Art. 45), the exchange of police liaison officers (Art. 47), mutual judicial assistance in criminal matters (Arts. 48–53; see also Arts. 54–58 concerning the principle of *ne bis in idem*), extradition (Arts. 59–66), execution of foreign criminal penalties (Art. 67–69), drugs and narcotics (Arts. 70–76), weapons and ammunition (Arts. 77–91). Some critics are skeptical about the effectiveness of these measures; see, e.g., Bieber 1994, 295; and Bäumler 1995, 489. On the executive committee established by the treaty (see Art. 131–33), see Dörr 1993.

33. On the structure of the SIS and problems of the protection of personal data, see ch. J (by H. Bäumler), in Lisken and Denninger 1992, 556–58 nn. 275–87; Bäumler 1995; and Scheller 1992.

34. Again the competence to issue such ordinances rests with the Federal Ministry of the Interior, which can only act with the consent of the Bundesrat.

35. A child born within the territory of the FRG is not automatically a German national, as the German law on nationality applies the rule of jus sanguinis, not jus soli. In general, a residence permit is issued ex officio to the child if the child's mother has a residence permit (for details, see AuslG § 21[1], 29 [2], 31[2]). When this is not the case, an application for a residence permit must be made within six months of birth (§ 69[1], sentence 1) by the child's parents or guardian (see § 68[4]).
36. See n. 13, above. In this respect, the ordinance is based on AuslG § 40 (2).
37. The "new" *Länder* of East Germany were under an obligation to introduce *Meldegesetze* within one year after the unification. See annex 1, ch. 2, subject group C, section 3, no. 4, of the Treaty of Unification of 23 Sept. 1990 (*BGBl.* 2: 885).
38. Federal Framework Law on the Registration of Residence and Domicile of 16 Aug. 1980, new publication of the statute of 24 June 1994 (*BGBl.* 1: 1430), amended by the federal statute of 12 July 1994 (*BGBl.* 1: 1497). On the constitutionality of regulations of the registration laws, see Federal Constitutional Court, order of 15 Mar. 1993, 601–2.
39. Art. 75 of the Basic Law was most recently amended by the federal statute of 27 Oct. 1994 (*BGBl.* 1: 3146). According to its new section 3, in contrast to their constitutional obligations before the amendment, the *Länder* are now under a duty to legislate according to the "pattern of framework rules" within the time limit set up in the relevant federal framework law. However, it is up to the *Länder* to "fill out" the framework with details, especially because in principle it is their laws, not the federal guidelines, that can reach out into the sphere of the individual (see Art. 75[2] of the Basic Law as amended by the federal statute of 27 Oct. 1994).
40. If a person has more than one residence or domicile, each must be registered as either a main or a secondary residence (MRRG § 12).
41. Exceptions are made in favor of people enjoying privileges and immunities under international law, of soldiers, and finally of conscientious objectors performing nonmilitary service (MRRG § 14–15). Moreover, certain modifications are necessary with respect to the crews of seagoing vessels and ships operating on the internal waterways (MRRG § 13).
42. Simplified registration is possible in cases of married couples, families traveling together, or traveling groups (see MRRG § 16[2], sentence 2).
43. Especially, in this context, by the Ausländergesetz (see § 75[2] and 76).
44. Registration—of a similar nature, though with some modifications—is even required for patients in hospitals or nursing homes or similar institutions (MRRG § 16[3]). The data collected, however, is not automatically transferred to the registration offices; instead, it is given to competent authorities only when, according to their knowledge, it is necessary in a single, specific case for the prevention of a substantial and present danger, for criminal prosecution, or for investigation into the fate of missing persons or casualties of accidents (MRRG § 16[3], sentence 3).
45. What is more, specific public authorities may receive information on request without the registration office having to check the admissibility of transfer. In Baden-Württemberg, for instance, these authorities include the courts, the public prosecutor's offices, and the police, especially the last with regard to enforcing the law on aliens.

46. Verordnung über Datenübermittlungen an die Ausländerbehörden (Ausländerdatenübermittlungsverordnung; AuslDÜV) of 18 Dec. 1990 (*BGBl.* 1: 2997; corrected *BGBl.* 1 (1991): 1216), released on the basis of AuslG § 76[5].
47. Section 19 of the Federal Employment Promotion Act (Arbeitsförderungsgesetz) of 25 June 1969 (*BGBl.* 1: 582), most recently amended by the federal statute of 24 July 1995 (*BGBl.* 1: 962, 970).
48. AuslG § 75[1] and [2], sentence 1, and 80, in combination with the Federal Ordinance on the Aliens', Diplomatic and Consular Offices' Management of Files on Aliens of 18 Dec. 1990 (*BGBl.* 1: 2999). See Bäumler 1994, esp. 239–41.
49. The German authorities are under a duty to comply with the request (AuslG § 76[1]).
50. Federal Statute on the Central Aliens Register of 2 Sept. 1994 (*BGBl.* 1: 2265).
51. The AZR-Gesetz has, however, been criticized for intermingling causes of the internal control of aliens with those more closely related to criminal prosecution and public security. See Schriever-Steinberg 1994, 3276.
52. The information recorded basically consists of a so-called VISA-number (i.e., an identification number for use in correspondence with the register office), the name of the competent diplomatic or consular office abroad, data on the applicant, and the date of data transmission (AZR-Gesetz § 29 [1]; see also [3]). For reasons of internal (national) security, the kind of passport document, the number of the passport, and the issuing state are also registered where applications for visas are made by nationals of certain states determined by the Federal Ministry of the Interior in agreement with the Federal Ministry of Foreign Affairs (AZR-Gesetz § 29[2]).
53. Bundesamt für die Anerkennung ausländischer Flüchtlinge. See AsylVfG § 5.
54. An on-line data transmission connection to these public authorities can be installed (AZR-Gesetz § 33).
55. This information is to assist in warding off illegal immigration and preventing crime (statement of the reasons for initiating legislation in the case of the AZR-Gesetz was presented by the federal government, in *Bundesratsdrucksache* 217/94, 45 ["Zu § 2 Absatz 2 Nummer 5"]). On illegal entry, see AuslG § 8 (2); and AsylVfG § 18 (2), no. 3.
56. This is important where an alien has disappeared trying to evade deportation or where a final or preliminary order of detention is issued before the deportee's arrest (AuslG § 57). (See Detention Prior to Deportation, below.) As a result of AZR-Gesetz § 2 (2), no. 6, the General Register shows search notices of the police's INPOL information system as far as they concern aliens (see *Bundesratsdrucksache* 217/94, 46 ["Zu § 2 Absatz 2 Nummer 6"]).
57. See AsylVfG § 66; see also Internal Controls of Asylum Seekers and n. 131, below. On detention prior to deportation, see AuslG § 57 and Detention Prior to Deportation, below. See also n. 56, above.
58. On other public authorities who are allowed to receive information, see AZR-Gesetz § 14, 16–21.
59. See AZR-Gesetz § 22, on this as well as on other public authorities allowed on-line correspondence. See Heyder 1994, 156.
60. This feature of the law has been criticized as allowing a statement of reasons to be handed over to a public authority that is unaware of the larger context of the relevant administrative decision, which could lead to severe

misconceptions. See Schriever-Steinberg 1994, 3276. A notice that any such copies of statements of reasons in a single case are kept in the Bundesverwaltungsamt's files is to be entered in the General Register. In practice, however, this is often omitted, which diminishes the files' value.

61. Under certain stricter conditions, search notices can also be used by the federal and Länder Offices for the Protection of the Constitution (Verfassungsschutzbehörden), the Office for Military Counterintelligence (Militärischer Abschirmdienst), and the Federal Intelligence Service (Bundesnachrichtendienst) to gain other information (AZR-Gesetz § 5[2]).

62. Interestingly, all these regulations are in compliance with Art. 22 of the Second Treaty of Schengen, which calls for a system of registering aliens from third-party states to be established in every of the contracting states (see also Art. 45 of the treaty).

63. See Bäumler 1995, 240—41, where the author points out the subsidiary applicability of the general restrictions of the Bundesdatenschutzgesetz (Federal Statute on the Protection of Data) of 20 Dec. 1990 (*BGBl.* 1: 2954) as most recently amended by the federal statute of 14 Sept. 1994 (*BGBl.* 1: 2378); and, in Hassemer and Starzacher 1995, K. Starzacher (12), W. Hassemer (16–19), H. Fromm (50–53), H. Bäumler (66–71), and H. Bäumer (72–74). On the AZR-Gesetz in particular, see Bäumler 1995, 242–43; and Schriever-Steinberg 1994. See also Heyder 1994, 157. Recently, nine persons have raised constitutional complaints against AZR-Gesetz before the Federal Constitutional Court (*Frankfurter Allgemeine Zeitung*, 22 Sept. 1995, 11).

64. The immeasurable importance of ensuring efficient updates can be illustrated by a case that was orally reported to this author: An alien's identity was checked by a police patrol. The Central Aliens Register was routinely consulted by the officers. The register contained a search notice (see above) calling for the man's arrest. It was Friday afternoon, however, and the aliens' office was already closed for the weekend, so the police took the man into custody. On the following morning they found him dead in his cell; he had hanged himself. The search notice, it turned out, should have been erased long before. But when the man had moved and the local administrative competences had consequently changed, the newly responsible aliens' office had not been informed of the existence of the search notice and therefore had taken no steps to have it removed.

65. See, however, AuslG § 69—especially (3)—as to the status of an alien who applies for a residence permit after the expiration of his or her visa or former residence permit.

66. The same rules apply in cases where aliens are permitted to apply for residence permits after entry and make their applications within the time limit. See also Control Through Residence Permits and Notification of Residence to the Aliens' Office, above.

66. The ultimate deadline for departure is six months after the duty to leave the territory of the FRG has become noncontestable. It should be mentioned that according to AuslG § 42 (4) an alien can comply with the obligation to depart by entering a member state of the European Community only if his or her entry and sojourn there are legal according to the law of the member state concerned.

68. It might appear awkward to speak of the enforceability of an abstract legal obligation. But the terminology of the Ausländergesetz merely expresses that, as a rule, deportation of an alien involves no more than the enforcement of his or her obedience to AuslG § 42, rather than the enforcement of an administrative act explicitly ordering him or her to leave the country. As mentioned above, only the act of expulsion (*Ausweisung*) can be understood to contain the individual order to depart.
69. Federal Law on the Procedure of the Administrative Courts of 21 Jan. 1961, new publication of 19 Mar. 1991, as most recently amended by the federal statute of 1 Nov. 1996 (*BGBl.* 1: 1626). See also VwGO § 58 and 70 (2) as to the prolongation of the time limit when the person affected by an administrative act has not been informed of his or her right to file an objection.
70. See also VwGO § 80 (2), no. 3, which allows exceptions from the rule of VwGO § 80 (1) to be made by federal statute.
71. When an alien has illegally entered the territory of the FRG, he or she is to be directly returned to the state from which he or she departed by means of a *Zurückschiebung* (AuslG § 61[1]), which is basically governed by the same rules as *Abschiebung* (deportation; see AuslG § 61[3]) and therefore not specifically dealt with in the text.
72. On the fulfillment of the obligation to leave the country, see AuslG § 42 (3) and (4).
73. Kloesel, Christ, and Häußer (1993) interpret AuslG § 49 (2), sentence 1, as requiring surveillance even in cases where an alien is detained by the police without a court order (AuslG § 49, 4 nn. 11–12).
74. The constitutional principle of proportionality calls for a restrictive interpretation of this reason for deportation. At the least, the alien must be legally obliged to give the information concerned, and there must be a connection between the declarations and the alien's duty to depart (Kanein and Renner 1993, AuslG § 49, 202 n. 8).
75. See also the Basic Law, Art. 86, which defines the federation's powers in cases of direct federal administration, and Art. 87, which lists matters of direct federal administration.
76. One might well argue, however, that there would nevertheless be a way of achieving uniformity of execution, for the constitution does allow the federal government, with the consent of the Bundesrat—where the *Länder* execute federal laws as matters of their own concern—to issue pertinent general administrative rules equally binding on all the *Länder* (Basic Law, Art. 84[2]). Yet even then there is no safeguard against a *Land*'s authorities deviating from these general rules in specific single cases. It may be added that the Ausländergesetz follows a much-criticized practice by empowering not the federal government as a corporate body but the minister of the interior as a single member of the federal government to issue such administrative rules with the consent of the Bundesrat (AuslG § 104).
77. When a court ruling that deportation in a specific case is admissible becomes nonappealable, a stay of deportation is only possible when deportation is impossible for legal or factual reasons or when a general stay is ordered according to AuslG § 54 (AuslG § 55[4], sentence 1).
78. Randelzhofer 1985, 417, 422. But cf. Doehring 1985: "In the sphere of human rights a duty to admit a foreigner only exists if his/her life is clearly and directly threatened" (11 f).

79. Most recently signed were the multilateral treaty with Belgium, France, Italy, Luxembourg, the Netherlands, and Poland (see n. 28, above) and the bilateral treaties with Romania (24 Sept. 1992, with protocol of 28 Oct. 1992, publication of 9 Feb. 1993, *BGBl.* 2: 220), Switzerland (20 Dec. 1993, to replace the agreement of 28 Dec. 1954, *Bundesanzeiger* no. 19/55), Croatia (25 Apr. 1994), Bulgaria (9 Sept. 1994, with protocol, publication of 16 Jan. 1995, *BGBl.* 2: 99–104), the Czech Republic (3 Nov. 1994, with protocols, publication of 27 Jan. 1995, *BGBl.* 2: 133–44), and the Socialist Republic of Vietnam (21 July 1995, with protocol, publication of 6 Sept. 1995, *BGBl.* 2: 743). Other agreements exist with Austria (19 July 1961, *Bundesanzeiger* no. 169/61), Denmark (31 May 1954, *Bundesanzeiger* no. 120/54), France (22 Jan. 1960, *Bundesanzeiger* no. 63/60), Norway (18 Mar. 1955, *Bundesanzeiger* no. 84/55), and Sweden (31 May 1954, *Bundesanzeiger* no. 120/54). On the negotiations with Vietnam, see *Frankfurter Allgemeine Zeitung*, 12 Jan. 1995, 1, 2.
80. AuslG § 51 attempts to translate the phrase used in Art. 1 (2) and Art. 33 (1) of the Geneva Convention Relating to the Status of Refugees (189 U.N.T.S. 137; 606 U.N.T.S. 267; see Federal Administrative Court, judgment of 18 Jan. 1994, 42–53). The attempt is insufficient as *nationality* is translated by *Staatsangehörigkeit* (meaning nationality in the sense of the legal bond between a state and its national) and not, as would be correct, by *Nationalität* or *Volkszugehörigkeit* (meaning a person's belonging to an ethnic group). See Richter 1991, 40 f.
81. On the practical operation of AuslG § 51, see Federal Administrative Court, order of 5 July 1994, 391–93. In its judgment of 10 May 1994 (24–28), the Federal Administrative Court held that a judgment merely denying an applicant the right of asylum under Art. 16a (1) of the Basic Law has no binding effect (in the sense of res judicata) on a decision on the applicant's entitlement to protection under AuslG § 51 (1).
82. In case of a positive decision by the Federal Office, the alien is to be granted a residence permit according to AuslG § 5, no. 4, and 30 (*Aufenthaltsbefugnis*) if for legal or factual reasons his or her deportation is not merely temporarily impossible (AsylVfG § 70[1]). The impossibility of deportation results if no other state that is not banned as a "target" state by AuslG § 51, 53 is willing to admit the alien. In cases of temporary obstacles to deportation, it does not seem impossible for the aliens' office to issue a residence permit, again according AuslG § 5, no. 4, § 30, and to limit strictly its validity in time. However, AsylVfG § 70 (1), in connection with AuslG § 55 (2), does seem to imply that a short-term impossibility of deportation is to be dealt with by tolerating the alien.

Regarding the extent of protection under AuslG § 51 (1), it should be mentioned that according to AuslG § 51 (3) (see also AsylVfG § 70[2]) deportation is not hindered by the danger of persecution in the "target" state if there are powerful reasons to consider the alien a threat to the security of the FRG or if he or she presents a risk to the public as a result of having been convicted of an especially severe criminal offense without the possibility of appeal. This exception from nondeportability, the constitutionality of which is controversial, applies to asylum seekers who have not yet been recognized as privileged by Art. 16a of the Basic Law (AuslG § 52).

83. In these cases, extradition law applies, according to which extradition is forbidden if the receiving state does not guarantee that either there will be no death sentence or the death penalty, if imposed, will not be carried out. See § 8 of the Gesetz über die internationale Rechtshilfe in Strafsachen (Law on international Legal Assistance in Criminal Cases) of 23 Dec. 1982 (*BGBl.* 1: 2071); and the revised statute of 27 June 1994 (*BGBl.* 1: 1537).
84. Federal Law of 7 Aug. 1952 consenting to the European Convention for Human Rights and Fundamental Freedoms (*BGBl.* 2: 685, 953).
85. Interestingly, AuslG § 53 (5) expressly declares that no legal obstacle to deportation exists when there is a general danger of an alien's being exposed to criminal prosecution or punishment or, subject to the provisions of § 53 (1) through (4), the alien faces the concrete danger of suffering a penalty in accordance with the legal order of the relevant foreign state.
86. In favor of this stance, see Cremer 1994, 426, as well as 255–309 and 405–11. For contrary arguments, see Hailbronner 1995b, 137.
87. According to AuslG § 53 (6), sentence 2, dangers in a target state to which the (whole) population or the population group to which the alien belongs is exposed are to be dealt according to AuslG § 54.

    When a court ruling that deportation in a specific case is admissible becomes nonappealable, a stay of deportation according to § 53 (6) is only possible when the act warning the alien of deportation has made a provision to this effect (AuslG § 55[4], sentence 2).
88. On the constitutionality of AuslG § 54, see Bäuerle and Kleindiek 1995 and Bryde 1994.

    Political controversies arose between several *Bundesländer* and the Federal Ministry of the Interior over the question of generally staying the deportation of Turkish citizens of Kurdish nationality when six-month stays ordered by these *Länder* were about to expire. Only after eight Kurdish members of the Turkish parliament were sentenced by a Turkish court to prison terms for being militant representatives of the Labor Party of Kurdistan (PKK) and as such supporters of a separatist movement and terrorists, did the federal government recommend that the *Länder* abstain until 20 January 1995 from deporting to Turkey Kurds illegally staying in the FRG. Simultaneously, the federal minister of the interior consented to a postponement (*Aufschub*) of all such deportations until that date and later recommended the prolongation of the standstill (except for criminals) until mid-March 1995. Whether this was a consent to a general stay of deportation under AuslG § 54—at least for those Kurds who are suspected to be members of the PKK—is not quite clear (see Hessian High Administrative Court, 70–71; see also *Frankfurter Allgemeine Zeitung*, 22 Nov. 1994, 2; 14 Dec. 1994; 31 Jan. 1995, 2; 13 Dec. 1994, 1, 7; 23 Feb. 1995, 1, 5; 24 Feb. 1995, 6; 2 Mar. 1995, 4; 16 Mar. 1995, 5; 17 Mar. 1995, 1; 18 Mar. 1995, 1; and 27 Oct. 1995, 8). The stay of deportation of principally all Turkish nationals of Kurdish ethnicity issued by the Hessian minister of the interior on 13 June 1995 has been ruled null and void by the Hessischer Verwaltungsgerichtshof (68–72).

    On the so-called Autobahn incident (during which Kurdish protesters blocked the Autobahn Stuttgart-Munich), see Bayerischer Verwaltungsgerichtshof, order of 6 May 1994, 941–43; order of 18 July 1994, 59–60.

The exchange of letters between the Turkish and German ministers of the interior, in which an agreement was reached on the treatment of unsuccessful asylum seekers returned to Turkey, is quoted by the Federal Constitutional Court, order of 23 Mar. 1995, 51–52; see also *Frankfurter Allgemeine Zeitung*, 11 Jan. 1995, 1; 18 Jan. 1995, 5; and 11 Mar. 1995, 1.

89. AuslG § 50 (4) determines the consequences of a (court) order suspending the duty to depart or the warning of deportation and thereby interrupting the time limit set for departure: should the suspension be lifted, a new deadline need not be fixed even if the original limit has elapsed.

According to AuslG § 50 (5), when an alien, by judicial order, has been imprisoned or otherwise taken into public custody (§ 49[2], sentence 1), a deadline need not be fixed at all, but deportation should be announced a week before its execution.

90. However, according to the statement of reasons for initiating legislation in the case of the Gesetz zur Neuregelung des Ausländerrechts (see n. 1, above) (*Bundestagsdrucksache* 11/6321, 76, "Zu § 57"), preparatory detention was intended to be limited without exception to six weeks.

91. (Federal) Statute on the Court Procedure in Cases of Deprivation of Liberty of 29 June 1956 (*BGBl.* 1: 599), as most recently amended by federal statute of 24 June 1994, *BGBl.* 1: 1325.

92. The court, however, is restricted to determining whether the alien's former right of sojourn has been effectively terminated by an administrative act, with the court largely being unable to adjudicate on the legality of such act (that being a matter of the administrative courts' jurisdiction), and whether the duty to leave the country has been lifted as a result of an application for asylum (see Hailbronner 1995a, AuslG § 57, 16–19 nn. 45–53; Bundesgerichtshof, decision of 12 June 1986, 112).

93. See AuslG § 42 (1) and (2), sentence 1, no. 1. An exception from ordering detention can be made when an alien has substantiated by prima facie evidence that he or she will not elude deportation (AuslG § 57[2], sentence 3).

94. For details, see Hailbronner 1995a, AuslG § 57, 23–24 n. 64. During a prison term or pretrial custody, an (additional) order of detention under AuslG § 57 (2) can be made, but this will go into effect no sooner than the alien otherwise would have to be released (*Überhaft nach Untersuchungs- oder Strafhaft*). However, even such an order of detention securing deportation requires the fulfillment of the specific conditions of AuslG § 57 (2) (see Hailbronner 1995a, AuslG § 57, 23–24 nn. 64–67; Oberlandesgericht Düsseldorf, 7; Oberlandesgericht Frankfurt/Main, 8).

95. In these cases, an oral hearing before the decision is not necessary when any delay would increase the danger, for example, of the alien's absconding; however, a hearing must follow as soon as possible.

96. See Federal Constitutional Court, order of 13 July 1994, 57–58; see also Bundesgerichtshof, decision of 12 June 1986, 112–44; cf. decision of 6 Dec. 1979, 382–83. As the constitutional principle of proportionality calls for a careful evaluation of the facts of the case, the urgent necessity of hearing the person to be detained in each and every case before the issuance of a final order of detention, as declared obligatory by FEVG § 5, becomes evident. See Detention Securing Deportation, above.

97. It should also be kept in mind that the administrative courts have the power to make their orders reactivating the suspensive effect of an admin-

istrative objection or the filing of a claim (see The Enforceability of the Obligation to Depart, above) dependent on judicial bond (VwGO § 80[5], sentence 4; see below, Important Modifications). When administrative acts activating AuslG § 42 (1) are suspended, the duty to depart becomes unenforceable (see AuslG § 42[2], sentence 2, and The Enforceability of the Obligation to Depart, above), and thus an order of preparatory detention—although it is not inadmissible (see Kanein and Renner 1993, AuslG § 57, 229 n. 11)—at least becomes more difficult to justify. See also VwGO § 123 in connection with § 921 of the Code on Civil Procedure (Zivilprozeßordnung of 30 Jan. 1877 [*Reichsgesetzblatt* (Journal of the German Reich), 83]), as most recently amended by federal statute of 18 Dec. 1995 (*BGBl.* 1: 1959).

98. Probably most spectacular was the revolt in the prison in Kassel, in the Bundesland Hessia. On 24 July 1994, only a few days after a visit to the prison by the Hessian minister of justice, Ms. Hohmann-Dennhardt, about forty inmates threatened to blow up a (fake) bomb and took a prison officer hostage, demanding safe passage to a neighboring state (*Frankfurter Allgemeine Zeitung*, 25 July 1994, 1; 29 July 1994, 3). See also Windgasse 1994, 167.

99. See the report by the Commission on Questions Concerning Foreigners and Ethnic Minorities in Rat der Evangelischen Kirche in Deutschland 1994, 27–30; and Windgasse 1994, 159–72. See also D. Deckers, in *Frankfurter Allgemeine Zeitung*, 29 July 1994, 3; and the report by H. Prantl in *Süddeutsche Zeitung*, 10/11 Dec. 1994, 10. Quite positive, however, is the report by the Committee for the Prevention of Torture and Inhuman or Degrading Treatment or Punishment (Council of Europe 1993, 23–25, II.B., nos. 46–58; 64, III.B., nos. 210–11; and appendix 1, 71, I.B].

100. Bundesministerium des Innern 1994, 61–63. The penal institutions thus act on behalf and under the supervision of the aliens' offices and merely render administrative assistance. On the execution of detention by penal institutions, see FEVG § 8 (2) and § 2–122, 171, and 173–75 of the federal statute on the Execution of Prison Sentences and Measures for the Prevention of Crime and the Reformation of Offenders (Gesetz über den Vollzug der Freiheitsstrafe und der freiheitsentziehenden Maßregeln der Besserung und Sicherung—Strafvollzugsgesetz—StVollzG) of 16 Mar. 1976 (*BGBl.* 1 [1976]: 581, 2088; *BGBl.* 1 [1977]: 436), most recently amended by the federal statute of 17 Dec. 1990 (*BGBl.* 1: 2847).

101. Therefore, StVollzG § 171, in connection with FEVG § 8 (2), can be understood to demand the separation of convicts and aliens detained under AuslG § 57.

102. In Baden-Württemberg, however, three detainees share a three-bed container shelter of 12.5 square meters (about 13 2/3 square yards) with a bath compartment.

103. In Berlin, the average duration of detention is reported to be 116 day for Algerian, 97 days for Lebanese, and 17 days for Polish deportees (see H. Prantl, in *Süddeutsche Zeitung*, 10/11 Dec. 1994). At the detention center in Büren, North-Rhine Westfalia, the average duration is said to be 60 days (see D. Deckers, in *Frankfurter Allgemeine Zeitung*, 29 July 1994). These numbers somewhat differ from those given by the Bundesministerium des Innern 1994, 58–61.

104. Doubts as to the proportionality of this provision are expressed by Kanein and Renner 1993, AuslG § 42, 160–61 n. 19; an opposing viewpoint can be found in Hailbronner 1995a, AuslG § 42, 11–12 n. 38; see also Kloesel, Christ, and Häußer 1993, AuslG § 42, 8 n. 27.
105. This is intended to prevent the alien from hiding or destroying the passport, which could obstruct deportation. While public international law forbids a permanent withdrawal of the passport (as this would amount to a cancellation of the sovereign act of a foreign state), the enforcement of a temporary deposit is admissible (Kanein and Renner 1993, AuslG § 42, 160 n. 18, 40, 154 n. 3, and 4, 23 n. 8; Hailbronner 1995a, AuslG § 4, 2 n. 4).
106. The Gesetz über das Zentralregister und das Erziehungsregister (Bundeszentralregistergesetz, or BZRG) (federal statute on the Central Register and the Correctional Register of Juvenile Delinquents) of 18 Mar. 1971 (*BGBl*. 1: 243), new publication of 21 Sept. 1984 (*BGBl*. 1: 1229, corrected *BGBl*. 1 [1985]: 195 most recently amended by federal statute of 15 July 1996 [*BGBl*. 1: 980]); especially § 10 (1), nos. 1 and 2, 19, 32 (1), and 41 (1), no. 7.
107. The same can be said of cases of factual impossibility of deportation. These cases can, however, be set aside when discussing judicial remedies against deportation.
108. See The Enforceability of the Obligation to Depart, above.
109. Furthermore, an alien's obligation to leave the country is enforceable inter alia if the alien, after the expiration of his or her residence permit, has not applied for its prolongation or for some other residence permit or if the alien has failed to apply for the first grant of a necessary residence permit and the legally limited time for such application has elapsed (AuslG § 42 [2], nos. 2 and 3). If in these cases the alien does (within one year) apply for a residence permit, the competent aliens' office can use its discretion under AuslG § 97 to decide that the temporary interruption of the legality of sojourn is irrelevant. Under this condition, the application itself will bring into effect the fiction of the alien's sojourn being legal according to AuslG § 69 (3).

However, if an alien has not left the country who (1) has illegally entered the territory of the FRG, (2) has been expelled, or (3) is obliged to leave the country by any other administrative act or if such an alien's former application for a residence permit has been rejected, he or she does not even enjoy the privilege of fictitiously being tolerated according to AuslG § 69 (2) if he or she applies for a residence permit.
110. However, see VwGO § 80 (2), no. 4.
111. See also AsylVfG § 5 (1); and Legal Impossibility of Deportation, above.
112. See n. 7, above. In three judgments of 14 May 1996 (case nos. 2 BVR 1507, 1508, 1516, 1938, 2315/93), the Federal Constitutional Court rejected as unfounded the constitutional complaints of five unsuccessful asylum seekers claiming that substantial parts of the AsylVfG were unconstitutional. The court held that the regulations concerning the so-called airport procedure (see n. 116, below), safe third states (see nn. 135, 137, and 141, below), and safe countries of origin (see n. 115, below), as well as Art. 16a of the Basic Law, a recent amendment to the constitution, were in conformity with the constitution. On the material problems concerned, see Schoch 1993; Wollenschläger and Schraml 1994.

113. AuslG § 73 (2) imposes on professional carriers of aircraft, seagoing vessels, or land vehicles the duty to take out of the country (on possible destinations, see AuslG § 73[3]) all aliens whom they have brought into the territory of the FRG without the necessary papers (passport or visa) legally required of nationals of their respective home states and who are not rejected at the border because they have alleged that they are politically prosecuted, that they would be in danger of torture if deported (AuslG § 53 [1]), or that their deportation would be in violation of the European Convention for Human Rights and Fundamental Freedoms (AuslG § 53[4]). This obligation lasts three years at the longest; it is terminated by the alien's receiving a residence permit (AuslG § 5) under the Ausländergesetz. Doubts as to the constitutionality of this provision are expressed in Kanein and Renner 1993, AuslG § 73, 275–76 n. 12.
114. Only photographs and fingerprints can be taken (AsylVfG § 16[1], sentence 2). The records are collected by the Federal Bureau of Criminal Investigation (Bundeskriminalamt) in files that are kept strictly separate (AsylVfG § 16[4]). On the bureau's Automated Fingerprint Identification System (Automatisiertes Fingerabdruckidentifizierungssystem, or AFIS), see Bundesministerium des Innern 1994, 37–39.
115. Annex 2 is based on Art. 16a (3), sentence 1, of the Basic Law. AsylVfG § 29a (3) allows the federal government, with the consent of the Bundesrat, to issue an ordinance declaring that a state listed in annex 2 to the AsylVfG is no longer to be considered a safe home state when changes in the legal or political situation of the state give reason to assume that the conditions required by Art. 16a (3), sentence 1, of the Basic Law have ceased to be met, i.e., freedom from political persecution and inhuman and degrading treatment is no longer guaranteed. Such a federal ordinance loses its validity six months after entering into force at the latest. Therefore, striking Gambia off the list of safe home states (federal ordinance of 6 Oct. 1994, *BGBl.* 1: 2850) was merely a temporary measure. Meanwhile, Gambia has been excluded (by federal statute of 31 Mar. 1995, [*BGBl.* 1: 430]).
116. See AsylVfG § 18a (4) and 36 (4) for details. See also Bundesministerium des Innern 1994, 26–34; Hailbronner 1994, 85–89. Doubts as to the fairness of the administrative and judicial proceedings have led to a discussion over the constitutionality of AsylVfG § 18a; see Kugelmann 1994; and Marx 1995, § 18a, 198 n. 4, 209 n. 36. In one of its judgments of 14 May 1996 (case no. 2 BvR 1516/93), the Federal Constitutional Court ruled that, under AsylVfG § 18a (4), the administrative court must on request grant those asylum seekers who applied for interim judicial relief within the three-day deadline another four days in which to present their arguments (283).
117. AsylVfG § 22a deals with aliens who have, under an international treaty, been taken over by the FRG in order to conduct an asylum procedure. Such aliens are to be considered equal to asylum seekers and are under the duty to report to the competent office (which is determined by the Federal Ministry of the Interior or by the competent authority appointed by it) on entry or immediately after entry. This provision stands in the context of the Treaty on the Determination of the State Competent to Examine an Application for Asylum Made in One of the Member States of the European Communities (Treaty of Dublin) of 15 June 1990 (federal statute consenting to the treaty of 27 June 1994, *BGBl.* 1: 791). The Treaty of Dublin aims at

reducing the possibilities for asylum shopping. See also the so-called Bonn Protocol of 26 Apr. 1994 (*BGBl.* 2 [1995]: 739) on the Consequences of the Entering into Force of the Dublin Convention on Some Provisions of the Second Treaty Schengen (federal statute consenting to the Protocol of 11 Sept. 1995, *BGBl.* 2: 738).
118. Where he or she will be accepted or will, after identification measures have been taken (if possible), be directed to the competent admission center. See AsylVfG § 22.
119. The police are to deal with aliens much the same as the border-control offices do (AsylVfG § 19).
120. Exceptions to this rule are made by AsylVfG § 14 (2) when

- a foreigner possesses a residence permit whose total duration of validity exceeds six months;
- he or she is in prison or has otherwise been taken into custody by public authorities, is in a hospital or nursing home or a child or youth welfare institution; or
- he or she is not yet sixteen years old and has a parent or guardian not obliged to live in an admission center.

121. However, a written application for asylum made at the aliens' office must be transferred to the Federal Office immediately (AsylVfG § 14[2], sentence 2).
122. AsylVfG § 19 and 22 imply that these asylum seekers are neither required nor even expected to know the competent center but rather are free to report to any admission center, to an aliens' office, or to the police.
123. According to AsylVfG § 15 (3), the relevant documents and papers include documents necessary for personal identification and verification of nationality; visas, residence permits, and other documents necessary for crossing borders; travel tickets; documents containing information on the route and means of travel taken from the alien's home country and on times of sojourn in other states en route; and documents to which the alien refers in his or her application or that contain information relevant to the asylum procedure, especially as to possibilities for returning the alien to any third state.
124. The asylum seeker can demand to receive copies of the documents. All documents and papers—especially the passport or substitute passport document (AsylVfG § 65)—will be returned when they are no longer needed for the asylum procedure or the administrative procedures leading to the alien's removal from the territory (AsylVfG § 21[4] and [5]).
125. When the asylum seeker illegally enters the FRG from a third state in the sense of AsylVfG § 26a and Art. 16a (2), sentence 1, of the Basic Law, the *Aufenthaltsgestattung* comes into existence when the application for asylum is made (AsylVfG § 55[1], sentence 3).
126. When the alien can directly apply for asylum at the Federal Office (AsylVfG § 14[2]), the *Aufenthaltsgestattung* is restricted to the district of the aliens' office of his or her residence (AsylVfG § 56[1], sentence 2).
127. An asylum seeker who is required to live in an admission center can without special permission leave the district in order to attend a hearing by an administrative authority or a court if his or her presence is necessary; he or she must, however, notify the admission center and the Federal Office in advance (AsylVfG § 57[3]). This duty of notification does not extend to other aliens not, or no longer, required to live in an admission center (AsylVfG § 58[3]).

128. When the asylum seeker is required to live in an admission center, the Federal Office can give such permission if there are urgent reasons (AsylVfG § 57[1]) and should do so immediately when the alien must keep an appointment with his or her legal representative, with the UN High Commissioner for Refugees, or with organizations dealing with the welfare of refugees (AsylVfG § 57[2]). Other asylum seekers can more easily receive permission to leave the district from the competent aliens' office, either in single cases or, with the consent of the aliens' offices whose districts are concerned, in general (for details, see AsylVfG § 58[1], [2], [4], and [5]). By ordinance, each government of a *Bundesland* can give these aliens general permission to stay temporarily in more than one office's district (AsylVfG § 58[6]).

129. Where an application has been successful before the Federal Office or a court has ordered the Federal Office to acknowledge an alien as entitled to asylum (this court decision not having to be noncontestable), the possibility of an asylum seeker earning wages must not be excluded (AsylVfG § 61[2]).

130. Cases of the *Aufenthaltsgestattung* losing its validity earlier are listed in AsylVfG § 67[1], nos. 1–5 (see also [2]).

131. AsylVfG § 66 (1), according to which the alien can be searched for when he or she

> having been directed to an admission center, has not arrived there within one week;
> has left the admission center and has not returned within a week;
> has not obeyed an order to live in an admission center or a directive under AsylVfG § 60 (2) to take up residence in a specified town or place within one week; or
> has not been reachable at the address that he or she has given or at the address of the quarters in which he or she has been ordered to take up residence (an alien is considered unreachable whenever he or she has failed to take possession, within two weeks, of any document served on him or her at the address in question).

It should be mentioned that, for the course of the asylum procedure, the asylum seeker is under the duty to make provisions ensuring that he or she will receive any information or document from the Federal Office, the competent aliens' office, and any court before which he or she has taken action; in particular, he or she must immediately give these institutions notice of every change of address (AsylVfG § 10[1]; see also [3]–[4]). Attached to this obligation is the legal fiction that the alien has received any document served on him at the last known address and any piece of information otherwise delivered to this address (for details, see AsylVfG § 10[2]). On the influence of the constitutional rules of due process on these provisions, see Federal Constitutional Court, order of 10 Mar. 1994, 2 BvR 2371/93, 25–26; and order of 10 Mar. 1994, 27.

132. On the special treatment of aliens who have possessed residence permits, see AsylVfG § 43.

133. According to AsylVfG § 36 and 38, the time limits allowed differ depending on whether the application has been dismissed as irrelevant (see § 29) or obviously unfounded (see § 30) or the asylum seeker has for other reasons not been acknowledged to be privileged by Art. 16a (1) of the Basic Law.

134. See also AsylVfG § 39 (on this, see n. 135, below). When the unsuccessful asylum seeker is to be deported to a safe third state, in the sense of AsylVfG § 26a, the Federal Office is to order the deportation (with no need for a warning or for setting a deadline for departure) as soon as it is clear that deportation is possible (AsylVfG § 34a[1], sentences 1 and 3). The Federal Office is to proceed likewise when the alien has restricted the application for asylum to the claim of there being a legal obstacle to deportation under the—one might say—"nonrefoulement provision" of AuslG § 51 (1) or has withdrawn his or her application for asylum before the Federal Office's decision (AsylVfG § 34a (1), sentence 2).

It is important to note that in these cases AsylVfG § 34a (2) precludes any measures of interim judicial relief. The constitutionality of this provision is being debated in the light of Art. 19 (4) of the Basic Law; see, e.g., M. Funke-Kaiser, in Fritz and Vormeier 1995, § 34 (a), 14–15 n. 31; Huber 1993, 741; Marx 1995, § 34 (a), 416–17 nn. 47–49; and Schoch 1993, 1168. In one of its decisions of 14 May 1996 (case nos. 2 BvR 1938 and 2315/93), the Federal Constitutional Court held that AsylVfG § 34a (2) was basically in conformity with Art. 16a (2), sentence 3, of the Basic Law and that the constitutional amendment introducing Art. 16a was valid. The court emphasized the concept of "normative reassurance" underlying Art. 16a of the Basic Law, according to which it was the parliamentary legislator's task to define safe third states. The court concluded that interim judicial relief was only admissible under exceptional circumstances, especially as far as the legislator's judgment on the safe situation in the third state, because of the abstract, general, and prognostic standard applied (see Art. 16a (2), sentences 1 and 2, of the Basic Law), could not take into account the specific facts of an individual case (2 BvR 1938, 2315/93, 251–51; see also 255).

135. See AsylVfG § 31, ¶¶ 2–5, which also specifies exceptions to this general rule. The most important exception is allowed when the Federal Office recognizes the applicant as an asylee privileged under Art. 16a (1) of the Basic Law. When such a (positive) decision is lifted by the judgment of an administrative court, the Federal Office must issue a warning of deportation fixing a one-month deadline for departure, and, when it has not done so before, it must decide whether there are legal obstacles to deportation under AuslG § 53 (AsylVfG § 39).

136. Similarly, the Federal Office informs the competent aliens' office of any order of deportation under AsylVfG § 34a (AsylVfG § 40[3]).

137. The aliens' office has no power to decide whether there is an obstacle to deportation under AuslG § 51 (1), as this matter is dealt with by the Federal Office exclusively (see n. 82, above). However, the aliens' office must decide whether, after the Federal Office's decision, an obstacle to deportation stemming from proceedings pending extradition (AuslG § 53[3]; see Legal Impossibility of Deportation, above) has arisen (AsylVfG § 42, sentence 2).

Furthermore, when the Federal Office has affirmed that there is an obstacle to deportation under AuslG § 53 (6) (cases of a substantial concrete danger to limb, life, or liberty in the target state), its decision leads to a three-month stay of deportation (for details, see AsylVfG § 41[1]). The aliens' office can, however, repeal the decision of the Federal Office, and, after the three months have elapsed, it is competent to decide on its own whether there is, or continues to be, an obstacle under AuslG § 53 (6) and it is therefore willing to tolerate the alien. See AsylVfG § 41 (1), sentence 1, and (2).

Finally, it should be mentioned that, when a married couple, or parents and children of minor age, simultaneously or respectively but immediately after their entry into the country, have applied for asylum, the aliens' office can temporarily stay deportation in order to allow the family to depart together (AsylVfG § 43[3]).

138. The initiation of court proceedings further suspends the administrative act when the decision by which recognition as an asylee is repealed is contested (AsylVfG § 75, in connection with § 73). In all other cases (thus especially when a successive or second application for asylum does not induce the (re)initiation of an asylum procedure; on these cases, see AsylVfG § 71, 71a), the suspensive effect of court proceedings (in the form of the *Anfechtungsklage*) must be expressly ordered by the court.
139. According to AsylVfG § 67 (1), no. 4, the *Aufenthaltsgestattung* becomes invalid when a warning of deportation has become enforceable; however, this is prevented by the suspensive effect of judicial proceedings.
140. But see AsylVfG § 34a (2), which excludes such measures when an alien is to be deported to a safe third state.
141. Postponement of the decision is restricted. See AsylVfG § 36 (3), sentences 5–7. As to doubts concerning the constitutionality of these restrictions, see Schoch 1993, 1169. Generally, oral hearings are not be held, and, when held, they are restricted to the motion for interim judicial relief; the principal claim is not to be dealt with (AsylVfG § 36[3], sentence 4). The verdict of unconstitutionality might well have to be attached to AsylVfG § 36 (3), sentences 8–9, whose provisions permit the deportation of an unsuccessful applicant for interim judicial relief as soon as the operative part of the court's decision (denying relief), signed by the judge, is available (!) at the office of the clerk of the court. In other words, the applicant can be deported before the decision has been formally served on him. See Schoch 1993, 1169–70; but see also Marx 1995, § 36, 434 n. 31).

In one of its judgments of 14 May 1996 (case no. 2 BvR 1516/93), however, the Federal Constitutional Court held that AsylVfG § 36 (4), sentence 9, was constitutional in the light of Art. 16a (4) of the Basic Law and its intention to accelerate the asylum procedure. The court pointed out that rules of due process were not infringed as the administrative court's decision on interim judicial relief was nonappealable. Furthermore, it denied that AsylVfG § 36 (4), sentence 9, was in discord with Art. 93 (1), no. 4a, of the Basic Law as this constitutional provision did not in every case guarantee a person affected by an act of the state the right to have the Federal Constitutional Court decide on his or her constitutional complaint before the contested act was enforced (283–87, with the jointly dissenting opinions of judges Limbach, Böckenförde, and Sommer on 288–92).
142. In particular, this would mean enabling users to insert or update data directly into the General File (AZR-Gesetz § 7, in connection with § 6; see Heyder 1994, 155).
143. Statistics of the Federal Ministry of the Interior for 1988 through 1990 show that the whereabouts of roughly 11 percent of all asylum seekers were not traceable ("Verbleib ehemaliger Asylbewerber für den Zeitraum 1988 bis 1990—Bundesministerium des Inneren, BMI-V II 4," appendix 7

of Hailbronner 1994, 145). See also Bundesministerium des Innern 1994, 54–56.

The chief of the Bezirksstelle für Asyl Nordbaden (Central Office for Asylum Matters for the Region of North Baden) at Rastatt estimates that presently 30 to 40 percent of all unsuccessful asylum seekers at the Bezirksstelle disappear before deportation. The head of the Ausländerreferat (aliens department) at the Landratsamt Rhein-Neckar-Kreis (Office of the Rhine-Neckar-District) assumes that 50 to 60 percent of unsuccessful asylum seekers evade deportation. This number was judged to be generally realistic by an official of the Ministry of the Interior of Baden-Württemberg. This information was provided to the author in personal interviews.

144. Incentives to leave the country have been offered to non-EU aliens from states from which the FRG formerly recruited workers. These incentives include (1) paying cash bonuses to foreign workers agreeing to return to their home countries (Rückkehrhilfegesetz, Art. 1 of the Gesetz zur Förderung der Rückkehrbereitschaft von Ausländern of 28 Nov. 1983, *BGBl.* 2: 1377), (2) enabling those who agree to leave the country permanently to make use of building-and-loan-association loans (*Bauspardarlehen*) in their home states (Gesetz über eine Wiedereingliederungshilfe im Wohnungsbau für rückkehrende Ausländer of 18 Feb. 1986, *BGBl.* 1: 280), and (3) assisting them with reintegration (*Wiedereingliederungshilfen*) into their home states, such help ranging from supplying information to sending German teachers to Turkish schools and supporting vocational qualification programs (see Bundesministerium des Innern 1994, 45–48, 78–81). Offers of financial aid may be of considerable short-term efficiency and can especially be regarded as "fair" when the aliens concerned are not under the legal duty to depart. However, in times of tight state budgets, such incentives cannot be considered as adequate long-term means of persuasion. The financial offers of the first and second programs have expired, and the federal government does not seem to be inclined to renew them. In no way, it should be stressed, have such incentives ever been used to induce the fulfillment of the obligation to leave the country under AuslG § 42 (1).

145. An intention to violate the duty under public international law to admit one's own nationals to one's territory can only seldom be established or proven as any state can easily claim that an alien's passport has been forged and he or she is not really one of its nationals.

146. Neither the Catholic nor the Protestant churches believe that the church has a right to grant asylum that the state is under a duty to respect. Rather, they consider this act to be a breach of law that can nonetheless be morally justified.

147. See Art. 17 of the Basic Law and parallel norms of the *Länder* constitutions.

148. Apart from this, within the webs of international relations, German immigration policies will always be a delicate balancing act. This is illustrated by the recent scandal at Frankfurt on the Oder, a town roughly thirty-five miles east of Berlin on the border to Poland. A large number of Polish nationals was lured to Germany by a businessman's offer of short-term jobs. The job seekers crossed the border at Frankfurt, possessing neither valid resident's nor work permits, which under German law each of them was required to have. Having thus entered the FRG illegally, they were arrested. News reports spoke of rounding up a great number of Polish

nationals—some of whom claimed to be tourists or shoppers in the *Kleinen Grenzverkehr* (see n. 28, above)—and keeping them confined in some large hall for identification and interrogation. Subsequently, they were all expelled and deported to Poland, their passports stamped *"Ausgewiesen"*— "Expelled." In Poland both the media and the public reacted with shock and rage. Wounds inflicted during World War II, only superficially healed, seemed to break open once more.

The German authorities quickly repealed the expulsions, and the case is presently being investigated (especially as the justice of the measures taken could be debated); however, neither the expulsions nor the deportations prima facie appear to have been unlawful: the Polish nationals concerned had truly been job seekers who had entered Germany illegally.

149. An example of this is visible in the recent escalation and sudden collapse of excitement over seven unsuccessful asylum seekers from the Sudan (see Federal Constitutional Court, order of 23 Aug. 1995,65–66, with editor's note; *Frankfurter Allgemeine Zeitung*, 14 Sept. 1995, 1–2; 15 Sept. 1995, 4; 21 Sept. 1995, 1–2). Furthermore, the Hessia and Rhineland-Palatinate *Bundesländer* have lately issued general stays of deportation for certain asylum seekers who have resided in the FRG for very long periods of time (*Altfallregelung*), an approach the federal minister of the interior has declared to be a breach of (federal) law (*Frankfurter Allgemeine Zeitung*, 11 May 1995, 2). See also *Frankfurter Allgemeine Zeitung*, 7 Nov. 1994, 4; 10 Nov. 1994, 4; 16 Mar. 1995, 5; 20 May 1995, 2; and n. 88, above.

150. The total number of unsuccessful asylum seekers deported has steadily risen from 5,583 in 1990, through 8,232 in 1991 and 10,798 in 1992, to 35,915 in 1993 (Bundesministerium des Innern 1994, 51). Simultaneously, the influx of asylum seekers into the FRG increased from 193,063 in 1990, through 256,112 in 1991, to 438,191 in 1992 (Bundesministerium des Innern 1993, 45–48, 58, 78–81); then, with the new asylum law entering into force on 1 July 1993, it dropped dramatically from the first (224,099) to the second half (98,500) of 1993, that year's numbers totaling 322,599 (Bundesministerium des Innern 1994, 5).

References

Bäuerle, Michael, and Ralf Kleindiek. 1995. "Der generelle Abschiebestopp gem. AuslG § 54." *Neue Zeitschrift für Verwaltungsrecht*: 43–46.

Bäumler, Helmut. 1995. Datenschutz für Ausländer, 239–43. *Neue Zeitschrift für Verwaltungsrecht*. Munich: Beck.

———. 1994. "Schengener Abkommen und Wirtschaftskriminalität: Informationelle Zusammenarbeit der Sicherheitsbehörden." *Computer und Recht*: 487–92.

Bieber, Roland. 1994. "Die Abkommen von Schengen über den Abbau der Grenzkontrollen." *Neue Juristische Wochenschrift*: 294–97.

Bryde, Brun-Otto. 1994. "Gutachten zur Zulässigkeit einer wiederholten generellen Aussetzung der Abschiebung bestimmter Ausländergruppen durch oberste Landesbehörden" (Expert opinion on the admissibility of repeated general stays of deportation issued by the highest administrative authorities), delivered on behalf of the parliamentary group Bündnis 90/Die Grünen in the *Landtag* of Hessiaerstattet. Photocopy.

Bundesministerium des Innern. 1994. "Bericht des Bundesministeriums des Innern über erste Erfahrungen mit den am 1. Juli 1993 in Kraft getretenen Neuregelungen des Asylverfahrensrechts—Asyl-Erfahrungsbericht 1993-." A 3—125 415/10. 25 Feb.

———. 1993. "Aufzeichnung zur Ausländerpolitik und zum Ausländerrecht in der Bundesrepublik Deutschland." A 1 1993—937 020/15. July.

Council of Europe, ed. 1993. "Report to the Government of the Federal Republic of Germany of 20 Oct. 1992 on the Committee's visit to Germany Carried out by the European Committee for the Prevention of Torture and Inhuman or Degrading Treatment or Punishment (CPT) from 8 to 20 December 1991." CPT/Inf (93) 13.

———. 1993. "Bericht des CPT über den Besuch in Deutschland vom 8–20 Dezember 1991." Trans. Federal Government. *Europäische Grundrechte Zeitschrift*: 329–58.

Cremer, Hans-Joachim. 1994. *Der Schutz vor den Auslandsfolgen aufenthaltsbeendender Maßnahmen*. Baden-Baden: Nomos.

Doehring, Karl. 1985. "Aliens, Admission." In *Encyclopedia of Public International Law*, vol. 8, *Human Rights and the Individual in International Law, International Economic Relations*, ed. Rudolf Bernhardt, 11–13. Amsterdam: Elsevier Science.

Dörr, Oliver. 1993. "Das Schengener Durchführungsübereinkommen: Ein Fall des Art. 24 Abs. 1 GG." *Die Öffentliche Verwaltung*: 696–705.

Finkelnburg, Klaus, and Klaus Peter Jank. 1986. *Vorläufiger Rechtsschutz im Verwaltungsstreitverfahren*. 3d ed. Munich: Beck.
Fritz, Roland, and Jürgen Vormeier, eds. 1995. *Gemeinschaftskommentar zum Asylverfahrensgesetz*. Loose-leaf ed. Neuwied, Germany: H. Luchterhand.
Hailbronner, Kay. 1995a. *Ausländerrecht, Kommentar*. Loose-leaf ed. Heidelberg: C. F. Müller.
———. 1995b. "Ausweisung und Abschiebung in der neueren Rechtsprechung und Gesetzgebung." *Juristenzeitung*: 127–38.
———. 1994. *Reform des Asylrechts, Steuerung und Kontrolle des Zuzugs von Ausländern*. Konstanz: Universitätsverlag Konstanz.
Hailbronner, Kay, and Günter Renner. 1991. *Staatsangehörigkeitsrecht, Kommentar*. Munich: Beck.
Hassemer, Winfried, and Karl Starzacher. 1995. *Datenschutz—auch für Ausländer*. Baden-Baden: Nomos.
Heyder, Udo. 1994. "Zum Gesetz über das Ausländerzentralregister." *Zeitschrift für Ausländerrecht*: 153–57.
Huber, Bertold. 1993. "Das Asylrecht nach der Grundgesetzänderung." *Neue Zeitschrift für Verwaltungsrecht*: 736–43.
Kanein, Werner, and Günter Renner. 1993. *Ausländergesetz*. 6th ed. Munich: Beck.
Kloesel, Arno, Rudolf Christ, and Otto Häußer. 1993. *Deutsches Ausländerrecht, Kommentar zum Ausländergesetz und zu den wichtigsten ausländerrechtlichen Vorschriften*. Loose-leaf ed. Stuttgart: W. Kohlhammer.
Kopp, Ferdinand O. 1994. *Verwaltungsgerichtsordnung*. 10th ed. Munich: Beck.
Kugelmann, Dieter. 1994. "Verfassungsmäßigkeit der Flughafenregelung des § 18a AsylVfG." *Zeitschrift für Ausländerrecht*: 158–67.
Lisken, Hans, and Erhard Denninger. 1992. *Handbuch des Polizeirechts*. Munich: Beck.
Makarov, Alexander N., and Hans von Mangoldt. 1993. *Deutsches Staatsangehörigkeitsrecht, Kommentar*. 3d loose-leaf ed. Neuwied, Germany: Alfred Metzner.
Marx, Reinhard. 1995. *Kommentar zum Asylverfahrensgesetz*. 3d ed. Neuwied, Germany: H. Luchterhand.
Pitschas, Rainer. 1993. "Europäisches Polizeirecht als Informationsrecht." *Zeitschrift für Rechtspolitik*: 174–77.
Randelzhofer, Albrecht. 1985. "Nationality." In *Encyclopedia of Public International Law*, vol. 8, *Human Rights and the Individual in International Law, International Economic Relations*, ed. Rudolf Bernhardt, 416–24. Amsterdam: Elsevier Science.
Rat der Evangelischen Kirche in Deutschland, ed. 1994. "Bericht der Kommission für Ausländerfragen und ethnische Minderheiten

('Asylsuchende und Flüchtlinge—Zur Praxis des Asylverfahrens und des Schutzes vor Abschiebung')." Presented at the fifth meeting of the Eighth Synod of the Protestant Church in Germany, Halle/Saale, Nov., Büro der Synode. Drucksache No. III/1, 27–30.

Richter, Stefan. 1991. "Selbstgeschaffene Nachfluchtgründe und die Rechtsstellung von Konventionsflüchtlingen nach der Rechtsprechung des Bundesverfassungsgerichts zum Grundrecht auf Asyl und dem Gesetz zur Neuregelung des Ausländerrechts." *Zeitschrift für ausländisches öffentliches Recht und Völkerrecht* (Heidelberg journal of international law) 51: 1–45.

Saage, Erwin, and Horst Göppinger. 1994. *Freiheitsentziehung und Unterbringung—Materielles Recht und Verfahrensrecht—Kurzkommentar.* 3d ed. Munich: Beck.

Scheller, Susanne M. 1992. "Das Schengener Informationssystem: Rechtshilfeersuchen 'per Computer.'" *Juristenzeitung*: 904–11.

Schmitt Glaeser, Walter. 1989. "Schutz der Privatsphäre." In *Handbuch des Staatsrechts*, vol. 6, *Freiheitsrechte*, ed. Josef Isensee and Paul Kirchhof, 41–107. Heidelberg: C. F. Müller.

Schoch, Friedrich. 1993. "Das neue Asylrecht gemäß Art. 16a GG." *Deutsches Verwaltungsblatt*: 1161–70.

Schriever-Steinberg, Angelika. 1994. "Das Ausländerzentralregistergesetz." *Neue Juristische Wochenschrift*: 3276–77.

Windgasse, Annette. 1994. "Bericht zur Abschiebehaft in NRW (Nordrhein Westfalen)." In "Bericht der Kommission für Ausländerfragen und ethnische Minderheiten ('Asylsuchende und Flüchtlinge—Zur Praxis des Asylverfahrens und des Schutzes vor Abschiebung')," ed. Rat der Evangelischen Kirche in Deutschland. Presented at the fifth meeting of the Eighth Synod of the Protestant Church in Germany, Halle/Saale, Nov., Büro der Synode. Drucksache No. III/1a, 159–72.

Wollenschläger, Michael, and Alexander Schraml. 1994. "Art. 16a GG, das neue 'Grundrecht' auf Asyl?" *Juristenzeitung*: 61–71.

Table of Cases

Bavarian High Administrative Court (Bayerischer
   Verwaltungsgerichtshof). Order of 18 July 1994. 11 CS 94.1887.
   Neue Zeitschrift für Verwaltungsrecht, supp. 8 (1994): 59–60.
Bavarian High Administrative Court (Bayerischer
   Verwaltungsgerichtshof). Order of 6 May 1994. 11 CS 94.1429.
   Deutsches Verwaltungsblatt (1992): 941–43.
Bavarian Supreme Court (Bayerisches Oberstes Landesgericht).
   Order of 31 Jan. 1991. BReg. 3 Z 6/91. *Neue Zeitschrift für
   Verwaltungsrecht* (1992): 300–302
European Court of Human Rights (ECHR). Judgment of 7 July 1989
   (*Soering*), with concurring opinion of Judge de Meyer. In
   *Publications of the European Court of Human Rights, Series A:
   Judgments and Decisions*, ed. Registry of the Court, Council of
   Europe, 161:8–50, 51 f. Strasbourg. Cologne: Carl Heymanns.
European Court of Human Rights (ECHR). Judgment of 20 Mar. 1991
   (*Cruz Varas*). In *Publications of the European Court of Human
   Rights, Series A: Judgments and Decisions*, ed. Registry of the
   Court, Council of Europe, Strasbourg, 201:8–41. Cologne: Carl
   Heymanns.
European Court of Human Rights (ECHR). Judgment of 30 Oct. 1991
   (*Vilvarajah and others*), with partly dissenting opinion of Judge
   Walsh joined by Judge Russo and dissenting opinion of Judge
   Russo. In *Publications of the European Court of Human Rights,
   Series A: Judgments and Decisions*, ed. Registry of the Court,
   Council of Europe, Strasbourg, 215:6–40, 41–43, 44. Cologne: Carl
   Heymanns.
Federal Administrative Court (Bundesverwaltungsgericht). Judgment
   of 23 June 1981. BVerwG 1 C 78.77. In *Entscheidungen des
   Bundesverwaltungsgerichts*, ed. members of the court, 62:325–30.
   Berlin: Carl Heymanns.
Federal Administrative Court (Bundesverwaltungsgericht). Order of 5
   July 1994. 9 C 1/94. *Neue Zeitschrift für Verwaltungsrecht* (1995):
   391–93.
Federal Administrative Court (Bundesverwaltungsgericht). Judgment
   of 18 Jan. 1994. BVerwG 9 C 48.92. In *Entscheidungen des
   Bundesverwaltungsgerichts*, ed. members of the court, 95:42–53.
   Berlin: Carl Heymanns.
Federal Administrative Court (Bundesverwaltungsgericht). Judgment
   of 10 May 1994. BVerwG 9 C 501.93. In *Entscheidungen des
   Bundesverwaltungsgerichts*, ed. members of the court, 96:24–28.
   Berlin: Carl Heymanns.
Federal Constitutional Court (Bundesverfassungsgericht). Judgment
   of 15 Dec. 1983. 1 BvR 209,269,362,420,440,484/83. In

Entscheidungen des Bundesverfassungsgerichts, ed. members of the court, 65: 1–71. Tübingen, Germany: J. C. B. Mohr (Paul Siebeck), 1984.

Federal Constitutional Court, First Chamber of the First Senate (Bundesverfassungsgericht, 1. Kammer des Ersten Senats). Order of 15 Mar. 1993. 1 BvR 1296/92. *Deutsches Verwaltungsblatt* (1993): 601–2.

Federal Constitutional Court, First Chamber of the Second Senate (Bundesverfassungsgericht, 1. Kammer des Zweiten Senats). Order of 2 Dec. 1993. 2 BvR 1475/93. *Neue Zeitschrift für Verwaltungsrecht*, supp. 2 (1994): 11–13.

Federal Constitutional Court, First Chamber of the Second Senate (Bundesverfassungsgericht, 1. Kammer des Zweiten Senats). Order of 10 Mar. 1994. 2 BvR 2371/93. *Neue Zeitschrift für Verwaltungsrecht*, supp. 4 (1994): 25–26.

Federal Constitutional Court, First Chamber of the Second Senate (Bundesverfassungsgericht, 1. Kammer des Zweiten Senats). Order of 10 Mar. 1994. 2 BvR 2450/93. *Neue Zeitschrift für Verwaltungsrecht*, supp. 4 (1994): 27.

Federal Constitutional Court, First Chamber of the Second Senate (Bundesverfassungsgericht, 1. Kammer des Zweiten Senats). Order of 28 Apr. 1994. 2 BvR 2709/93. *Neue Zeitschrift für Verwaltungsrecht*, supp. 7 (1994): 51–53.

Federal Constitutional Court, Third Chamber of the Second Senate (Bundesverfassungsgericht, 3. Kammer des Zweiten Senats). Order of 13 July 1994. 2 BvL 12,45/93. *Neue Zeitschrift für Verwaltungsrecht*, supp. 8 (1994): 57–58.

Federal Constitutional Court (Bundesverfassungsgericht). Order of 23 Mar. 1995. 2 BvR 492,493/95. *Neue Zeitschrift für Verwaltungsrecht*, supp. 7 (1995): 50–52.

Federal Constitutional Court, First Chamber of the Second Senate (Bundesverfassungsgericht, 1. Kammer des Zweiten Senats). Order of 23 Aug. 1995. 2 BvR 1906, 1907, 1908, 1909, 1910, 1911, 1912/95. *Neue Zeitschrift für Verwaltungsrecht*, supp. 8 (1994): 65–66.

Federal Constitutional Court (Bundesverfassungsgericht). Judgment of 14 May 1996. 2 BvR 1938, 2315/93. *Europäische Grundrechte Zeitschrift* (1996): 237–56.

Federal Constitutional Court (Bundesverfassungsgericht). Judgment of 14 May 1996. 2 BvR 1507, 1508/93. *Europäische Grundrechte Zeitschrift* (1996): 256–68, judges *Limbach (268–70), Böckenförde (270), and Sommer (270–71)* jointly dissenting.

Federal Constitutional Court (Bundesverfassungsgericht). Judgment of 14 May 1996. 2 BvR 1516/93. *Europäische Grundrechte*

Zeitschrift (1996): 271–92, judges Limbach, Böckenförde, and Sommer jointly dissenting (288–92).

Federal Court [of Ordinary Jurisdiction] (Bundesgerichtshof). Order of 6 Dec. 1979. VII ZB 11/79. In *Entscheidungen des Bundesgerichtshofs in Zivilsachen*, ed. members of the court and the Bundesanwaltschaft, 75:375–83. Cologne: Carl Heymanns.

Federal Court [of Ordinary Jurisdiction] (Bundesgerichtshof). Judgment of 12 June 1986. V ZB 9/86. In *Entscheidungen des Bundesgerichtshofs in Zivilsachen*, ed. members of the court and the Bundesanwaltschaft, 98:109–15. Cologne: Carl Heymanns.

Federal Court [of Ordinary Jurisdiction] (Bundesgerichtshof). Order of 1 July 1993. V ZB 19/93. *Neue Juristische Wochenschrift* (1993): 3069–70.

Hessian High Administrative Court (Hessischer Verwaltungsgerichtshof). Order of 27 July 1995. 12 TG 2342/95. *Neue Zeitschrift für Verwaltungsrecht*, supp. 9 (1995): 67–72.

High Court of Düsseldorf (Oberlandesgericht Düsseldorf). Order of 30 May 1994. 3 Wx 305/94. *Neue Zeitschrift für Verwaltungsrecht*, supp. 1 (1995): 7.

High Court of Frankfurt/Main (Oberlandesgericht Frankfurt/Main). Order of 7 Nov. 1994. 20 W 493/94. *Neue Zeitschrift für Verwaltungsrecht*, supp. 1 (1995): 8.

Chapter 3

The New Techniques for Managing High-Volume Asylum Systems

Stephen Legomsky*

As the world refugee population has grown, governments around the world have had to balance humanitarian aspirations against economic, social, law enforcement, and political imperatives. In the United States and several other Western nations, the primary battleground has been political asylum. It is in this arena that national values have been most severely tested, for the sheer numbers of asylum claimants have raised the stakes for all concerned.

Recent efforts to reconcile these frequently conflicting goals have generally focused more on process than on substance. This is not surprising given that, as discussed below, the number of asylum claimants has far outpaced the available adjudicative resources. War, poverty, and human rights violations have become routine components of daily life. At the same time, technological advances in both communication and transportation have made migration a realistic option for more and more of the world's victims. The inevitable result—growing numbers of asylum seekers—collides with the increased public awareness of finite national resources and unmet needs.

This article identifies, evaluates, and synthesizes the major asylum process reforms recently adopted or considered in the

---

Notes for this chapter begin on page 152.

United States. It examines both the benefits those reforms are intended to bring and the human price they would exact. As the article will show, the various reforms follow common patterns: all of them aim to reduce the backlog of undecided cases and to speed the disposition of future claims. Almost all reflect a willingness—unremarkable in a climate of growing public hostility toward immigrants—to accept an increased risk of erroneous denials in exchange.

The Background[1]

U.S. law distinguishes, first, between the admission of overseas refugees and the treatment of those refugee claimants who have already reached U.S. territory. The former are outside the United States, either still in their countries of origin or in third countries. They are processed overseas and admitted under annual presidential quotas (INA § 207, 8 U.S.C. § 1157). This article does not attempt to cover those procedures.[2]

For those refugees who have reached U.S. shores—either ports of entry or the interior—two distinct remedies are potentially available. Nonrefoulement prohibits a claimant's return to the country of persecution but not to a third country. It is mandatory under Article 33 of the 1951 U.N. Convention Relating to the Status of Refugees and, since 1980, under the Immigration and Nationality Act (INA).[3] Asylum is a stronger remedy, resulting in permission to remain in the United States at least temporarily and in most cases permanently.[4] Asylum is not required by the U.N. Convention but is authorized by the INA (8 U.S.C. § 1158). It is available to any refugee at the discretion of the attorney general.

The procedures for applying for asylum and for nonrefoulement, laid out in the Justice Department regulations, are the same.[5] In this article, references to asylum procedure should be understood as encompassing the procedures for applying for both remedies.

If the Immigration and Naturalization Service (INS) has already instituted either exclusion or deportation proceedings, then an alien's initial application must be filed during those proceedings (8 C.F.R. § 208.4[c][1]). There will be an evidentiary hearing before an "immigration judge," who is within the Justice Department's Executive Office for Immigration Review (EOIR) (8 C.F.R. § 3.10). Either the alien or the INS may appeal the immigration judge's decision to the Board of Immigration Appeals (BIA) (8 C.F.R. § 3.1[b][1,2]), which is also within EOIR. The BIA decision is then subject to judicial review (INA §§ 106 [a] [deportation order reviewable by petition for review in the court of appeals], 106[b] [exclusion order reviewable by habeas corpus in the district court]).

If no exclusion or deportation proceedings have been instituted, then the initial application (usually described as an "affirmative application") is filed with the INS. About 90 percent of initial asylum claims are filed in this way (*Interpreter Releases* 1994d, 1577, 1578). Regulations issued in 1990 established a specialized, geographically dispersed corps of INS asylum officers to adjudicate these cases (*Fed. Reg.* 55 [27 July 1990]: 30674–87; 8 C.F.R. §§ 208.1[b], 208.4[a]). Under those regulations, the asylum officer conducts a nonadversarial interview (8 C.F.R. § 208.9). Until recently, the officer would either grant or deny the application (8 C.F.R. §§ 208.14[a], 208.16, 208.17 [1994]). Denials were not appealable, but applications could be renewed de novo in any subsequent exclusion or deportation proceedings that the INS chose to initiate (8 C.F.R. § 208.18[b]). Decisions reached in those proceedings were then (and still are) subject to BIA and judicial review as described earlier.

In recent years the resources that the government has chosen to allocate to asylum adjudication have failed to match the demands of what has become a huge caseload. Apart from what the size of the caseload evidences about the world conditions from which the claimants have fled, the gap between filings and dispositions has been worrisome from a management perspective. Preliminary INS estimates for fiscal year 1994 (ending 30 September 1994) showed 147,605 asylum applications filed but only 54,196 dispositions.[6] The excess of filings over dispositions increased the already bloated INS backlog to 420,794 cases as of 30 September 1994.[7]

To address the numbers problem, the Justice Department made major changes to the INS asylum officer procedure. Effective 4 January 1995, the asylum officers no longer deny applications outright; instead, they either grant them or refer them to immigration judges, who then adjudicate them in deportation proceedings.[8] Together with other changes described below, the new procedure has reduced the INS processing time considerably.

To supplement those efforts, Congress in September 1994 appropriated $64 million for fiscal year 1995 (more for years 1996–98) to expedite the adjudication of asylum claims and the removal of rejected claimants (*U.S. Statutes at Large* 1994, § 130005, 2028). The department is in the process of using those funds to add both INS asylum officers and immigration judges, as discussed below.

The combination of speedier adjudication, expanded resources, and a drop in filings has lessened the management problem. In calendar year 1995, INS dispositions exceeded new claims filed (*Interpreter Releases* 1996, 45–47). Still, a huge INS backlog persists. Moreover, the vast majority of INS "dispositions" were referrals to immigration judges; consequently, final adjudication is still pending.

The Problems

People who talk about the "asylum problem" are not always referring to the same thing. From a geopolitical standpoint, the roots of "the problem" run deep. They include human rights violations, armed conflict, economic disparities among nations, family separation, and all the other conditions that impel people to cross international boundaries in search of better lives.

To others, the problem is one of procedural justice. Critics of U.S. asylum procedures have voiced concerns that range from foreign policy bias[9] to notification of rights, access to counsel, adequacy of foreign language translations, and law-enforcement-oriented adjudicators.[10]

To still others, the problem is one of case management, and it is that subject to which this article is devoted. Here, two separate problems have been primary: the sheer volume of asylum claims and the time and government resources that each individual claim consumes.

From each of those two primary problems, several others flow. First, and most obviously, there is the problem of money. The more claims there are, and the more each one costs to adjudicate, the greater will be the total fiscal cost.

Second, with finite resources, the combination of high case volumes and significant time per case spells long delays. Delay, in turn, is harmful in several ways: It impedes the final approval of valid asylum claims, thus aggravating the insecurities and hardships of planning and beginning a new life. It makes the evidence less accessible. And, many would say (e.g., Martin 1990), it furnishes an incentive for those with unfounded claims to file asylum applications in order to receive work authorization or other interim benefits. To the extent that that incentive generates unfounded claims, it worsens the backlog, which further increases the delay, which further enlarges the incentive to file unfounded claims, which worsens the backlog still further, and so on.

Third, the combination of limited resources, high case volumes, and substantial resources per case undermines the effectiveness of the process. Ideally an asylum system should promptly grant meritorious applications and reject and remove those whose applications have been finally denied. But in fiscal year 1992 deportation charges were filed against only 54 percent of rejected asylum claimants, and only a fraction of these were actually deported (*Interpreter Releases* 1994a, 445, 446).

The Solutions

The problems outlined above are large ones that no society can conscionably ignore. But any and all responses must be built on one central premise: the raison d'être of political asylum is to provide refuge for the persecuted. While sound policy and political reality make tradeoffs inevitable, any institution that forgets its guiding mission will lose its bearings quickly. The challenge is to devise practical solutions that will not unacceptably impair the quality and accuracy of the results.

What solutions are in sight? The ideal ones, of course, are those that address the root causes of forced migration: war, human rights violations, and poverty. Eliminating the need to seek refuge would surely be preferable to merely refining the adjudication process. National and international efforts to influence world conditions and government practices thus hold the greatest promise for achieving long-term results.

I leave those broader initiatives in the hands of the diplomats and the economists. My goal here is less ambitious. On the assumption that the world will never obliterate all the causes of forced migration, the immediate task is to tend, after the fact, to the needs of the world's twenty million refugees. To that end, this article will focus on some of the newer procedural devices for managing high-volume asylum adjudication.

These techniques are numerous, and they could be organized in any number of ways. I group them here into four categories: (1) reducing the number of cases that require adjudication; (2) prioritizing among filed cases so as to dispose of unfounded claims promptly; (3) streamlining procedures; and (4) enlarging and improving the adjudicative staff. Some strategies, of course, aim simultaneously at two or more of these objectives.

Reducing the Number of Cases

Techniques that fall under this heading can be subcategorized into three groups: denying access to the nation's domestic asylum system; discouraging the filing of claims; and legalizing cases in the backlog.

Denying Access

Interdiction

In recent years, the United States and other nations have resorted increasingly to interdiction, or "pushback," programs as a response to refugees fleeing by boat. By intercepting vessels on the high seas, a nation prevents people from gaining access to its domestic asylum system and acquiring the bundle of substantive and procedural rights that such access entails.

Pushbacks gained their first major foothold when Malaysia repelled forty thousand Vietnamese boat people in 1979. Several other members of the Association of Southeast Asian Nations followed suit (Frelick 1993, 682). The United States since 1981 has been interdicting Haitian vessels[11] and, more recently, boats from China and Cuba. Italy began interdicting Albanian vessels in 1991 (Frelick 1993, 691).

Interdiction programs are subject to important variations. A country might turn back all passengers—refugees and nonrefugees alike—as the United States did with Haitian boat people from May 1992 to May 1994 (*Interpreter Releases* 1994b, 743–44; Executive Order 12807 [23 May 1992]), or it might attempt to ascertain which passengers are refugees and return only the others. If it chooses to adjudicate refugee claims, it might do so onboard ship, or it might transport the passengers to the shores of the intercepting country, to its foreign territories (such as Guantánamo), or to the land or territorial waters of cooperating third countries. Adjudication procedures could range from informal interviews to quasi-formal evidentiary hearings, and the determination could proceed with or without specialized adjudicators, with or without counsel, and with or without appeal rights.

In the United States, legislation that would specifically ratify interdiction has been introduced more than once. Different bills would authorize the attorney general, at his or her unreviewable discretion, to invoke a special summary process whenever the government interdicts foreign vessels on the high seas and escorts the occupants to the United States or when it interdicts vessels in U.S. territorial waters and escorts the occupants to ports of entry (e.g., S. 1333 [substitute version] [1993], § 1; S. 269 [1995], introduced by Sen. Simpson [R-Wyo.], §§ 141 [summary exclusion], 148 [detention or parole]).

The legality of the Haitian interdiction program was seemingly resolved in *Sale v. Haitian Centers Council* (113 S.Ct. 2549 [1993]). There, the Supreme Court held that both INA § 243 (h) and Article 33 of the 1951 U.N. convention, which prohibit the refoulement of refugees, are inapplicable on the high seas. Since the program upheld in *Sale* entailed the return of aliens without *any* adjudication of refugee claims, the legal barriers to *summary* procedures for interdicted aliens would seem fewer still.

Interdiction holds great appeal for governments of destination states. It is normally both faster and cheaper than waiting for people to arrive by boat and then processing their asylum claims through regular channels. The latter option can involve investigation, adjudication, detention, and removal. The adjudication component can occupy both prosecutorial and adjudicative staff, and it can do so at both trial and appellate levels. Interdicting nations also hope that the very existence of an interdiction program will deter boat people from leaving in the first place, thus preventing both loss of life at sea and domestic and political costs for the interdicting nations. Finally, interdiction spares the government having to choose between detaining the arriving passengers and risking their absconding.

But the moral costs of interdiction are compelling. In the process of deterring nonconvention refugees from fleeing, interdiction can also deter genuine refugees. When it does, the baby is thrown out with the bathwater. For those who attempt the journey despite the interdiction policy, there is a further cost: if the interdicting nation makes no attempt to decide which passengers are refugees, then a certain number of genuine refugees will inevitably be returned. When that happens, the harm—possible persecution, including death—would be just as great as if a nation practiced more clearly prohibited refoulement from its own shores. And if, in contrast, the interdicting nation makes some attempt to decide which passengers are refugees, there can be, depending on the adjudication procedures, practical barriers to the fairness and accuracy of the determinations. Will the interviews be lengthy enough to permit meaningful presentation of evidence and meaningful deliberation? Will there be access to counsel? Will there be enough privacy that claimants feel secure in providing information? Will there be an opportunity for review of an initial denial?

There is another kind of moral cost. World refugee policy relies heavily on the willingness of nations—especially those that neighbor refugee source countries—to serve as countries of first asylum. For that reason, the U.S. government urges other countries to fill that role. The United States criticized Hong Kong and the United Kingdom for forcibly repatriating those Vietnamese boat people who had been found not to qualify as refugees. As some have argued (e.g., Frelick 1993, 682–83, 690–92), the moral authority to make those criticisms eroded when the United States began interdicting Haitians on the high seas and returning refugees and nonrefugees alike to the country of persecution.

Designating Safe Countries of Origin

In recent years several European nations have adopted or considered proposals to designate "safe" countries of origin: i.e., countries that neither engage in persecution themselves nor return refugees to other countries that engage in persecution (for a survey of state practices, see generally Hailbronner 1993). Variables might include the criteria and procedures for identifying safe countries and the action to be taken when the country of claimed persecution is on the safe list. The latter could include automatic denial of the claim (in which case discussion of the technique belongs in this section) or merely the triggering of a more abbreviated procedure (in which case the technique is better classified under any of several headings discussed below; for example, Discouraging Unfounded Claims, Prioritizing among Cases, Fast Track for Unfounded Cases, or Streamlining Procedures).

Kay Hailbronner has thoroughly discussed the pros and cons of the safe country of origin approach (1993, 49–58).[12] The assumption is that asylum claims filed by people fleeing countries on the safe list are generally unfounded. Under that assumption, the argument runs, it makes sense to avoid the delay and expense of adjudicating each case individually (or at least some of that delay and expense if the consequence of being on the list is a summary procedure rather than automatic denial). The inclusion of a country on the safe list might also serve to discourage the filing of applications in the first place. These advantages are significant when a nation receives a large number of asylum claims from nationals of countries thought to be safe.

The dangers of this approach are, however, considerable. The most obvious is the difficulty of deciding whether a given country is safe. That challenge alone can create errors, especially when a country is large. There can also be foreign policy pressures to include countries whose human rights records are marginal. Moreover, there will be difficult questions as to who should decide which countries to put on the list. And even if a list is perfect at the time it is drawn up, rapid changes in human rights conditions might destroy its accuracy well before its use is discontinued.

Apart from those considerations, there is a fundamental policy question as to whether the interests of justice inherently demand individualized consideration. No country is 100 percent free of persecution. Under a safe country of origin approach, therefore, a certain number of genuine refugees—and the number might be small—will inevitably face real persecution in countries listed as "safe." The savings in time and money must therefore be balanced against the human cost of more frequent error. That cost will depend, of course, on both the likelihood and gravity of error. These factors, in turn, will hinge on the care with which the lists are prepared and on the inclinations of the drafters in instances where the calls are close.

Safe Third Countries

Many nations have adopted, and the United States is considering, safe third country constraints. The idea is that a person with designated connections to a safe third country should be required to seek asylum there rather than in a country to which he or she later travels.

Again there are several variables. One concerns the closeness of the applicant's connection to the safe third country. In the United States, Justice Department regulations bar asylum if the applicant has been "firmly resettled" in another country.[13] An additional regulation, finalized on 5 December 1994, authorizes discretionary denials of asylum to aliens who would be deported to safe third countries through which they traveled en route to the United States, even in the absence of firm resettlement, provided the United States and the third country have entered into an agreement governing that subject (8 C.F.R. § 208.14[e]). A comprehensive immigration reform bill introduced by Representative Lamar Smith (R-Tex.) would apply the safe third country limitation to any safe country willing to accept the alien; no prior connection would be required (H.R. 2202, § 526[a] [1995], adding INA § 208[b][3][vi]).

A second variable is, what consequence occurs once the specified connection is found? Under the new regulation just mentioned, the existence of a safe third country becomes a negative discretionary factor. A bill introduced by former Representative Romano Mazzoli (D-Ky.) would have gone further, barring asylum entirely (H.R. 3363, introduced 26 Oct. 1993, § 201[a], which would have added INA § 208[a][2][C][V], 8 U.S.C. § 1158 [a][2 [C][V]). The Smith bill would allow the attorney general to waive the safe third country limitation "in the public interest" (H.R. 2202, § 526[a], adding INA § 208[b][3][vi]). Yet another possibility would be to trigger a fast-track procedure, although that could be problematic when there is a factual dispute over whether the third country is safe or whether it would accept the person.

A third variable is whether the restriction is made dependent on the existence of a standing agreement with the safe third country. Under the regulation cited above, the restriction depends explicitly on such an agreement being reached. At this writing, the United States has no such agreement, but negotiations with Canada are proceeding (see generally Helton 1993). In contrast, neither the Mazzoli bill nor the Smith bill would require a standing agreement; the safe third country's willingness to receive the particular applicant would be enough.

As with the safe country of origin strategy, the theory behind the safe third country approach is that, when it applies, protection is simply unnecessary because another country is already willing to provide it. The twin goals are to deter filings and to adjudicate more speedily the applications that are filed.

The difficulties of deciding which countries of origin are safe also apply here. In addition, at least when the law requires some prior connection between the alien and the safe third country, there are some practical questions as to what the safe third country disqualification will accomplish after its existence becomes widely known. The answers to those questions depend on at least two variables: whether the cooperating nations have harmonized their asylum criteria and how easy it is for nationals of third countries to cross the common borders of the cooperating nations.[14]

Some asylum claimants have practical choices of travel routes; others do not. Possible constraints include the urgency of escape, the terrain, the distances involved, the available commercial carrier routes, and the transportation expense. To the extent that itineraries are beyond the control of the applicants, a safe third country rule can influence the distribution of asylum claims among the receiving nations. In the absence of such a rule, some claimants might well decide not to apply for asylum in the country of first arrival. Presumably applicants would take numerous factors into account: the standards of living in the various receiving countries, the presence of family members or supportive ethnic communities, the comparative stringency of the various receiving countries' asylum criteria, and the ease with which third country nationals can cross the borders of the cooperating countries. Market forces would therefore largely determine the distribution of asylum claims among receiving countries.

A safe third country limitation, however, not only constrains the applicants' choices but also enables geography and commercial carrier practices to dictate filing patterns. For asylum claimants who have some control over their itineraries, a safe third country rule furnishes an incentive to avoid passing through a second-choice country en route to a first-choice country. The marginal impact of that incentive depends, of course, on the choices that such applicants would have made in the absence of a safe third country limitation. Those choices, in turn, would again reflect a range of competing incentives to remain in the country of first arrival, such as the stringency of other countries' asylum criteria and the difficulty of crossing into the territories of other nations.

A prerequisite to a safe third country arrangement is a clear common understanding among the cooperating nations. Without that, there will always be a danger of "refugees in orbit" (Hailbronner 1993, 58–59).

Finally, if passing through—as distinguished from firm resettlement—is the applicable criterion, then it is essential that the cooperating nations adopt asylum procedures that are practically accessible to aliens in transit. The difficulty of devising such procedures is itself a good reason to limit the safe third country rule to firm resettlement or something comparable (Hailbronner 1993, 59).

Regional Agreements for Common Adjudication

Countries within a given region might pool adjudication resources by agreeing that each contracting party will have the right to deny an asylum claim on the grounds that it has already been rejected by another of the contracting parties. Normally one would expect such an agreement to be part of a larger treaty that created safe third country limitations, which is in fact the case in Western Europe.[15] In theory, however, it would be possible to have a stand-alone agreement in which the contracting parties make no attempt to allocate responsibility for adjudicating asylum claims but agree nonetheless that, once one of them finally denies an asylum claim, the other(s) may decline to hear it. For that matter, one country could simply amend its municipal law to authorize the denial of asylum claims on the grounds that they had already been rejected by other specified countries.

The goal of each of these strategies would be to avoid the wasteful duplication of resources.

Again, however, there are serious issues. Justice demands some assurance that the adjudication process used by the other country is full, fair, and sufficiently accurate. Justice also requires carefully crafted exceptions for cases in which either the applicant's personal circumstances or the conditions in the country of origin have materially changed. In addition, any of these strategies would pose problems if the contracting parties have not already achieved a reasonable degree of both substantive and procedural harmonization. If applicants perceive that their chances of success are better in some of the cooperating countries than they are in others, then a rule that disqualifies applicants who have been rejected elsewhere would simply drive many claimants to apply in the most lenient country first.

In-Country Processing and Preinspection

The refugee definition contained in the 1951 U.N. Convention Relating to the Status of Refugees covers only someone who "is outside the country of his nationality" or who, not having a nationality, is "outside the country of his former habitual residence" (Article 1.a[2]). But U.S. municipal law allows the president to admit refugees who are within their countries of nationality or habitual residence (INA § 101[a][42][b]), 8 U.S.C. § 1101[a][42][b]). In recent years, such "in-country processing" in Moscow and Ho Chi Minh City has in fact accounted for the bulk of the U.S. overseas refugee admissions.

In-country processing in an embassy or other office of the receiving country is a useful supplement to asylum. For those who fear persecution but can travel safely to the designated processing center and afford some delay before departure, in-country processing can be beneficial. It can avoid uncertainty, temporary homelessness, and loss of employment during the waiting period. Depending on the surroundings, in-country processing can also be physically safer. For those who would have been denied nonrefoulement and returned, in-country processing also saves the time, expense, and physical danger of a futile voyage.

From the standpoint of the receiving country, in-country processing can also be simpler and less costly than the domestic asylum procedure. It also involves less incentive to file unfounded applications because normally there are no interim benefits during the adjudication phase. For all these reasons, the in-country processing programs in Russia and Vietnam have been generally beneficial (Frelick 1993, 689–90).

Problems have arisen, however, when in-country processing has been used as a substitute for nonrefoulement, as in Haiti, where it has been accompanied by interdiction. The dangers of interdiction have already been considered, but the issue here is whether in-country processing makes nonrefoulement unnecessary and interdiction defensible.

As others have pointed out (Frelick 1993, 689–90; Inzunza 1990, 421–22), in-country processing, though a useful option for some, is inadequate for others. First, delay might be dangerous. As Bill Frelick has said, "real refugees can't wait" (Frelick 1993, 689). Second, traveling to the relevant embassy or office can be unsafe. Applicants can be noticed and arrested en route, on the way home, or later. Third, full and fair procedures, including access to counsel and the availability of review, are generally less likely in a foreign embassy or office than in a domestic system that provides administrative tribunals and formal courts. Fourth, unlike nonrefoulement, in-country processing permits the rejection of genuine refugees on discretionary grounds. Fifth, success depends on the willingness of the host government to cooperate in the emigration arrangements.

A related strategy is preinspection of passengers at foreign airports. As with in-country processing, the idea is to make the admissibility decision before the person has left for the intended destination country. In the United States, the Smith bill would require the attorney general to establish preinspection stations in at least ten foreign airports over a period of four years. These airports would have to be located in countries whose practices conform to the 1951 Convention or the 1967 Protocol (H.R. 2202, § 703, introduced by Rep. Smith in 1995; see also H.R. 3363, introduced by Rep. Mazzoli in 1993). In that important respect preinspection differs from in-country processing.

The pros and cons of preinspection generally parallel those of in-country processing, with some differences. On the benefit side, preinspection can bring efficiencies that are not confined to refugees; other prospective immigrants and nonimmigrants can be screened out at an earlier stage. Moreover, the dangers are somewhat less than with in-country processing of refugees, at least when the designated airports are in countries that are truly safe. On the other side of the ledger, one might assume that the logistical barriers to full and fair adjudication would be even more formidable at crowded and busy airport facilities than at processing centers designed specifically for adjudication.

Time Limits on Applying for Asylum

One other device for reducing the number of asylum applications is to place time limits on filing. Under the Smith bill, an alien would have to file, within thirty days of arrival, a "notice of intention" to apply for asylum. Then, within sixty days after arrival, the alien would have to file the actual application (H.R. 2202, § 526, adding INA § 208[f][1][a][i]). In its original form, the only exception to these strict time limits would have occurred in response to changes in country conditions that affect the applicant's eligibility for asylum (§ 208[f][1][a][ii]).

The House Judiciary Committee, however, approved an amendment by Representative Frank (D-Mass.) that would expand the exception to embrace relevant post-entry changes in the alien's own personal circumstances (*Interpreter Releases* 1995, 1449).

Even with those exceptions, this is drastic medicine. One experienced asylum practitioner, Philip Schrag, believes that these changes would be practically tantamount to repealing asylum. For various reasons, which he lays out in detail, Schrag suggests convincingly that only a rare applicant is able to file a serious application so soon after arriving. The immediate priorities of most refugees, he points out, are to find U.S. relatives or other contacts and to find food and lodging, often without a command of English and often while traumatized by the horrors from which they are fleeing. Refugees will normally need counsel to help them complete the long application forms and assemble the necessary supporting documentation. Finding counsel is not easy for indigent aliens. Even if counsel is obtained, gathering the documents and otherwise preparing the case can take weeks or months. The short deadlines imposed by the Smith bill are simply not realistic (*Washington Post*, 12 Nov. 1995, C-7). But even if the filing deadline were more generous and an asylum claimant who should have been able to meet the deadline negligently failed to do so, is not the sanction grossly disproportionate to the failing? Is the torture or death that persecution can entail really the appropriate penalty for a missed deadline?

Presumably, the rationale for time limits is to weed out unfounded claims. The premise appears to be that bona fide claimants would have no reason to delay filing. But the premise is flawed. Some aliens might simply be unaware of their legal rights and the procedural limits on those rights. Others might be unable either to understand the application or to prepare their claims and might be further unable to find help. Still others might harbor continuing fear of authority, particularly of government officials. And some might fear that their claims, though valid, will be denied erroneously and that filing the application will trigger deportation to the country of persecution. For all these reasons, one cannot equate delay with bad faith.

Discouraging Unfounded Claims

Detention Pending Disposition

U.S. law makes no provision for detaining people who file affirmative asylum applications with the INS. Detention becomes an issue only in the contexts of exclusion and deportation proceedings. As to exclusion, the literal wording of INA § 235 (b) (8 U.S.C. § 1225) seems to require detention pending the outcome of the proceeding. Justice Department regulations, however, permit discretionary release as long as the alien arrives at an authorized port of entry with documents that do not appear to be fraudulent. In such a case, the INS is to consider "the likelihood that the alien will abscond or pose a security risk" (8 C.F.R. § 235.3[b, c]). As for deportation, there is a general discretion to detain, release on bond, or release without bond (INA § 242[a], 8 U.S.C. § 1252[a]; 8 C.F.R. § 242.2).

A bill introduced in 1993 by Representative Becerra (D-Calif.) would have explicitly authorized the discretionary release of asylum applicants who have been taken into custody in connection with either exclusion or deportation proceedings (H.R. 3223, § 4 [1993]). To be eligible for discretionary release, an alien would have been required to show that either (a) the asylum application is nonfrivolous, he or she is not a threat to abscond or a danger to the community, and he or she has posted a reasonable bond or has reliable ties to the community; or (b) detention is otherwise not in the public interest. The bill would also have authorized the use of closed military bases as detention centers if they were located within fifty miles of major metropolitan areas.[16]

To the extent that people file unfounded asylum claims in order to delay deportation and work during the interim, detention is seen as a way to remove that incentive. Detention also assures that applicants will show up for hearings, not pose a danger to the community, and not compete with Americans for jobs. Yet increased resort to detention would have real drawbacks. For genuine refugees fleeing traumatic persecution, detention—particularly if it is lengthy—can prolong the suffering. Even with a fifty-mile or other geographic limit, the remoteness of detention centers would shut off practical access to counsel for many applicants. And, of course, detention is an expensive drain on public resources. The fear that aliens will either abscond or threaten the community could be diminished, though not eliminated entirely, by selective detention of those who seem likely to pose such dangers.

Denying or Delaying Work Authorization

Until 4 January 1995, the rule in the United States was that an asylum claimant could simultaneously or subsequently apply to the INS for interim work authorization, which would be granted within 90 days as long as the person was not detained and the asylum claim was found not to be frivolous (8 C.F.R. § 208.7[a] [1994]). The interim work authorization would be renewed annually while the asylum claim was pending (§ 208.7[b]). Once asylum was granted, work authorization would automatically follow (§ 208.20).

The new regulations have altered that scheme. Now an asylum claimant may not apply for interim work authorization until 150 days have elapsed since the INS's receipt of a complete asylum application. The INS then has 30 days in which to grant or deny work authorization; if it fails to act within that time frame, the applicant will be permitted to work (*Fed. Reg.* 59 [5 Dec. 1994]: 62284, amending 8 C.F.R. § 208.7[a][1]). Thus the total wait will be up to 180 days. If the asylum officer or immigration judge denies asylum within the 180-day period, the applicant will not receive work authorization.[17] If asylum is granted at any time, work authorization will be automatic, although the applicant must apply for the necessary documentation (8 C.F.R. § 208.20).

The new regulatory scheme deliberately delays the issuance of work authorization. The central purpose is to discourage aliens from filing unfounded applications solely to obtain interim permission to work. Keeping asylum claimants out of the workforce for a longer period also lessens competition for jobs with U.S. workers. The department could have chosen to base work authorization on assessments of the merits of individual asylum claims and the economic needs of the applicants, but it rejected that course because of the adjudicative resources required (commentary to final regulations, *Fed. Reg.*, 62284, 62290–91).

The Justice Department argued that the hardships of a 180-day wait were unlikely to materialize once the new package of reforms became fully operational, because it expected a 60-day turnaround by asylum officers (*Fed. Reg.*, 62290). In fact, in January 1996, the INS reported that 84 percent of asylum claims are now heard within 60 days (*Interpreter Releases* 1996, 46). The department also suggested that the new scheme would add an extra inducement for asylum officers and immigration judges to decide asylum claims within 150 days: avoiding the need to adjudicate work authorization requests.[18] If this added incentive spurs harder work, it will be a positive force. If it spurs sloppier work, its effects will be negative.

The principal argument against denying or delaying work authorization is that doing so will inevitably create economic hardship (59 *Fed. Reg.*, 62290 [5 Dec. 1994]). Many asylum applicants, including those whose claims are ultimately granted, arrive with precious little. They are generally ineligible for public benefits. Some have U.S. sponsors on whom they can rely, but many do not. For those left without funds, the choices are starvation, illegal work, crime, or returning to the country where they have alleged a likelihood of persecution (unless they are admissible to a third country). The claimant might also be unable to afford an attorney to assist in preparing the application.

Application Fees

At present there is no fee for filing an asylum application in the United States. Nor is there a fee for filing an initial application for work authorization, although there is a fee for renewing such an authorization (8 C.F.R. § 103.7[b]; *Fed. Reg.* 59 [30 Mar. 1994]: 14779, 14781 [proposed rule]). In 1994 the INS proposed charging a $130 fee for an asylum application and a $60 fee for an initial application for employment authorization, with a waiver provision for those unable to afford the fees.[19]

While an asylum application fee can be viewed as another device intended to discourage unfounded claims, the impetus behind this Justice Department proposal was revenue. The hope was that the extra funds would permit the department to hire additional adjudicators and thus speed the processing of cases. In addition, as a matter of equity, it was felt that applicants should generally pay for the services they receive if they are able to do so. Estimating that the average asylum application costs $615 to adjudicate and pointing out that the Justice Department surcharges other users of immigration services to subsidize asylum adjudication, the department argued that a $130 fee would cover at least a portion of the cost (*Fed. Reg.*, 14781; see also 31 U.S.C. § 9701[a], requiring that each service provided by a federal agency be "self-sustaining to the extent possible").

Many problems and objections were raised, and in the end the department decided not to impose the suggested fees. The main objection was philosophical: to many, protection against alleged persecution is something for which one simply should not have to pay. Only two other countries are known to impose asylum application fees, and in each of those countries the fee is small.[20]

Philosophy aside, there were concerns that a substantial application fee might discourage even bona fide refugees from filing claims. As it is, opponents stressed, serious applicants frequently have to spend great sums of money on attorneys, translators, and other services.[21] There were also real worries about both the accuracy and the efficiency of the proposed system for adjudicating fee waivers. Some predicted that the expense and delay associated with this extra layer of bureaucracy would make the proposed program self-defeating, especially if denials of fee waivers generated litigation (*Fed. Reg.*, 62286).

Sanctions for Frivolous Claims

Interim regulations in force since 1992 authorize disciplinary sanctions against attorneys or accredited representatives who engage in "frivolous behavior" before immigration judges, the BIA, or "any other administrative *appellate* body under [the INA]."[22] Whether by design or through oversight, the quoted language does not seem to cover actions taken before INS asylum officers.

Without speculating about the exact percentage of asylum claims that could fairly be described as legally frivolous, most would agree that some significant number fit that description. Are sanctions against the attorneys and representatives who file them appropriate? The principal purpose of sanctioning attorneys and representatives is to discourage them from engaging in the specified behavior in the first place. If the sanctions have teeth—i.e., if the enforcement is serious and evenhanded and the penalties are meaningful—and they are well enough publicized that attorneys and representatives understand the risks, then sanctions could be an appropriate and effective vehicle for discouraging the filing of unfounded claims. Attorneys and representatives should be held to the highest professional standards. Moreover, when an attorney or representative does file a frivolous claim or take other inappropriate delaying action, justice would seem to demand that he or she—not the alien, who might well be innocent—suffer the punishment.

An attorney sanctions program poses dangers, but careful drafting and sensitive enforcement can minimize them. If sanctions are not to chill vigorous advocacy, there must be a clear line between the frivolous and the creative. Both the language and the enforcement of the regulations should make clear, for example, that good faith arguments for a change in the law are not frivolous. Without that clarity, representation might be harder to obtain, and reasonable arguments might be withheld out of an excess of caution. In addition, both fairness and effective government demand that any sanctions program be applied with equal vigor to private attorneys and government attorneys. With those qualifications, attorney sanctions seem appropriate for both EOIR and INS filings.

An alternative strategy would be to impose sanctions on the alien claimant. Under the Smith bill, for example, if an asylum officer finds an application frivolous, the applicant would be permanently ineligible for all benefits under the Immigration and Nationality Act.[23]

Sanctions on the claimant and sanctions on the attorney trigger very different policy tradeoffs. The claimant will normally be a nonlawyer who relies on his or her counsel for advice. The claimant will also, often, be unable to speak English. There is thus a high probability, though admittedly less than 100 percent, that the claimant will be innocent of moral wrongdoing. In such cases, substantial penalties seem not only unfair but also unlikely to deter unfounded claims. Moreover, asylum officers can make mistakes. If an officer wrongly concludes that an application is more likely than not frivolous, the claimant loses not only a potential asylum grant but all future benefits as well.

Even when an alien in fact knows or should have known that the claim is frivolous, one must again try to match the wrong to the penalty. Without trivializing the substantial impact of unfounded asylum claims on all concerned, one might ask whether a permanent bar to all future immigration benefits is not excessive. Under the provision in question, U.S. citizens could be separated permanently from their spouses or their children because of a momentary lapse in judgment decades earlier.

Legalizing Cases in the Backlog

The backlogs described earlier have meant long waits for many thousands of asylum claimants. Since the INS uses a last-in-first-out system (discussed below), the oldest cases will not be adjudicated for quite some time. One option, therefore, would be to legalize the status of all aliens whose unadjudicated asylum claims were filed before a specified date, subject to criminal, national security, and other selected disqualifications. It would not be the first time Congress has enacted a legalization program for aliens.[24]

The main benefit of legalization would be to enable large numbers of asylum claimants and their families to end the long periods of uncertainty that have left them insecure and unable to plan their futures. In addition, legalization would reflect a recognition that, through no fault of the claimants, long delays have nurtured roots that the passing years make increasingly painful to sever. Further, for many, apprehension and removal after all these years is unrealistic; a more likely scenario, proponents of legalization would argue, is the long-term maintenance of an underground subculture that bodes ill for everyone. Finally, at least if the eligibility criteria for legalization are made clear and simple, processing times should be considerably less than those for disputed asylum claims. Consequently, there is potential for saving vast resources.

In the present climate, the political obstacles to legalization would be monumental. On the merits, the greatest fear would probably be that legalization would send the wrong signal, suggesting that someone who enters without inspection or overstays and then seeks asylum stands a chance of eventual legalization. The risk could be reduced but not eliminated by continuing to decide current claims first. Some would argue, too, that legalizing the status of those who entered without inspection or overstayed would unfairly allow them to bypass those who have been waiting lawfully in the queue. Further, any litigation over the meaning of the eligibility criteria could push back the statutory time deadlines, thus prolonging the very uncertainty that legalization would be aimed at ending. Finally, there would be the vexing question of what to do about the family members of legalized asylum claimants.

Prioritizing among Cases

Several modern asylum management strategies have focused on taking cases out of order.

Ordering Cases Generally

Prioritizing Asylum Cases over Other Cases

It is of course possible to divert resources from other immigration or nonimmigration cases to asylum adjudication. This could be accomplished either by shifting staff from other responsibilities to asylum processing or by establishing case priorities that require individuals who adjudicate both asylum cases and other cases to decide the asylum cases first.[25]

The main purpose of prioritizing asylum cases would be, again, to reduce the incentive for aliens to file unfounded claims solely to achieve delay. Both the INS and the EOIR have immigration responsibilities other than asylum. The problem, as always, is that shifting resources to asylum adjudication would aggravate other backlogs. In addition, arguments can be made for prioritizing other, competing needs. Those exclusion and deportation cases in which aliens are in detention command high priority because of the aliens' liberty interests and the heavy costs to the government. Criminal aliens also receive expedited treatment (INA §§ 242[i], 242A, 8 U.S.C. §§ 1252[i],

1252A). Many would assign a higher priority to visa petitions and other cases in which aliens apply for lawful status. There are only so many categories that one can prioritize before priorities become meaningless.

Last-In-First-Out (LIFO)

INS practice is to adjudicate first those asylum claims that are filed last, to the extent resources permit. Those new cases that cannot be reached are added to the backlog (*Interpreter Releases* 1994a, 445, 446). For reasons discussed below, the combination of increased staffing and other reforms leaves the INS hopeful that over the long term it will be able to keep pace with new filings and steadily reduce the backlog.

The goal of LIFO is to discourage new filings of unfounded claims by eliminating the delay incentive. The obvious disadvantage is that increasing numbers of old applications lie dormant indefinitely. This means hardship and uncertainty for genuine refugees and windfalls for those who filed unfounded claims many years ago. At some point, the more senior claimants deserve decisions.

Fast Track for Unfounded Cases

Summary Exclusion at Ports of Entry

One problem recently highlighted by media reports has been the arrival of asylum claimants at U.S. airports with false travel documents or none at all. In response, several bills have been introduced to provide what has come to be called "summary exclusion." The details vary, but most of the bills specify that, if an alien arrives at a port of entry without proper documents and he or she applies for asylum, a summary procedure would be invoked (e.g., S. 1333 [1994], introduced by Sen. Kennedy [D-Mass.]; H.R. 3363 [1993], introduced by Rep. Mazzoli; H.R. 1355 [1993], introduced by Rep. McCollum [R-Fla.]; H.R. 2202, §§ 302, 306; S. 269, §§ 141, 142, 171). In such a case, an INS official would conduct an on-the-spot interview to determine whether the applicant has a strong enough case to warrant a full-fledged exclusion hearing before an immigration judge. If not, the alien would be returned expeditiously. Depending on the bill, there might or might not be administrative review, and there would be no judicial review of the merits of the asylum claim.

Some bills go further (e.g., H.R. 1355; S. 269, § 171). In addition to abbreviating the procedures, they would disqualify from asylum anyone who arrives with fraudulent documents that were not needed to effectuate escape or has destroyed or lost the documents presented to the commercial carriers—even if the person is a genuine refugee.

The central purpose of summary exclusion is to dispose quickly of those unfounded asylum claims that are filed at ports of entry. Proponents hope that doing so will discourage nonrefugees from flying to the United States with false documents, destroying the documents onboard the airplane, applying for asylum at the port of entry, and then absconding before the exclusion hearing. In addition, the hope is that the time saved from both the smaller caseload and the shorter processing time per case will enable adjudicators to cut into the backlog or at least stunt its growth.

The greatest reservations about summary exclusion flow from the increased likelihood of error and the magnitude of the interests at stake. In the short time frame allowed, it will be difficult for many aliens to assemble the witnesses and documentary evidence necessary to prove their claims. The short time frame will also make it harder to obtain counsel or other assistance. As Representative Nadler (D-N.Y.) has observed, the INS determines in another context whether an asylum applicant has demonstrated a "credible fear" of persecution, and those decisions sometimes prove to be wrong (*Interpreter Releases* 1993, 1397, 1398, referring to INS decisions on whether to release asylum seekers from detention). Former American Immigration Lawyers Association President Hope Frye has described the particular difficulties that summary exclusion would pose for women refugees fleeing sexual assault.[26]

By how much would the probability of error increase? Much would depend on the substantive standard that the law required the applicant to meet to avoid summary exclusion. Suggestions have ranged from a lack of frivolousness to a "credible fear" of persecution. The latter, in turn, could be defined in any number of ways. One bill would define it to require a "substantial likelihood" that the alien's statements were true and a "reasonable possibility" that the alien would be found eligible for asylum (S. 1333 [as amended by Committee on the Judiciary, 1994], § 1, which would have added INA § 235[d][5]). Another bill would set a more demanding standard, denying an exclusion hearing unless the asylum officer finds it "more likely than not" that the statements are true (H.R. 2602 [1993]).

Provisions that deny an exclusion hearing when an asylum claimant possesses false documents that were not necessary for escape are both arbitrary and extraordinarily harsh. That the documents are fraudulent does not mean the claimant is not a genuine refugee, even if the fraud is later found not to have been essential to the escape. As others have pointed out, some adjudicators in fact view possession of valid travel documents as evidence that the fear of persecution is not well founded; the theory is that persecutors are unlikely to issue travel documents to their intended victims.[27] Even if Article 33 of the 1951 Convention Relating to the Status of Refugees were interpreted to permit it, returning a genuine refugee to his or her persecutors is surely disproportionate to the degree of culpability evidenced by the fraud.

Apart from its dangers, there is some question as to whether summary exclusion would even bring about the intended benefits. The entire backlog of 420,000 asylum claims represents only about 11 percent of the estimated undocumented alien population in the United States.[28] In turn, aliens who file asylum claims directly with immigration judges constitute only about 10 percent of all asylum claimants (*Interpreter Releases* 1994a, 445, 446). And aliens who file their asylum claims at ports of entry (as distinguished from those who apply during deportation proceedings) make up only a fraction of the latter. Finally, even within that last subcategory, only in those cases where the threshold is found not to be met would the benefits of shorter proceedings be felt. In just a small percentage of asylum cases (and a minuscule percentage of total undocumented alien cases), therefore, would there be any benefit at all.

Moreover, it is not clear that summary exclusion would generate any net administrative benefit. In those cases that are screened out, there will presumably be savings. But in cases that are screened in, costs will increase, since the initial screening by an asylum officer would be in addition to the exclusion hearing already required. Whether the net result would be to save or to lose administrative resources would thus depend on the average savings per case screened out, the average loss per case screened in, and the percentage of cases in each category.

Summary Dismissal for No-Shows

The Smith bill would require summary dismissal of an asylum claim whenever the claimant failed to appear for the hearing, absent "exceptional circumstances" (H.R. 2202, § 526, adding INA § 208[f][2][a][iii]; see also H.R. 3223, § 4). Like the strategy of summary exclusion for those who fail to present valid entry documents, this approach requires one to compare the transgression to the sanction. No-shows are a serious problem; they delay removal in cases where applications are unfounded, and they disrupt the tightly packed schedules of the adjudicators. Whether the sanction should include delivering genuine refugees to their persecutors, even for first offenses, is another question.

Other Forms of Prescreening

A preceding subsection dealt specifically with summary exclusion at ports of entry. Similar issues and tradeoffs arise in any system that makes use of prescreening or other tracking devices. There will always be concerns about the accuracy of the prescreening process and the potential for erroneously returning genuine refugees to their persecutors. From an efficiency standpoint, it will always be necessary to balance the savings from the screened-out cases against the losses from the screened-in cases. In all instances, this will mean trying to predict what both those differentials will be (per case) and what proportions of cases will in fact be screened out. Canada's experience suggests that prescreening can actually waste resources (Hailbronner 1993, 40), but that country's exceptionally high screen-in percentage and other variables preclude meaningful extrapolation.

There are several variations to consider. Prescreening might be employed at the initial hearing stage, at the administrative review stage, or at the judicial review stage. Prescreening could be used to make either administrative or judicial review discretionary. The cost savings per case screened out will be greatest when the screening function is performed by a single individual per case and the full adjudication is done by a multimember panel. Still another possible form would be to adjudicate fully all cases on their merits, but only after channeling "easy" cases to single adjudicators and "hard" cases to multimember panels. Law clerks could be used to separate the cases. False negatives in the cursory initial screening would be more tolerable if they resulted only in cases being adjudicated by a single person rather than in negative final dispositions. With any of these approaches, policymakers would need to consider whether the net result would be to increase or to decrease costs and, if a decrease is expected, how the resource savings stack up against any loss in accuracy.

Streamlining Procedures

One Bite at the Apple

As noted earlier, U.S. asylum procedure currently affords applicants "two bites at the apple." The first bite is a relatively informal adjudication by an INS asylum officer. If the asylum officer does not approve the application, there follows a more formal, de novo evidentiary hearing before an immigration judge.[29]

The two-bites feature has two advantages, the more obvious being that the second bite adds one further opportunity to detect error. Some have questioned whether the second adjudicator is any more likely than the first to form an accurate picture of the facts (e.g., Martin 1990, 1344). To that, one might respond that the second adjudicator has the benefits of the first adjudicator's insights in addition to his or her own, provided the first adjudicator prepares written reasons for the denial.[30]

The other rationale for the two-bites feature is that the bites are of different kinds. On the one hand, in a nonadversarial interview a reticent applicant might feel more comfortable relating sensitive facts. On the other hand, the traditional U.S.-style adversarial, trial-type hearing affords opportunities for the two sides to rebut each other's evidence through cross-examination and responsive documents. Each bite, therefore, adds something to the other.

David Martin has argued persuasively for a one-bite system in which trained, specialized[31] asylum adjudicators conduct nonadversarial hearings. He sees the second bite as a source of unnecessary delay and expense. In any event, he believes that, because the government seldom calls witnesses, asylum claimants rarely utilize the primary benefit of adversarial proceedings: cross-examination (for these and other rationales, see Martin 1990, 1324, 1346–52). Pending legislation would establish a one-bite system in which INS asylum officers issue administratively final decisions (H.R. 2202, § 526, adding INA § 208[f][2]).

INS Referrals to Immigration Judges

As detailed above, under Background, the procedures that went into force on 4 January 1995 alter the roles of INS asylum officers. Now they normally either grant asylum applications or refer them to immigration judges for deportation proceedings, rather than deny them outright.

The new arrangement has several advantages. Since a decision not to approve an application normally means that it will be taken up fully by an immigration judge, the asylum officer can now be thought of as serving a kind of reverse screening function. Applicants who prove their claims can receive asylum promptly, while others—both clearly ineligible applicants and close calls—will receive fuller hearings. Under those circumstances, the nonfinal nature of a negative decision makes certain procedural components less crucial. In particular, the new regulations eliminate Notices of Intent to Deny, commonly known as NOIDs, and written reasons for denials (both discussed below).

The new grant-or-refer procedure also makes it easier to remove rejected claimants. In part it does this by automatically referring the person to deportation proceedings, an essential first step toward removal. In addition, the application itself might contain information that the government can use to establish deportability.[32] Finally, the knowledge that filing an asylum application could ultimately result in deportation proceedings might dissuade the filing of unfounded claims.

There are some drawbacks, however. The risk of deportation proceedings might discourage bona fide asylum claims. That is, someone who feels his or her case is close or fears that it might not be believed even though it clearly merits approval might withhold a bona fide application to avoid apprehension and deportation. The Justice Department points out that such a person would have the opportunity to file an asylum claim with the immigration judge if apprehended later (*Fed. Reg.*, 62284, 62296). In the meantime, though, the lives of the alien and his or her family are in limbo.

The grant-or-refer procedure also adds vast numbers of cases to the already overburdened dockets of the immigration judges. In turn, this will mean many more cases for the INS trial attorneys to prosecute, more appeals to the BIA, and more petitions for judicial review.

A final drawback to the new arrangement is that it has enabled the INS to eliminate some procedural steps that have real value, as the following discussion will show.

Deleting Selected Components of the Hearing Procedure

As noted, the new INS regulations eliminate NOIDs (*Fed. Reg.*, 62284, 62293–94, 62300, amending 8 C.F.R. § 208.12[a]) and, in all but a few cases, written reasons for denials.[33] Those changes save asylum officers the time previously spent drafting the NOIDs, reviewing the applicants' responses to them, and drafting reasons for denial.[34] In addition, the time allowed for rebuttal exacerbated overall delays.

Still, eliminating NOIDs and reasons for denial has costs. Their combined deletion means that applicants will enter deportation proceedings without a clear understanding of the (possibly remediable) obstacles they need to overcome. They may acquire that understanding as the deportation hearing progresses, but learning earlier could save the time needed to gather the requisite proof. Moreover, the very process of having to articulate written reasons for a tentative or final denial can help an asylum officer decide what the result should be. There might well be cases in which an officer who has to justify a decision in writing realizes that, on reflection, a particular application should be granted after all. Finally, written reasons for denials help INS trial attorneys to prepare their cases and immigration judges to decide them. When asylum officers don't reduce reasons to writing, the time and thought they have invested is lost; their insights can never be passed on.

The 1995 regulations also eliminate one other ingredient. Until then, the asylum adjudicator in every case requested an advisory opinion from the State Department's Bureau of Human Rights and Humanitarian Affairs (BHRHA). The final decision was withheld until the BHRHA opinion had been received. The resulting delay would be as long as sixty days.[35]

Mainly to speed the process, the Justice Department's new regulations no longer require adjudicators to request BHRHA opinions or delay their decisions pending receipt of those opinions. Instead, BHRHA now has the discretion whether to comment. In any given case it may still submit information on general conditions in the applicant's country and/or comments specific to the applicant's case, but those comments will not be solicited routinely, and the decision will not be held off in the meantime. The adjudicator may also affirmatively request a BHRHA opinion in an individual case (8 C.F.R. § 208.11 [1995]). In addition, the adjudicators will have easy access to the State Department's published *Country Reports*, which contain the department's general assessments of human rights conditions.

The advantage of receiving BHRHA opinions is that the State Department has information about country conditions, as well as highly specialized professional expertise, that can be of great potential relevance in asylum cases. At a time when the department is anxious to minimize delay, however, BHRHA opinions are a logical target, especially because the State Department's *Country Reports* are already accessible to adjudicators and the public (annual *Country Reports on Human Rights Practices*, mandated by 21 U.S.C. § 2151n[d]).

Apart from the problem of delay, the State Department has a foreign policy mission that many feel taints its opinions (see, e.g., *Kasravi v. INS*, 400 F.2d 675, 677 n.1 [9th Cir. 1968]; Aleinikoff 1984, 194–95; and the periodical *Human Rights Watch and Lawyers Comm. for Human Rights, Critique—Review of the Department of State's Country Reports on Human Rights Practices*). There are also related concerns about the procedural fairness of receiving an opinion on an ultimate issue (such as the probability of persecution) without giving the applicant a chance to confront the writer of the opinion.

Limiting Administrative or Judicial Review

Appellate review of government agency decisions is traditionally described as serving two separate functions: a retrospective error-correcting function and, at least in common law systems, a prospective guidance function (see, e.g., Carrington, Meador, and Rosenberg 1976; Leonard 1984, 299–302). To these, one might add a third, prophylactic function: encouraging care and thought in the preparation of the initial decision (Legomsky 1989, 1210–11).

But why have both administrative and judicial review? Are the two processes duplicative?

As discussed elsewhere (Legomsky 1984, 280–98; Martin 1990, 1355–56), eliminating either step entirely would be inadvisable, for each has its advantages. Administrative review (relative to judicial review) supplies fast, cheap, accessible, informal justice informed by specialized expertise. Judicial review adds both actual and apparent insulation from the executive branch and, at least as currently constituted, a generalist perspective. The U.S. Constitution might also require judicial review, at least by way of habeas corpus.[36]

Nevertheless, the combination adds delay and expense to a system for which speed and efficiency are sorely needed. Consequently, reform of the review structure raises many of the issues already discussed.[37] In addition, any such reforms must take account of the criteria by which adjudicative systems are generally evaluated: accuracy, efficiency, acceptability to the public, and consistency (see Cramton 1964, 111–12; Legomsky 1986, 1313–14).

One possibility that merits specific mention is substituting a single specialized court for the current combination of the BIA and the general courts. In 1980 Former BIA chairman Maurice Roberts floated the idea of a specialized immigration court; a specialized asylum court would raise numerous analogous issues. They include questions on the pros and cons of specialization (discussed below), the issue of one centralized court versus a system of courts geographically dispersed, and the constitutional status of the resulting tribunal. Thorough discussion of these issues can be found elsewhere (Roberts 1980; Legomsky 1986, 1386–96; and Levinson 1981).

Faster Removals

One last component of modern streamlining efforts has been the emphasis on speedy removal of rejected applicants. The Justice Department's recent switch from a grant-or-deny system to a grant-or-refer system is one element in that strategy. Pending legislation would reinforce that strategy by generally mandating deportation within ninety days of an administratively final order or, when applicable, a court order (H.R. 2202, § 305).

Enhancing Adjudicative Staff

Resource Levels

The Justice Department faces a numbers crunch, as discussed earlier (see Background, above). To cope with those numbers, the INS is in the process of expanding its asylum officer corps from 150 to 330. It hopes that this expansion, when combined with the speedier grant-or-refer system already discussed, will enable it to complete 150,000 cases per year (interview with Gregg Beyer, then INS director of asylum, 28 Nov. 1994). If that prediction proves right, and if the denial rate does not change appreciably, the immigration judges can expect to receive some 120,000 referrals per year.[38] Since roughly one-half of all immigration judge asylum denials are appealed to the BIA, the BIA can realistically expect its total caseload to multiply.[39] To meet those expectations, both the immigration judge corps and the BIA are undergoing expansion.

Even with the recent changes, however, it will be a challenge for the INS to cut deeply into the backlog. It is possible that the 1995 drop in filings noted earlier will continue and the INS will be able to eliminate the backlog eventually just by staying the present course. But there is no guarantee that the new trend will persist, the backlogged claimants have now been waiting many years, and even under the rosiest assumptions several more years would be required. The question, therefore, is what to do with the backlog.

In theory, one option is to do nothing. Unadjudicated claims could be kept in file drawers forever. That course, however, would leave hundreds of thousands of people—some significant percentage of them genuine refugees—permanently insecure and unable to plan their futures.

Another option would be to legalize the status of the backlogged applicants. As noted earlier, that course has both benefits and costs but is in any event politically unlikely.

If the backlogged cases are to be neither ignored nor legalized, then the only remaining option is to adjudicate them. The problem, as always, is resources.

One approach would be a "quick hit," a dramatic infusion of short-term resources to knock out the backlog. Detailed elsewhere (Legomsky 1994, 191), the idea here is to set a time period—say, one or two years—during which an expanded corps of INS asylum officers would complete all backlogged cases plus all those filed in the interim. The department would calculate how many additional adjudicators it would need to complete the task, hire that number for the agreed-upon period, and provide the necessary training. At a time when law jobs are relatively scarce, the expectation is that more than enough highly capable law school graduates would be eager to take Justice Department fellowships of this kind.[40]

For a one-year program, the costs have been estimated at about $50 million.[41] Even though the United States spends much less per case than do almost all other major asylum countries (see, e.g., U.S. Committee for Refugees 1993, 6 [table]), the current climate of fiscal belt-tightening makes a new appropriation of this magnitude unlikely. There is still a strong case to be made, however. Since the backlogged cases will have to be adjudicated eventually (again assuming they are neither ignored nor legalized), the only question is when to do so: now or later.

Once it is accepted that this is the proper question, the arguments for a quick hit become compelling. It should cost much less to adjudicate the cases now rather than later, and for two reasons. First, to the extent that a backlog generates delays that attract unfounded claims, erasing the backlog should reduce the total number of cases filed. Second, for those cases that are filed, experienced attorneys employed on a permanent basis would be more expensive than temporary department fellows fresh out of law school. Thus a quick hit should reduce the cost per case adjudicated.

Specialization

Whatever the subject matter, questions can arise over the optimal degree of judicial specialization. In the present context, the least specialized adjudicators are the general courts. After that, in order of increasing degree of specialization, the jurisdiction of an adjudicative tribunal might be defined as immigration cases, or as asylum cases, or as asylum cases from a particular world region or even country.

In his report for the Administrative Conference of the United States, David Martin strongly urged the creation of a specialized corps of asylum adjudicators in the United States (1990, 1338–44). The INS soon adopted that approach for its own asylum adjudication (*Fed. Reg.* 55 [27 July 1990]: 30674–87). At the EOIR, asylum continues to be the province of the immigration judges and the BIA.

Observing that most other Western countries employ asylum specialists, Martin argued that specialization would improve the accuracy, fairness, and speed of the asylum process (1990, 1338–39). The expertise that the adjudicators would bring (and develop), he suggested, would particularly help them to formulate questions, judge credibility, and assess the ultimate risks (1342).

One might add other benefits. Since so many asylum cases present common issues (the meaning of persecution, the human rights conditions prevailing in particular countries, the meaning of political opinion, etc.), entrusting the decisions to a relatively small group of specialists would promote both efficiency and consistency. The high level of specialization would make it possible to sustain relevant professional associations vital to continued growth. Because both asylum law and country conditions change so rapidly, specialists would be better situated to keep up with current developments. Specialized expertise would make adjudicators less dependent on the information and opinions of the State Department. And there are easily enough cases for asylum specialists to be deployed, and kept busy, at geographically dispersed locations.[42]

To be sure, reliance on asylum specialists would have disadvantages as well. The generalist perspective, already heavily sacrificed when decisions are entrusted to immigration specialists, would recede further if the specialty were narrowed to asylum. An "immigration generalist" might be better equipped to assure the conformity of asylum rules with more general principles of immigration law. There is, moreover, the danger that someone who handled a steady stream of asylum cases and nothing else would become hardened, inclined to discount the severities of common forms of persecution. Finally, it might be that a mix of cases would minimize monotony and thereby enhance the attractiveness of the positions to potential candidates.

Many of these same issues arise when the question is whether asylum adjudicators should subspecialize by region or country. Subspecialization can bring real benefits, including knowledge of cultural norms and country conditions (see Aleinikoff 1984, 234; and Kalin 1986, 239). In a country the size of the United States, however, the widespread use of such subspecialized adjudicators (and possibly staff) would pose serious logistical problems (Martin 1990, 1342). In addition, the main disadvantages of specialization noted earlier—the loss of the generalist perspective, the risk of callousness or other natural biases, and the potential for monotony—magnify as the degree of specialization increases.

Conclusion

From a case management perspective, few would deny that asylum reform has become a matter of some urgency. All the major reform proposals recently adopted or considered in the United States require tradeoffs. Most require decision makers to balance fairness and accuracy against speed and efficiency.

In the present political climate, lawmakers have placed overriding emphasis on speeding up asylum adjudication, clearing out the backlog, removing rejected claimants, and, in the process, deterring those who would abuse our generosity. All those goals are legitimate and important. Too often, however, elected officials have pursued those objectives in ways that relegate to the periphery what ought to be the central mission of asylum: providing refuge for the persecuted. So radical a change in the philosophy of asylum is unnecessary, for there are ways to combat the illness without killing the patient.

One major change would probably accomplish the most, with the least sacrifice of accuracy and procedural fairness and the least long-term pain: the infusion of huge short-term resources to attack the backlog of unadjudicated claims and some proportion of current filings. The United States ranks very low on the international list with respect to adjudicative resources per asylum case. By investing in the short term, the nation could achieve substantial efficiency gains in the long term. More important, it could do so without jettisoning procedural justice, substantive compassion, or other shared moral aspirations.

Notes

* This article appeared in *Iowa L. Rev.* 81, no. 671 (1996) (reprinted with permission). I thank the American Academy of Arts and Sciences and the German-American Academic Foundation for sponsoring this project and Corinne Schelling for organizing it. I also appreciate the thoughtful comments of the other participants at the Cambridge and Ladenburg workshops, especially those of David A. Martin and Kay Hailbronner, as well as those of my colleague Ronald Mann. The views expressed in this article are my own.

1. See generally Legomsky 1992, ch. 9.
2. See Lawyers Committee for Human Rights 1990. For a proposed restructuring of those procedures, see Legomsky 1995.
3. 8 U.S.C. § 1253 (h). This provision is sometimes called "withholding of deportation," but since 1980 it has been available in exclusion proceedings as well.
4. INA § 209 (b), 8 U.S.C. § 1159 (b), authorizes adjustment of status after one year.
5. See generally 8 C.F.R. § 208. In fact, anyone who applies for asylum is automatically treated as having filed an alternative application for nonrefoulement (§ 208.3[b]).
6. United States Immigration and Naturalization Service (USINS) 1994d; *Interpreter Releases* 1994d, 1577, 1578. Of the 147,605 filings, well over half were from Central Americans, Mexicans, and Haitians (USINS 1994a). The leading country of nationality was Guatemala, with 34,630. El Salvador was second with 18,543 (ibid.).
7. USINS 1994c. The backlogs at the ends of the two preceding fiscal years— 1992 and 1993—were 219,014 and 327,385, respectively (ibid.).
8. *Federal Register* 59 (5 Dec. 1994): 62284, 62300, amending 8 C.F.R. § 208.14. The only exception is for applicants in valid nonimmigrant status; since there is no ground for deportation proceedings in their cases, asylum officers would either grant or deny asylum (ibid.).
9. See the sources cited in Legomsky 1992, 952–53.
10. See sources cited in ibid., 955–57.
11. Much has been written on the Haitian interdiction program. For a small sampling, see Frelick 1993; Koh 1994; Legomsky 1990a; and Motomura 1993.
12. Almost all the pros and cons discussed in this subsection are drawn from Hailbronner. Page citations for specific points are omitted.
13. 8 C.F.R. § 208.14 (c) (2) (1994). See also INA § 207 (c) (1), 8 U.S.C. § 1157 (c) (1) (admission under overseas refugee program also requires "firm resettlement"); INA § 209 (b) (4), 8 U.S.C. § 1159 (b) (4) (asylee who is firmly resettled in another country may not receive adjustment of status to permanent residence).
14. This question differs from that concerning free movement by nationals of the cooperating countries. See, e.g., Treaty of Rome, Article 48–51 (1957) (free movement of workers); Single European Act, Article 13 (1986), adding Article 8A to the Treaty of Rome, reproduced in *International Legal Materials* 1986, 510–11.

15. The best-known example is the "Convention Determining the State Responsible for Examining Applications for Asylum Lodged in one of the Member States of the European Communities" (the Dublin Convention)], Art. 10.1 (e) (15 June 1990), reproduced in *International Journal of Refugee Law* 1990. See also Convention on the Application of the Schengen Agreement of 14 June 1985 relating to the Gradual Suppression of Controls at Common Frontiers, between the Governments of States Members of the Benelux Economic Union, the Federal Republic of Germany and the French Republic (Schengen, 19 June 1990), excerpted in *International Journal of Refugee Law* 1992.
16. A more recent bill would require the attorney general and the secretary of defense to study that last possibility. See S. 269, § 152.
17. If the denial occurs during the first 150 days, there will have been no application for work authorization. If the denial occurs during the next 30 days, the new regulations mandate denial of work authorization (*Fed. Reg.* 62284, amending 8 C.F.R. § 208.7[a][1]).
18. *Fed. Reg.* 59 (30 Mar. 1994): 14779, 14780 (commentary to proposed rule). Actually, the added incentive extends for 180 days, because, as noted earlier, the regulations provide that work authorization must be denied if asylum is denied during the 30-day window.
19. *Fed. Reg.*, 14781, 14784. Pending legislation would expressly authorize the attorney general to impose filing fees for asylum, work authorization, and adjustment of status of asylees (H.R. 2202, § 526, adding INA § 208[f][1][c] [introduced by Rep. Smith, 1995]).
20. Australia and the Netherlands charge fees of $30 and $25, respectively (59 *Fed. Reg.*, 62284, 62286 [5 Dec. 1994]).
21. An alternative possibility would be to treat the processing costs as a loan, to be repaid by successful claimants when they apply later for adjustment of status and by others if they ever seek immigration benefits in the future. Recouping some of the cost would be better than recouping none. See 59 *Fed. Reg.*, 62287.
22. 8 C.F.R. § 292.3 (a) (15) (emphasis added), mandated by INA § 242B (d), 8 U.S.C. § 1252B (d). "Frivolous behavior" will be found when the attorney or representative "knows or reasonably should have known" that his or her argument, application, motion, or appeal "lack[s] an arguable basis in law or in fact" or is "taken for an improper purpose, such as to cause unnecessary delay" (8 C.F.R. § 292.3[a][15][i]).
23. H.R. 2202, § 526, adding INA § 208 (h) (1) (1995). For purposes of that provision, any "willful misrepresentation or concealment of a material fact" will automatically render the application "frivolous" (§ 208[h][2]).
24. *The Immigration Reform and Control Act of 1986* (IRCA) (*U.S. Statutes at Large*, 1986), among other things, created three different ad hoc legalization programs: a general program, a program for agricultural workers, and a program for Cubans and Haitians. See generally Legomsky 1992, 547–53. In addition, two permanent provisions for regularizing the status of undocumented aliens with long-term residences in the United States are suspension of deportation (INA § 244[a], 8 U.S.C. § 1254[a]) and registry (INA § 249, 8 U.S.C. § 1259).
25. *The Violent Crime Control and Law Enforcement Act of 1994* (*U.S. Statutes at Large*, 1994) specifically authorizes the attorney general to "provide

generally for the expeditious adjudication of asylum claims" (§ 130005, 2028). In addition to appropriating funds (§ 130005[c]), that language might be read as endorsing a policy of prioritizing asylum cases vis-à-vis other immigration cases.

26. As she eloquently puts it: "You are given minutes to cross language, cultural and religious barriers to describe how and when and how often you were touched, probed or penetrated. You must tell this to a border cop, almost always male, often with badges and uniforms—tokens you recognize as danger signals, not beacons of safety" (Frye 1993).
27. See the arguments of Robert Rubin and Warren Leiden, testifying before the House immigration subcommittee in April 1993, reported in U.S. Committee for Refugees 1993, 4.
28. See testimony of Hon. Doris Meissner before the Senate Judiciary Committee (15 June 1994), reported in *Interpreter Releases* 1994c, estimating 3.8 million undocumented aliens.
29. As I discuss in the next subsection, the 1994 regulations have reduced but not eliminated the separation between these two steps.
30. The new regulations continue to require written reasons for INS denials of asylum claims (8 C.F.R. § 208.17), but under new § 208.14 (b) only a few exceptional categories of applications are subject to denial; the others must be either granted or referred to immigration judges.
31. I discuss the specialization issue separately below.
32. This possibility is expressly approved by the new regulations. See 8 C.F.R. § 242.17 (e).
33. See n. 30, above.
34. About 50 percent of the NOIDs generated rebuttals, but only about 2 percent of the rebuttals produced reversals (*American Immigration Lawyers Association Monthly Mailing* 1993).
35. 8 C.F.R. § 208.11 (1994); *Interpreter Releases* 1994a, 445, 448. Over the years the BHRHA opinions became gradually less detailed and Justice Department adjudicators began assigning them correspondingly less weight. See generally Legomsky 1992, 931–34.
36. I thank Gerald Neuman for raising this question. See generally Hart 1953.
37. E.g., detention, denying or delaying work authorization, filing fees, attorney sanctions, legalization, fast tracks for unfounded cases, discretionary review, case priorities, LIFO, and deleting selecting procedural ingredients. Removal speed, resource allocation, and degree of specialization, discussed below, are also relevant to review. The time period for initiating review is also worthy of consideration, but at present there is not much that could be shaved. One has only ten days to file a notice of appeal with the BIA (8 C.F.R. § 3.38[b]) and ninety days to petition for judicial review of a deportation order (thirty for aggravated felons) (INA § 106[a][1], 8 U.S.C. § 1105a [a][1]). The time limit on petitions for review was recently shortened from six months. It could be shortened further, but the efficiency gains would be small because nothing requires the INS to wait the full ninety days before removing an alien who has been ordered to be deported and has not filed a petition for review.
38. In January 1996 the INS estimated that it was approving 20 percent of all asylum claims. Eighty percent of 150,000 is 120,000. See *Interpreter Releases* 1996, 45–47.

39. *Interpreter Releases* 1996, 45–47. The expected increase in the BIA workload is hard to estimate. Unknowns include the percentage of claims that the immigration judges will approve (probably very low because they will hear only those cases that the INS has already declined to approve) and the percentage of immigration judge denials that will be appealed to the BIA (presumably lower than the historical one-half because these will all be cases that have already been rejected twice).
40. Pending legislation would take a similar tack but utilize retired federal employees and retired military officers rather than recent law school graduates. See H.R. 2202, § 523; S. 269, § 173.
41. Legomsky 1994, 193–94. The bill would now be higher: the backlog has grown, and, with the inauguration of the new grant-or-refer system, the proposal would also now require more immigration judges and more BIA and judicial resources.
42. For a more general study of specialized adjudication, see Legomsky 1990b, ch. 2 of which considers the criteria for determining whether a given subject would benefit from specialized adjudication.

References

Aleinikoff, T. Alexander. 1984. "Political Asylum in the Federal Republic of Germany and the Republic of France: Lessons for the United States." *University of Michigan Journal of Law Reform* 17: 183–241.

American Immigration Lawyers Association Monthly Mailing. 1993. Sept., 649.

Carrington, Paul D., Daniel J. Meador, and Maurice Rosenberg. 1976. Justice on Appeal 2–3 (St. Paul, Minn.: West, 1976).

Cramton, Roger C. 1964. "Administrative Procedure Reform: The Effects of S.1663 on the Conduct of Federal Rate Proceedings." *Administrative Law Review* 16: 108–54.

Frelick, Bill. 1993. "Haitian Boat Interdiction and Return: First Asylum and First Principles of Refugee Protection." *Cornell International Law Journal* 26: 675–94.

Frye, Hope M. 1993. "Message from the President, From Bad to Worse." *American Immigration Lawyers Association Monthly Mailing*, Sept., S-1.

Hailbronner, Kay. 1993. "The Concept of 'Safe Country' and Expeditious Asylum Procedures: A Western European Perspective." *International Journal of Refugee Law* 5: 31–65.

Hart, Henry. 1953. "The Power of Congress to Limit the Jurisdiction of the Federal Courts: An Exercise in Dialectic." *Harvard Law Review* 66: 1362–1402.

Helton, Arthur C. 1993. "Toward Harmonized Asylum Procedures in North America: The Proposed United States–Canada Memorandum of Understanding for Cooperation in the Examination of Refugee Status Claims from Nationals of Third Countries." *Cornell International Law Journal* 26: 737–51.

Interpreter Releases. 1996. Vol. 73 (10 Jan.). Washington, D.C.: Federal Publications.

———. 1995. Vol. 72 (23 Oct.). Washington, D.C.: Federal Publications.

———. 1994d. Vol. 71 (5 Dec.). Washington, D.C.: Federal Publications.

———. 1994c. Vol. 71 (27 June). Washington, D.C.: Federal Publications.

———. 1994b. Vol. 71 (6 June). Washington, D.C.: Federal Publications.

———. 1994a. Vol. 71 (4 Apr.). Washington, D.C.: Federal Publications.

———. 1993. Vol. 70 (25 Oct.). Washington, D.C.: Federal Publications.

International Journal of Refugee Law. 1992. Vol. 3.

———. 1990. Vol. 2. *International Legal Materials*. 1986. Vol. 25, no. 3 (May): 506–18.

Inzunza, Ricardo. 1990. "The Refugee Act of 1980 Ten Years After—Still the Way to Go." *International Journal of Refugee Law* 2: 413–27.

Kalin, Walter. 1986. "Troubled Communication: Cross-Cultural Misunderstandings in the Asylum-Hearing." *International Migration Review* 20: 230–41.

Koh, Harold H. 1994. "The 'Haiti Paradigm' in United States Human Rights Policy." *Yale Law Journal* 103: 2391–2435.

Lawyers Committee for Human Rights. 1990. *The Implementation of the Refugee Act of 1980: A Decade of Experience*. New York: Lawyers Committee for Human Rights.

Leonard, David P. 1984. "The Correctness Function of Appellate Decision-Making: Judicial Obligation in an Era of Fragmentation." *Loyola of Los Angeles Law Review* 17: 299–352.

Legomsky, Stephen H. 1995. "The Making of United States Refugee Policy: Separation of Powers in the Post–Cold War Era." *Washington Law Review* 70: 675–714.

———. 1994. "Reforming the Asylum Process: An Ambitious Proposal for Adequate Staffing, in Immigration Law." *Immigration Law: United States and International Perspectives on Asylum and*

Refugee Status, joint issue of *American University Journal of International Law and Policy* and *Loyola of Los Angeles International and Comparative Law Journal* 9: 191–94.
———. 1992. Immigration Law and Policy, ch. 9 (with 1994 supp.). Westbury, N.Y.: Foundation.
———. 1990a. "The Haitian Interdiction Programme, Human Rights, and the Role of Judicial Protection." 2 *International Journal of Refugee Law* (special issue) 2: 181–89.
———. 1990b. *Specialised Justice—Courts, Administrative Tribunals, and a Cross-National Theory of Specialisation*. Oxford: Oxford University Press, Clarendon.
———. 1989. "Political Asylum and the Theory of Judicial Review." *Minnesota Law Review* 73: 1205–16.
———. 1986. "Forum Choices for the Review of Agency Adjudication: A Study of the Immigration Process." *Iowa Law Review* 71: 1297–1403.
———. 1984. *Immigration and the Judiciary—Law and Politics in Britain and America*. Oxford: Oxford University Press, Clarendon.
Levinson, Peter J. 1981. "A Specialized Court for Immigration Hearings and Appeals." *Notre Dame Lawyer* 56: 644–55.
Martin, David A. 1990. "Reforming Asylum Adjudication: On Navigating the Coast of Bohemia." *University of Pennsylvania Law Review* 138: 1247–1381.
Motomura, Hiroshi. 1993. "Haitian Asylum Seekers: Interdiction and Immigrants' Rights." *Cornell International Law Journal* 26: 695–717.
Roberts, Maurice A. 1980. "Proposed: A Specialized Statutory Immigration Court." *San Diego Law Review* 18: 1–24.
United States Committee for Refugees. 1993. *Refugee Reports* 14, no. 5 (31 May).
United States Immigration and Naturalization Service. 1994a. "Asylum Applications Filed with INS by Selected Nationality Preliminary FY 1994." 28 Oct. Washington, D.C.: GPO.
———. 1994b. "Asylum Applications Filed with INS by Office—Preliminary FY 94." 28 Oct. Washington, D.C.: GPO.
———. 1994c. "Asylum Office Workload, Asylum Data Comparison, FY 1992–94." 28 Oct. Washington, D.C.: GPO.
———. 1994d. "Asylum Office Workload, Preliminary FY 94." 28 Oct. Washington, D.C.: GPO.
United States Statutes at Large. 1994. Vol. 108, 1796–2151. *Violent Crime Control and Law Enforcement Act of 1994*. U.S. Public Law 103-322.
———. 1986. Vol. 100, 3359–3445. *The Immigration Reform and Control Act of 1986* (*IRCA*). U.S. Public Law 99-603.

Chapter 4

New Techniques for Rendering Asylum Manageable

Kay Hailbronner

Introduction

Recent Developments

The numbers of asylum seekers reached a peak in 1992, with 682,639 asylum seekers in Western Europe, as compared to 103,500 in the United States. According to a survey based on United Nations High Commissioner for Refugees (UNHCR) and EU (European Union) figures, however, in 1994 there was a substantial decrease in the numbers registered in Western Europe, clearly a result of new legislative and administrative measures adopted in Germany the previous July and similar legislation and practice in various other EU countries.[1] In 1994 (and again in 1995) the numbers in Germany went down to 130,000, where they had been in the late eighties, while in some neighboring countries an increase was noted. In the Netherlands, for example, 48,400 persons applied for asylum and even more were expected in 1995. The Dutch government reacted quickly by submitting legislation very similar to the German asylum law reform. According to this new legislation, Dutch border control authorities will be authorized to reject asylum seekers arriving via safe third countries (member states of the Council of Europe, including East European countries) without putting

---

Notes for this chapter can be found on page 200.

them through an asylum procedure. In addition, legal asylum seekers are to be excluded from financial subsidies (*Frankfurter Allgemeine Zeitung* 1994).

In Switzerland, new laws entered into force in 1994 allowing for detention of criminal asylum seekers or those failing to obey administrative orders to remain within a specified area (see Federal Law on Enforcement Measures of 18 Mar. 1994). A general reform of the asylum act of 1990 streamlining the procedure is on the way. Under Swiss law, a list of safe third countries is already used in the asylum procedure, which allows speedy rejection of some asylum claims, though the procedure is still based on an individual examination of every claim. In 1990 the Swiss legislature also introduced special airport procedures permitting a summary exclusion of asylum seekers, with the consent of UNHCR.

In Germany, the asylum law reform of July 1993 introduced the safe third country concept, by which a person entering the country from a member state of the EU or a country deemed a safe third country by legislation is excluded from the right of asylum. An asylum seeker arriving via a safe third country determined by law may be rejected at the border or deported without being permitted to enter, judicial remedies have no suspensive effect.

By statutory law, countries may also be specified as "safe countries of origin" if the legal situation and general political circumstances justify the assumption that neither political persecution nor inhuman or degrading punishment or treatment is to be expected. It is presumed that a refugee from such a country is not subject to persecution on political grounds so long as the person does not present facts to the contrary. EU countries are designated as safe countries of origin by constitutional law.

The constitutional amendment also provides for international agreements among member states of the European Communities and with third countries to establish jurisdiction for the consideration of applications for asylum, including the mutual recognition of decisions on asylum. The Dublin Convention determining the state responsible for examining applications for asylum lodged in one of the member states of the European Communities (*International Journal of Refugee Law* [1990]: 469) was expected to enter into force in spring 1995; as of this writing, this has still not come to pass.

Finally, the new German law introduced a number of essential innovations in the asylum procedure act, based on a special constitutional authorization.[2] Asylum procedures are accelerated by prescribing time limits for administrative decisions and judicial control. The procedure applies when the Federal Office for the Recognition of Foreign Refugees (henceforward Federal Office) rejects as manifestly unfounded an alien's application for asylum. The alien may apply within one week to the administrative court for provisional legal protection, and as a rule the administrative court must decide within one week. An expulsion decision may only be set aside when there are "serious doubts" as to the legality of the decision.

Because of their rapidly growing numbers, asylum applicants from safe countries of origin arriving at international airports face a special airport procedure. Under section 18a of the Asylum Procedure Law, asylum proceedings are carried out before the applicant enters the country. The same rule applies to asylum seekers arriving at airports who are unable to establish their identities with valid passports or other documentation. The authorities accommodate such applicants at the airport during the proceedings, and the asylum seeker is not allowed to leave the transit area. He or she may apply for provisional legal protection within three days. The administrative court must rule on such an appeal within fourteen days, and if it fails to do so immigration authorities must allow the alien to enter the country (Hailbronner 1994, 165).

As noted, as a result of these new legislative and administrative measures, the number of asylum seekers went down considerably. It is in dispute whether this decrease is due primarily to the legislative reform or to the administrative measures in the Federal Office. By the end of 1993, 300,000 asylum claims were still pending. In addition, asylum proceedings hopelessly overburdened the judicial system: between January and July 1993, there were 60,700 asylum proceedings registered at administrative courts, along with 35,000 applications for preliminary injunctions. Following a substantial increase in the staff of the Federal Office in January 1994 (to 4,400), as well as the establishment of branch offices, the backlog was substantially reduced. While in July 1993 asylum claims were still pending for 460,000 persons, in July 1994 only 170,500 asylum applications were unresolved.

Although many predicted the restrictions Germany had introduced in July 1993 would inevitably lead to a significant increase in illegal entries, statistics indicate otherwise. Between July 1992 and 1 July 1993, 62,202 illegal entries were registered, whereas only 36,580 illegal entries were discovered between 1 July 1993 and 30 June 1994 (Federal Ministry of the Interior, press release, July 1994). The streamlining of asylum procedures, including a rather strict policy of return and deportation, has resulted in a substantial increase in the deportations of rejected asylum seekers. The number rose from 10,798 in 1992 to 36,358 in 1993 (Federal Ministry of the Interior, press release, July 1994).

Although the safe third country rule did not always function as originally envisaged, its mere existence has led to a substantial decrease in asylum applications. However, difficulties have resulted from the reluctance of third states to accept rejected or returned asylum seekers. Such refusal is often justified on the basis of formal requirements such as the time limits for filing readmission requests. Frequently, for example, asylum seekers make false statements concerning their journeys or apply for asylum months after illegal entry, which makes meeting the time requirements for deportation difficult. In addition, to prevent readmission, third countries frequently apply readmission agreements restrictively. As a result, Germany cannot always apply the safe third country clause, and the Federal Office has often decided on the merits of asylum claims from applicants entering via safe third countries instead of engaging in protracted and difficult attempts to achieve readmission under readmission agreements.

In spite of the difficulties with the application of readmission agreements, the number of deportations by air transport has increased considerably, from 15,408 in 1992 to 16,494 in 1993, amounting to 16.8 percent of all deportations in 1993. Despite this increase, there is no guarantee that rejected or deported aliens will not quickly return to Germany or some other EU country. In an effort to prevent this, Germany has introduced a reasonably effective system of data collection based on fingerprints. There are, however, considerable legal (data protection) and practical obstacles to establishing an EU-wide data collection and exchange system, which is one of the reasons the Convention of Schengen of June 1990[3] among nine EU member states only came into force in April 1995. It is clear that with the abolition of internal border controls, member states will have to solve these problems. Objections to the third safe country concept based on an expected breakdown of the administrative resources of third states did not turn out to be justified. Although the German-Polish readmission agreement of 7 May 1993 (*Bulletin of the Federal Government* 1993, 326), as well as the 3 November 1994, agreement between Germany and the Czech Republic,[4] did provide for substantial financial assistance (120 million deutsche marks for 1993 and 1994) to implement a program to build up the infrastructure for asylum proceedings and strengthen border protection, very few asylum seekers returned to Poland or the Czech Republic did in fact apply for asylum; instead, they returned to their home countries or "disappeared" elsewhere. In 1994 7,000 persons, including 3,496 Polish nationals, were returned under the readmission agreement; of these, only 1,191 were registered as asylum seekers.[5] Only 850 asylum seekers were registered in Poland in 1993, and in many cases procedures were suspended because asylum seekers left Poland during the process.

The safe country of origin clause provided for in Article 16a, paragraph 3, of the Basic Law has led to a substantial decrease in asylum applications from these countries. During the second half of 1993, the number dropped from 20,109 to 2,438 for Bulgaria; from 63,827 to 9,890 for Romania; and from 1,747 to 224 for Gambia.[6] This trend is clearly affirmed by the statistics for 1994. Refugees from safe countries of origin (Bulgaria, the Czech Republic, Gambia, Ghana, Hungary, Poland, Romania, Senegal, and Slovakia) accounted for only 22,365 asylum applications from 1 July 1993, to 30 June 1994, as compared to 198,183 from 1 July 1992, to 30 June 1993 (Federal Ministry of the Interior, press release, July 1994, 3). In 1995 Gambia was removed from the list.

In 1994 most people seeking asylum in Germany came from the former Federal Republic of Yugoslavia; the remainder were mostly from, in order of importance, Turkey and Romania, Bosnia-Herzegovina, Afghanistan, Sri Lanka, Bulgaria, Iran, Vietnam, and Togo (Federal Ministry of the Interior, press release, July 1994, 2).

In Western Europe, the large exodus that some expected to occur after the breakup of the Soviet Union did not materialize, although there are indications of a large number of would-be immigrants to Western Europe. Former Eastern bloc countries such as Hungary and Poland are witnessing an increase in illegal immigrants not registering as refugees.[7] A study on transit migration reports that up to two million immigrants living in central Europe want to move to the West. This number is continuing to grow because of the war in the former Yugoslavia and growing political and economic instability in the former Soviet Union. Over 70 percent of the migrants questioned about their future plans wanted to move to the West; 60 percent said they would go to any Western nation. Germany and Austria are the favored destinations for people from Eastern Europe, the United States is preferred by those from the former Soviet Union (*Migration News* 1995).

Legal and administrative responses to the influx of asylum seekers have been similar in most West European countries, based on a common assessment of the new situation caused by the increase in the annual numbers of asylum seekers from the late eighties to 1992.

The Problem

At a meeting of senior officials of fourteen states in Europe, North America, and Australia, to discuss long-term perspective and policies, held at Lyon on 12 and 13 March 1990, it was recognized that a considerable proportion of asylum seekers are not refugees. The report ("Informal Consultations" 1990) stemming from the meeting described the situation as follows.

As things stand now, receiving states are quickly heading for a serious crisis with regard to asylum. More and more asylum seekers arrive, but few turn out to be genuine refugees. In spite of heavy government investments in new staff for determining eligibility (a total of 2,300 new posts have been created in Europe and Canada since 1990), backlogs of unresolved cases continue to grow, now amounting to 400,000 in participating states. The costs for the asylum system in the whole OECD region now amount to approximately five billion U.S. dollars annually—i.e., ten times the total budget of UNHCR, devised for

15 million refugees, mostly from the third world—at a time when the UNHCR is facing a serious financial crisis.

According to a recent study, 75 to 85 percent of rejected asylum seekers in participating states remain in the country of reception (see "Information Consultations" 1990, 3). Taking into account the enormous costs involved, global refugee needs, and the end result of asylum procedures, the asylum system in the region seems to have become an ineffective aid to genuine refugees at the same time that it has turned into an inadequate and inadvertent immigration mechanism. It is obvious that current developments in the asylum area have to be analyzed not only in terms of the traditional and fully recognized perspective of providing asylum to persecuted persons but also the broader perspective of migration and development policies.

The report raises four fundamental questions:

1. What can be done to safeguard the institution of asylum and ensure that it does not degenerate into an inadequate and costly immigration mechanism?
2. How can some of the resources now used for taking care of asylum seekers be better used to help refugees in need of protection all over the world?
3. How can immigration mechanisms be made more efficient, and what is the future role of immigration in European states?
4. What can be done to mitigate and alleviate future migratory pressures, given that these will likely increase as a result of population increases, poverty, human rights abuses, internal wars, ecological disasters, and all of these factors in combination with the rapid evolution of global communication?

To respond to these questions, the senior officials attending the meeting envisaged a comprehensive strategy based on an understanding that the prevention of large irregular migration movements cannot be tackled efficiently with any traditional asylum instruments, because there is an interplay among national asylum policies, national migration policies, global refugee policies, and global development policies. They gave primary attention to accelerating procedures and to creating a more efficient method for implementing negative asylum decisions. In addition, they acknowledged in general the need for more efficient and targeted selection mechanism.

The participants also mentioned the desirability of agreements on country of first asylum and implementation mechanisms open for participation of all states in the region. Many conceded that such agreements involve some kind of burden sharing with countries of first asylum from which there are irregular flows of asylum seekers, although proposals to establish a joint crisis mechanism to achieve such sharing at the regional level in mass influx situations met with considerable skepticism. Also generally acknowledged is the need to prevent organized abuse of the asylum procedure and to take measures aimed at combating illegal immigration and irregular practices. This points up the need for harmonization of visa and entry control practices in connection with safe third country agreements and for information systems to avoid double applications.

Most believed that efforts in the area of return and repatriation policies are indispensable, considering that, as noted, 75 to 85 percent of rejected asylum seekers in the participating states remain in the country of reception (cited in "Informal Consultations 1990, 3). No consensus could be achieved, however, on a concept of a joint system for orderly resettlement policies and practices, although the senior officials did agree on the need for further joint measures to accommodate the voluntary repatriation of special groups of refugees and asylum seekers and to expedite the effective removal of asylum seekers.

Finally, there was a general though rather vague consensus on the need to develop new policies and mechanisms to avert new flows of refugees as a result of human rights abuses and demographic pressures, the need to revise present development assistance practices, and the need to mitigate the root causes of refugee and migratory flows.

All participants agreed that a fundamental revision of the existing asylum system is urgently required. Existing asylum systems are not adequate to distinguish those aliens who can be returned to their countries of origin from those aliens who cannot be returned because of the risks involved, taking into account the conditions in the home country. For many years states have granted protection to aliens who do not qualify as convention refugees, though frequently on legal grounds different from those governing recognized refugees. This suggests the need for a fast and efficient way to identify which aliens are in need of protection without putting immigration control at risk.

The Geneva Convention of 1951 turned out to be of little assistance in solving the problems raised by the influx of large irregular movements of asylum seekers. The individual rather than group-oriented approach of the convention and its preference for permanent external settlement over "protection" hardly makes it suitable for the management of large refugee movements. Governments of receiving states recognize that the existing legal system based on the Geneva Convention was constructed under a political system and global circumstances fundamentally different from those that reign today. Nevertheless, they—frequently in contrast to legal scholars—hesitate to embark on a revision of the convention. There is general support for the existing international legal system for the protection of conventional refugees. The possibility of classifying humanitarian refugees as conventional refugees or even revising the refugee definition contained in Article 1 (a) of the Geneva Convention is widely rejected, however, because of a belief that the asylum system developed on the basis of the convention is not suited to render large asylum movements manageable.

The concept of asylum must be understood in a larger sense of granting protection to people who do not have a right of entry and residence under regular immigration procedures. Thus, "protection," in contrast to asylum, denotes the need for more flexible and pragmatic solutions taking into account that permanent settlement in Western industrialized countries can hardly be a solution for economic underdevelopment, political instability, and civil war in many regions of the world. On the other hand, humanitarian considerations require action beyond the legal framework of the Geneva Convention. The refugees streaming from Haiti, Cuba, and the former Federal Republic of Yugoslavia represent just three examples of flows that—rightly or not—the governments of receiving states consider unmanageable by means of traditional asylum processing based on individual procedures, judicial remedies, and a right of entry and residence. New and even less manageable migration movements may present new challenges for the traditional international legal system based on the concept of persecution as laid down in Article 1 (a) of the Geneva Convention. The discussion on the addition of gender as a prohibited ground of persecution (Fullerton 1993, 505; Johnsson 1989, 221) only indicates the difficulties of applying traditional concepts of persecution when this may lead to unmanageable refugee flows. One aspect especially troubling Western Europe is the gap between West European political and social standards and rising Islamic fundamentalism. Will women unwilling to adjust to Islamic rules on social behavior automatically acquire a right of asylum? Will Western-oriented Algerians, for decades trained in French language and culture, gain the right to seek protection in France after an Islamic government has taken over? Should Somalis or Bosnians trying to escape war and chaos be allowed to move to Western countries?

The common response to these questions is to refer to the Geneva Convention of 1951. Whether somebody seeking asylum is entitled to receive protection depends on whether he or she qualifies as a conventional refugee, which means in effect that he or she must demonstrate a "well-founded fear" of individual persecution for the reasons laid down in Article 1 (a) of the convention. In other words, asylum is not to be granted to purely humanitarian refugees facing a concrete but general danger to life and liberty stemming from war or political unrest. Thus the solution to the problem appears to lie in a more effective administration of the Geneva Convention, clearer standards of interpretation, and a faster review procedure, not a revision of the basic premise to provide effective refuge for every person demonstrating a reasonable fear of persecution. More or less all international and national legal instruments and techniques recently introduced to render asylum more manageable are based on a declaration to guarantee adequate protection to conventional refugees and to stick to humanitarian traditions with respect to the protection of refugees.[8] The basic assumption that the raison d'être of political asylum is to provide refuge for the persecuted can hardly be challenged.[9] It cannot be ignored, however, that there is a certain hypocrisy, or at least a certain deliberate uncertainty, in official statements emphasizing the need for "adequate protection" for political refugees. While the numbers of refugees deemed conventional by present standards of individual political persecution do not really present a quantitative problem in Germany and elsewhere, it is the status of asylum seekers that frequently makes asylum systems unmanageable.

The issue is whether it is possible under the existing system to find out in a reasonable time and with a reasonable amount of administrative and financial resources who is entitled to political asylum or some other kind of temporary or permanent protection. The Geneva Convention specifies no such procedural requirements. It does however prohibit rejection, expulsion, or return (refoulement) to any country of persecution thus guaranteeing in effect a provisional right of entry and stay. The lacuna has been filled by UNHCR executive committee recommendations, in particular those in Resolution No. 30 on manifestly unfounded or abusive asylum claims (UNHCR 1983).

New techniques for rendering asylum manageable must reflect a different perception of "adequacy." They must be based on the recognition that a reasonable concept of asylum must represent a balance of interests. The interest of an asylum seeker to be granted political asylum cannot claim absolute priority over the interest to control immigration and keep the system as a whole manageable. Techniques to prevent access to a nation's domestic asylum system through visa requirements and carrier sanctions may well be indispensable even though they apply to bona fide asylum seekers as well as to economic refugees. Existing administrative and judicial standards will have to be examined for their suitability in processing large numbers of asylum seekers. More trust in the officials running the procedures, including granting them discretionary power, may be one of the answers to the problem (Martin 1990, 1247). "Navigating the coast of Bohemia" has definitely become even more difficult in the nineties. There is no alternative but to render asylum manageable. It is futile simply to deplore restrictive trends and lament "fortress Europe," asking for a return to the more liberal asylum system of the sixties. Circumstances have changed, and no return to the standards and procedures of the sixties will maintain the concept of political asylum.

Recent Legislative and Administrative Concepts for Rendering Asylum Manageable: A Survey

Western Europe

By the end of 1995 there seemed to have been little progress toward achieving a comprehensive strategy for handling asylum.

Most receiving West European states have reacted to increasing immigration pressure with administrative and legislative restrictions to the access of asylum seekers that streamline procedures and introduce new measures against the organized abuse of the asylum procedure. Significant steps toward an internationally coordinated management of large refugee movements were lacking.

Within the member states of the European Union a number of measures and proposals on the national as well as European level have been submitted or enacted to render asylum manageable. In a 23 February 1994 communication to the Council and the European Parliament, the commission attached primary importance to the control of migration flows to the EU and the prevention of illegal immigration. The report recommended that the member states of the EU

- improve procedures for the exchange of information on routes and carriers, and take appropriate follow-up measures of a preventive nature;
- adopt and implement the revised draft convention on the crossing of external borders;
- develop measures designed to identify people illegally resident in the EC, focusing in particular on combating illegal employment;
- define minimum standards for the treatment of those who have been found to be in irregular situations;
- develop guidelines for repatriation policies concerning particularly vulnerable groups, such as unaccompanied minors;
- harmonize national schemes for the voluntary repatriation of illegal immigrants, intensify mutual cooperation in order to facilitate repatriation in appropriate cases, and extend this cooperation to relevant third countries; and
- conclude readmission agreements with relevant third countries, linking these agreements as necessary with the corresponding external agreements of the EC and examining the consequences of such readmission agreements for certain relevant countries of origin or transit (Commission to the Council and the European Parliament, COM [94] 23 final, 23 February 1994, 42f).

On the question of international protection for convention refugees and humanitarian refugees the commission considers streamlining procedures as well as developing a new concept of protection, including the notion of temporary protection for people in need of it, to be a step essential to managing refugee movements. It identified the following items as part of a European refugee policy:

- Implementation of the plan of action approved by the European Council in December 1993 in regard to (1) the harmonized application of the definition of refugees in accordance with Article 1 (a) of the Geneva Convention; and (2) the development of minimum standards for fair and efficient asylum procedures
- The elaboration of a convention on manifestly unfounded asylum applications and the implementation of the third host country principle
- Harmonization of policies concerning people who cannot be admitted as refugees but whom member states would nevertheless not require to return to their countries of origin in view of the general prevailing situations there
- Harmonization of the schemes for temporary protection
- Development of a system to monitor absorption capacities and creation of a mechanism to support member states willing to assist other member states faced with mass influx situations and to support projects of member states or third transit countries suddenly faced with new pressures (Commission to the Council and the European Parliament, COM [94] 23 final, 23 February 1994, 42f).

The commission refers to the European Council Plan of Action approved in 2 December 1993 (Doc. 10655/93). The council, representing the governments of the EU's states, has decided to give priority, in the field of harmonization of substantive asylum law, to:

unambiguous conditions for determining that applications for asylum are clearly unjustified;
definition and harmonized application of the principle of first host country;

common assessment of the situations in countries of origin with a view both to admission and expulsion; and

harmonized application of the definition of refugee as given in Article 1 (a) of the Geneva Convention.

In addition, there is general agreement that aims of asylum and immigration policy are to be included in external relations with third states. The council has therefore decided to establish common principles to include in bilateral or multilateral agreements on readmission or return. A link of external relations with the EU's asylum policy on return and repatriation is also envisaged in association—and cooperation—with EU agreements with third states.[10]

In both the commission's and the council's proposals on a European asylum policy, the most progress seems to have been achieved in the area of migration control and special procedures for dealing with manifestly unfounded or abusive asylum claims. These procedures are also applicable to persons arriving via a safe third country or a safe country of origin. All member states view the introduction of a coordinated restrictive policy in the field of border control, visa requirements, and carrier sanctions as necessary to render asylum manageable.

A second major field of action concerns the introduction of asylum policy into external relations (return, readmission, and repatriation), starting with the Schengen states' return agreement with Poland in January 1993.[11]

Third, a new technique for rendering asylum manageable has been to emphasize regional and local protection and extend the first host country concept beyond the limits of the European Union. On 30 November and 1 December 1992 immigration ministers passed various nonbinding conclusions and recommendations, recommending them for incorporation into national law by a specified date. The most important of these resolutions concerns a procedure for handling manifestly unfounded applications for asylum (see Special Procedures for Manifestly Unfounded or Abusive Asylum Claims, below). A conclusion on countries in which there is generally no serious risk of persecution was also passed. Finally, the safe third country concept was addressed in the resolution on a harmonized approach to questions concerning host third countries. A decision establishing a clearinghouse set the framework for an exchange of information and the compilation of documentation on all matters relating to asylum.

To what extent recently introduced legal and administrative concepts have been successful is a matter of some debate. There are as yet no precise assessments of the resolutions and conclusions of the EU immigration ministers since member states have only begun to adapt their national law to these principles. In Germany, the amendment of the Basic Law modeled according to the principles recommended by the EU immigration ministers has substantially contributed to the calming of an extremely emotional debate. In 1994 and 1995 approximately 130,000 asylum seekers were registered, compared to 438,200 in 1992 and 322,600 in 1993. The reduction in numbers is largely attributed to the streamlining of the procedure, the new law's safe third country clause, and a relatively strict deportation and return policy.

The new instruments envisaged by national laws and the recommendations of the EU immigration ministers have provoked criticism from refugee advocates and scholars. In striking contrast to the public's broad acceptance, the "fortress Europe" label has become the most common criticism. It is argued that West European asylum policy is fundamentally restrictive, establishing a *cordon sanitaire* preventing entry into Western Europe by means of safe third country clauses and other barriers such as visa requirements and carrier sanctions.[12]

The United States

To a West European observer, the present U.S. asylum situation resembles that in Western Europe in 1989. Asylum claims in 1993 rose to 150,000, well above the expected number. The asylum system is frequently characterized as "increasingly fair but decreasingly timely" (Beyer 1994, 50). Without additional resources, administrative streamlining, and other reform, the U.S. asylum program is expected to fall further and further behind. The number of unadjusted cases grew from 114,000 in April 1991 to 354,000 by January 1994. Overburdened, the system is considered to be ripe for fraud and abuse. Migrants with little or no legitimate fear of persecution are claiming asylum primarily to gain entry into the United States. As in the old German system, increasing numbers of others are using the asylum system to get into the "work authorised backlog" (51).

There is general agreement that a fundamental reform of the asylum system is overdue. The reforms announced by the Justice Department and the INS in 1994[13] were intended to

- reduce spurious and abusive claims by "boilerplate" petitions (virtually carbon copy applications inadequate to support a claim) by returning them to the claimants for more detail and by providing for possible fines and criminal prosecution of those who prepare such applications.
- establish definitive identification, based on fingerprints, of asylum applicants to deter duplicate applications and to permit checking against the records of known criminals, terrorists, and other undesirable aliens.
- allow the deportation of criminal aliens convicted of serious crimes without having to go through costly and time-consuming hearings.
- make current the processing of applications by doubling the INS asylum corps from 150 to 334 in fiscal 1994. The INS assumed that by increasing the number of asylum officers and cutting the average time taken to decide cases it would be able to process the present level of 150,000 applicants per year as well as gradually eliminating the backlog of 420,794 by the end of 1994. To aid this process, a decision was made to have asylum officers expedite approvals and refer cases that were unclear or likely be rejected directly to immigration judges for determination.
- require applicants not granted asylum immediately to wait 150 days from the time of application before they could request a work permit (effective since 4 January 1995). The hope was that when asylum officers were current in their work—possibly by the end of 1994—most new cases would be decided within that time limit. If so, only bona fide applicants and persons with particularly difficult cases would receive work authorization, and the work permit would no longer serve as an attraction for baseless claims to asylum, as was currently the situation.
- reform regulations so that asylum seekers who have passed through a safe country of transit could be denied

asylum and returned to that safe country if the United States has a reciprocal agreement for return. The new regulations of 5 November 1994 authorized the discretionary denial of asylum to aliens who would be deported to safe third countries through which they traveled en route to the United States, provided the United States and the third country have entered into a return agreement.[14]
- increase resources and personnel to allow immigration judges to deal with current cases and their own asylum backlogs.
- charge a fee of $130 for processing asylum claims, except when poor claimants request a waiver. (This provision has been heavily criticized by immigration lawyers and human rights groups; as yet no standards have been proposed [*Immigration Review*, no. 17 (spring 1994): 4].) This proposal has been dropped.

Among the administrative methods to curb the growing number of asylum applications, interdiction at sea in combination with external examination procedures have marked a new stage in asylum policy. The United States has followed a zigzag path on its treatment of Haitian boat people. On 16 June 1994 the United States announced that henceforward Haitians picked up at sea and seeking asylum would be eligible to present to U.S. asylum officers onboard U.S. ships evidence that they faced persecution in Haiti. As a result, over 11,627 Haitians were picked up by the U.S. Coast Guard by 6 July, many of them hoping to be granted refugee status and allowed to go to the United States. Those turned down—about 70 percent of those requesting asylum—continue to be returned to Haiti. President Clinton changed the policy in July. After that date, Haitians picked up at sea were sent to the U.S. base at Guantánamo Bay, Cuba, to present their cases for asylum.[15] After the cessation of shipboard hearings, the number of Haitians picked up by the Coast Guard dropped dramatically (*Migration News* 1994b).

With regard to Cuba, in August 1994 a twenty-eight-year-old policy was reversed. Henceforward, people from the island nation heading for the United States on rafts and small boats were to be treated as illegal aliens, detained in centers outside the United States, and not permitted to enter the United States unless they could satisfy the criteria for refugee or immigrant status individually. After the policy changed on 19 August 1994, some 18,000 Cubans were picked up at sea and taken to safe haven at the U.S. naval base on Guantánamo Bay, where there are already almost 15,000 Haitians. On 24 August the United States announced plans to expand the tent camps at Guantánamo to hold up to 40,000 Cubans there. Panama and Honduras promised to take up to 15,000 Cubans for up to six months (*Migration News* 1994a).

In Congress three proposals for major immigration reforms and various individual bills dealing with illegal immigration have been introduced. In July 1994 the Clinton administration announced a legislative package including a special expedited exclusion procedure for bogus asylum applicants arriving at ports of entry. This proposal has been dropped, however, apparently because the number of bogus applications coming through JFK airport has been reduced substantially.

Streamlining Procedure

General Remarks

The need for a faster and more efficient asylum procedure is generally acknowledged. The delay in the traditional asylum system led almost inevitably to abuse. The bigger the backlog, the longer the average asylum procedure, and the greater the hope to make use of the asylum procedure to achieve some kind of residence status that would not be available under normal immigration rules. Once a certain time has passed, it becomes increasingly hard to enforce negative asylum decisions; the system has great difficulty sending anyone home (Martin 1990, 1377). There are different opinions on the evaluation of recognition rates. Even the most careful commentators, however, would not dispute that a large majority of asylum seekers do not have valid reasons for applying for asylum.

One of the main reasons for the failure of the system lies in its judicially oriented approach and disregard for the political and discretionary elements of the decision-making process. In addition, the particularities of the interests involved in an asylum procedure are neglected. Asylum seekers frequently are interested in delaying the procedure, especially if this improves their chances of qualifying for a legalization program or some other kind of residential status.

Substantially increasing the staff of adjudicators and immigration judges is essential to reducing the average time of procedures.[16] There may also be a need for sanctions against attorneys or representatives who engage in so-called frivolous behavior, although in the German legal system the attempt to draw a line between frivolous and creative would be doomed to failure.

The task of discovering whether somebody has a well-founded fear of persecution under alien political and social conditions in a remote country cannot be dealt with under the same rules as the right to build a house or operate a business. In the absence of witnesses and documentary proof, the success of an asylum claim often turns on intelligence and legal advice. The impossibility, in many cases, of carrying out a thorough examination of a purported danger of persecution calls for a stronger role for discretionary and even political elements in the decision-making process (although this is not to deny that individual expertise and special training also play an essential role). It should be recognized, however, that a system of extensive administrative and judicial review will not necessarily contribute to more justice. Even if one accepts the assumption that judicial review contributes to the protection of bona fide refugees, the costs of such a system are too high if it leads to a virtual unenforcement of immigration law. Thus preference should be given to a system of specially trained adjudicators deciding on asylum claims as well as any other temporary or permanent right of residence in a single procedure. Judicial review should be open within a certain time limit and be restricted to legal issues. If an asylum claim has been determined to be manifestly unfounded or abusive, judicial remedies should not necessarily suspend the effect of that decision.

A second element of traditional asylum procedure is its focus on the individual situation of an asylum seeker. Individual case-by-case determination seems to be a logical consequence of the individual persecution requirement under the Geneva Convention. In reality, however, the decision-making process frequently focuses on certain categories of cases and the likelihood of political persecution of a special group of applicants. The question may be raised regarding whether a group-decision process, made publicly known and used as a precedent in individual asylum procedures, might not contribute substantially to distinguishing, in a shorter procedure, between bona fide asylum seekers and those filing manifestly unfounded asylum claims. Experience shows that in many cases members of certain ethnic groups, such as, for example, the Roma and the Sinti in East European states, are submitting similar claims relating to the danger of political persecution. It would seem to be unnecessary to examine those claims in thousands of individual cases. A group-decision element could, of course, work both ways. A positive determination might attract everybody belonging to a certain group, an invitation that most governments would not be inclined to issue; indeed, this may be why governments continue to insist that asylum can only be granted on the basis of an individual examination process. The objections aside, however, general assessments of the political situation in a given country relating to a certain ethnic or religious group could contribute to preventing unfounded asylum claims. A beginning in this direction has been made with the safe country of origin concept (see the discussion on this subject below).

A third element of traditional asylum procedure has been its focus on the provisional rights of asylum seekers, which amounts to a temporary right of residence ensuing from the filing of an asylum claim, along with procedural rights and social privileges such as the right to work and to claim social benefits. It is clear that a provisional right of residence is necessary to pursue an asylum claim effectively. But how far should the right of provisional residence during the asylum procedure gain priority over the effective implementation of immigration legislation? Execution of negative asylum decisions is frequently impossible after a certain period of time has lapsed, because of a lack of documents and other factors. It is therefore necessary to draw distinctions between different types of asylum claims and the public and private interests involved. In the types of cases discussed in the next section, immediate deportation after an administrative procedure by trained adjudicators may well be acceptable to reconcile the conflicting interests of immigration control and individual protection needs.

Special Procedures for Manifestly Unfounded or Abusive Asylum Claims

In November/December 1992, in London, EU immigration ministers passed a resolution on manifestly unfounded asylum applications. This resolution provides that an application for asylum shall be regarded as manifestly unfounded if it clearly raises no substantive issue under the Geneva Convention either because there is clearly no substance to the applicant's claim to fear persecution in his or her country or because the claim is based on a deliberate deception or is an abuse of an asylum procedure. Furthermore, an application for asylum may not be subject to determination when it falls under the provision of the resolution on host third countries (see The Safe Third Country Concept, below). The accelerated procedure does not envisage full examination as an automatic necessity at every level of the procedure. It also provides for member states to operate admissibility procedures under which applications may be rejected quickly on objective grounds.

Under the resolution, member states will aim to reach initial decisions on relevant applications as soon as possible, at the latest within one month, and to complete any appeal or review procedures as soon as possible. Appeal or review procedures may be more simplified than those generally available for other rejected asylum applications. A decision to refuse an asylum application will be taken by a competent authority, at the appropriate level, who is fully qualified in asylum or refugee matters. The applicant should be given the opportunity for a personal interview with a qualified official. Every member state will ensure that an applicant whose application is refused leaves EC territory, unless he or she is given permission to enter or remain on other grounds.

The resolution deems manifestly unfounded claims for which the grounds are outside the scope of the Geneva Convention, those totally lacking in substance, and those manifestly lacking in any credibility (i.e., the story is inconsistent, contradictory, or fundamentally improbable). Member states may also consider as manifestly unfounded applications from asylum seekers living in geographical areas where effective protection is readily available in another part of the country. A consultation mechanism is provided for the application of this paragraph.

The resolution describes as deliberate deception or abuse of asylum procedures cases in which the applicant has without reasonable explanation

> based the application on a false identity or forged or counterfeit documents that he or she has maintained are genuine when questioned about them, thereby deliberately making false representations about the claim either orally or in writing, after applying for asylum;
> in bad faith destroyed, damaged, or disposed of any passport, other document, or ticket relevant to the claim, either in order to establish a false identity for the purpose of the asylum application or to make the consideration of the application more difficult;
> deliberately failed to reveal that he or she has previously lodged an application in one or more countries, particularly when false identities are used;
> submitted the application in order to forestall an impending expulsion measure, after having had ample opportunity to do so earlier;
> flagrantly failed to comply with substantive obligations imposed by national rules relating to asylum procedures; or
> submitted an application in a member state after having been rejected in another country following an examination comprising adequate procedural guarantees and in accordance with the Geneva Convention on the Status of Refugees. To this end, contacts between member states and third countries would, when necessary, be made through UNHCR.

The factors mentioned are indications of bad faith and justify consideration of a case under accelerated procedures. But according to the resolution, they cannot in themselves outweigh a well-founded fear of persecution under Article 1 of the Geneva Convention, and none of them carries any greater weight than any other.

The resolution does not define procedural rights in an accelerated procedure. At the Brussels meeting of the European Council in November 1994 consensus was achieved in substance, although a resolution was not formally adopted because of a dispute between Belgium and Spain on the admission of Spanish asylum seekers to the Belgium asylum procedure. The consensus related to the rights of asylum seekers in the procedure, judicial remedies, and the suspensive effect of remedies. Every asylum application is to be examined by a specialized authority fully competent in asylum and refugee matters and deciding on the basis of objectivity and neutrality. The asylum seeker must have a chance to present the individual circumstances of his or her case in a personal hearing. He or she may consult an attorney and must be informed about his or her rights and remedies. As a rule, he or she has a right of provisional residence until the asylum claim has been decided on.

In principle, the possibility of filing a remedy within an appropriate time is also recognized; however, the right of provisional residence during the review procedure is limited. Restrictions are possible under national law in specified circumstances. As a minimum standard, the asylum seeker is to be given the right to ask a court or an independent review authority for a stay of deportation. Additional restrictions are envisaged for manifestly unfounded asylum claims and for the examination of claims from asylum seekers entering from safe third countries. The right of judicial review can be restricted in case of manifestly unfounded asylum claims if an independent executive authority of higher level confirms the negative decision and its immediate execution.

Generally speaking, the introduction of special procedures for manifestly unfounded or abusive claims can be considered as an effective instrument for preventing the overburdening of the system. The crucial issue revolves around the fairness and accuracy of the procedure and the reasonableness of the criteria used. A common criticism is that some of the criteria are not convincing enough to permit a conclusion on the legitimacy of an asylum claim. The immigration ministers' resolution makes it clear, however, that the criteria used are not intended to replace an examination of the claim of well-founded fear of persecution. Accelerated procedures are not necessarily based on a negative prima facie assessment of an asylum claim but rather on the need to sanction effectively certain types of behavior such as the use of false documents or the failure to cooperate in the asylum procedure. An asylum seeker may well be forced to use falsified passports. There is, however, no convincing reason to conceal one's identity or use falsified documents when questioned by immigration authorities. A consequent and firm response to such practices will contribute to the elimination of established abuse that has long been used to escape rejection or deportation. One could even go a step further and ask whether the list of criteria should not be extended to apply to other cases where an urgent resolution of the claims is considered necessary. The need for accelerated procedure is particularly urgent if the applicant has committed a serious offense or if he or she is considered a danger for public security. The EU immigration ministers' resolution makes it clear that member states' national provisions for considering such cases under accelerated provisions would not be affected even though they are not included explicitly in the resolution.

As noted above, if an asylum seeker files an asylum application long after entering the country, this too may be considered to be an abuse of asylum. Frequently, asylum applications are filed as a reaction to expulsion or deportation or to enforce a prolongation of stay. In theory, there is no reason why an asylum seeker should not be obliged to present the reasons for an asylum claim within a certain time limit. In practice, however, it may be very difficult to find out when an asylum seeker actually entered the country. In addition, it is frequently argued that time prescriptions are of no use because asylum seekers must not be returned to a country in which they face persecution. Yet, although neither objection is altogether convincing, sanctioning such requirements seems to be difficult. One way could be the general use of accelerated procedures if an asylum seeker does not file an asylum claim within a prescribed time limit.

The Safe Country of Origin Concept

Under Article 16 (a) (3), German immigration authorities must refuse as manifestly unfounded an application for asylum from a citizen of a safe country of origin. The only exception to this policy occurs when the alien provides facts or evidence sufficient to justify the assumption that, despite the general situation in the country of origin, he or she remains in danger of political persecution. Using this method, German immigration authorities process applications under a shortened and accelerated asylum procedure.

According to the criteria Article 16 (a) articulates, safe countries of origin are countries in which, on the basis of their legal situations, their application of the law, and their general political environment, practice neither political persecution nor inhumane or degrading treatment. The law does not explicitly describe the conditions for determining safety. The draft bill, however, lists the following criteria:

> recognition rates for asylum applicants in previous years;
> general political situation (e.g., democratic structure of the state);
> observance of human rights (such as compliance with the International Covenant on Civil and Political Rights);
> readiness of the state of origin to allow independent international human rights organizations access in its territory; and
> stability of the country (Bundestagsdrucksache 12/4450, 2 Mar 1993).[17]

In an annex to Article 1, § 29 (a), of the Gesetz zur Änderung asylverfahrens-, ausländer- und staatsangehörigkeitsrechtlicher Vorschriften (*BGBl.* 1 [1993]: 1070), the legislature designated the following countries as safe states of origin: Bulgaria, the Czech Republic, Gambia, Ghana, Hungary, Poland, Romania, Senegal, and the Slovak Republic.

Objections to a list of safe countries of origin find no sufficient basis in either the Refugee or the European Convention. With respect to countries Germany deems safe, a refutable presumption requires an applicant to provide facts challenging the presumption of safety. Judicial review, although only to a limited degree, determines whether an applicant has offered relevant facts. These procedures fulfill the minimum requirements of the Refugee Convention, thereby ensuring that Germany does not violate the nonrefoulement clause.[18]

German administrative courts, however, have largely neglected to apply this new concept. The legislative presumption of safety has not significantly changed the individual case procedure; as before, claims of individual persecution are examined closely if precise facts are presented to the courts. Preliminary rulings of the Constitutional Court, to some extent, have supported this practice. Administrative court decisions have been quashed, however, for not sufficiently examining individual claims of persecution in safe countries of origin as a result of illegal participation in demonstrations and police harassment.[19]

Within the EU, no agreement has yet been reached on a common European decision-making process for the purpose of designating safe countries of origin. At their meeting in December 1992 the immigration ministers did not reject the idea as such; in fact, the resolution on manifestly unfounded applications for asylum includes a reference to the concept of countries in which there is in general no serious risk of persecution. It is left to each member state, however, to decide which countries qualify on the basis of the elements set out in the conclusions, although member states have an interest in reaching common assessment of certain countries in this context.

According to the conclusions of the immigration ministers, a country of origin is defined as safe if it "can be clearly shown, in an objective and verifiable way, normally not to generate refugees or ... it can be clearly shown, in an objective and verifiable way, that circumstances which might in the past have justified recourse to the 1951 Convention have ceased to exist" (*Report from Immigration Ministers to the European Council Meeting in Maastricht*, Doc. WGI 930, 38). This definition is intended to assist member states in establishing a harmonized approach to applications from nationals of countries that produce a high proportion of clearly unfounded applications and to reduce pressure on asylum determination systems. An appropriate framework of information exchange on relevant national decisions is envisioned.

Member states will take into account the following elements in any assessment of the general risk of persecution in a particular country:

(a) *previous numbers of refugees and recognition rates*. It is necessary to look at the recognition rates for asylum applicants from the country in question who have come to Member States in recent years. Obviously, a situation may change and historically low recognition rates need not continue following (for example) a violent coup. But in the absence of any significant change in the country it is reasonable to assume that low recognition rates will continue and that the country tends not to produce refugees.

(b) *observance of human rights*. It is necessary to consider the formal obligations undertaken by a country in adhering to international human rights instruments and in its domestic law and how in practice it meets those obligations. The latter is clearly more important and adherence or non-adherence to a particular instrument cannot in itself result in consideration as a country in which there is generally no serious risk of persecution. It should be recognized that a pattern of breaches of human rights may be exclusively linked to a particular group within a country's population or to a particular area of the country. The readiness of the country concerned to allow monitoring by NGOs of their human rights observance is also relevant in judging how seriously a country takes its human rights obligations.

(c) *democratic institutions*. The existence of one or more specific institutions cannot be a sine qua non but consideration should be given to democratic processes, elections, political pluralism and freedom of expression and thought. Particular attention should be paid to the availability and effectiveness of legal avenues of protection and redress.

(d) *stability*. Taking into account the above mentioned elements, an assessment must be made of the prospect for dramatic change in the immediate future. Any view formed must be reviewed over time in the light of events. (European Communities 1992, Doc. 10579/92, annex C to annex 2)

The conclusions of the immigration ministers explicitly provide that an individual member state's assessment of a country as one in which there is generally no serious risk of persecution should not automatically result in the refusal of all asylum applications from its nationals or their exclusion from individualized determination procedures. Rather, each state will consider the claims of all applicants from such countries, along with any specific individual factors presented by the applicant that might outweigh a general presumption. Criticisms that the safe country of origin concept represents a denial of the right to be judged on an individual case-by-case basis and constitutes an unacceptable restriction of the geographical scope of the Geneva Convention are thus clearly unfounded. The concept of countries of origin does not provide for an automatic rejection of asylum claims but only for a refutable presumption of safety and acceleration of individual procedure, as described in the resolution on manifestly unfounded applications

Less far-fetched are doubts as to whether the system can be of any practical effect given that most asylum seekers come from countries in which a general assessment of safety is difficult to make. Experience in Germany as well as in other European countries shows, however, that the concept as a whole has functioned efficiently. The number of applicants from countries determined as safe countries of origin has dropped substantially. Nevertheless, the concept has met some difficulties with regard to the evidence required to refute the presumption of safety. Administrative courts have frequently requested that authorities thoroughly examine assertions of individual persecution, in spite of the general presumption of safety of a country of origin. A chamber of the German Constitutional Court has upheld this interpretation of law, holding in preliminary injunction proceedings that the individual right of asylum, maintained in Article 16 (a) (1) of the Basic Law implies an individual right to present concrete assertions of individual persecution that an administrative court must examine.[20]

For the concept to work efficiently, it should be extended and diversified. Rather than making a general assessment about safety of a country of origin, general assessments could relate to the safety of special ethnic, religious, or linguistic groups within a certain country or a particular region within a specified country. Alternative possibilities of protection within a country of origin or a specified region or internationally controlled zone could also be included in a more general evaluation of safety.

Any general assessment of safety provokes the question of fairness and individual justice. There is a danger that a third state could be defined as a safe country of origin for political reasons. This danger can be reduced substantially, however, by the establishment of an objective assessment procedure and the participation of advisory committees in the determination process. The legitimacy of decisions could also be greatly increased by international cooperation. Within the European Union, common assessment procedures are envisaged but not yet established; the immigration ministers' conclusions only refer to the "goal to reach common assessment of certain countries that are of particular interest in this context."

The resolution on manifestly unfounded asylum applications also leaves it to every member state to decide whether no serious, general risk of persecution exists in a country of origin. In so deciding, however, member states are obliged to take into account the elements set out in the conclusions of the immigration ministers and must still consider the individual claims of all applicants from such countries and any specific indications presented by the applicant which might outweigh a general presumption.

Prescreening or Summary Exclusion Procedures

In general, prescreening procedures intended to establish whether a category of asylum seekers should be admitted to the asylum procedure have proved to be of little value in rendering asylum more manageable. The main purpose of such procedures is to dispose quickly of manifestly unfounded or abusive asylum claims. For the system to work, however, border or police authorities—generally not sufficiently trained to evaluate asylum claims—would have to decide on the spot as to whether asylum seekers should be admitted to the asylum procedure. But in order to avoid the danger of erroneous decisions inherent in such procedures, the possibility of judicial or at least administrative review cannot be excluded altogether. This could lead, in effect, to a procedure within the procedure. It makes more sense to decide on the merits of an asylum claim in a general accelerated procedure rather than to concentrate on admission to the asylum procedure.

There may however be a need for special procedures at ports of entry to prevent the entry and possibly disappearance of asylum seekers. Frequently, asylum seekers arriving at air- or seaports destroy their travel documents in order to prevent rejection or deportation. The rapidly growing number of asylum seekers arriving at airports led to the creation of a special airport procedure in cases where asylum applicants from safe countries of origin arrive via international flights. Under § 18 (a) of the German asylum procedure law, the Federal Office must carry out the asylum proceedings before the applicant enters the country. The same procedure applies to aliens requesting asylum at an airport who are unable to establish their identities with valid passports or other documentation. The authorities accommodate such asylum seekers at the airport during the proceedings, and the asylum seekers are not allowed to leave the transit area. They may apply for provisional legal protection within three days of a Federal Office decision rejecting their applications. The administrative court must rule on such appeals within fourteen days, and, if it fails to do so within this time frame, the government must allow the applicants to enter the country. This rule also applies when the Federal Office does not decide on asylum applications within two days of filing.

Within the European Union a draft resolution on minimum standards of asylum procedures on which consensus has been achieved in substance provides for a special procedure at ports of entry to discover whether asylum claims are manifestly unfounded. During the procedure, the asylum seeker is not rejected but can be detained. In case of a manifestly unfounded application the asylum seeker is refused entry. Suspensive effects of remedies may be excluded. In this case, refusal to grant entry must be authorized by the immigration minister or a central authority. The same rules are to apply in the case of asylum applications from asylum seekers entering via a safe third state.

The Safe Third Country Concept

Article 16 (a) (2) of the Basic Law represents a fundamental shift from the unqualified right to seek asylum in Germany, in that it precludes recourse to the right of asylum in the case of applicants arriving from safe third states.

By definition, safe third states include the members of the European Community and countries guaranteeing the application of the UN Convention Relating to the Status of Refugees (1951 Refugee Convention) and the European Convention for the Protection of Human Rights and Fundamental Freedoms (1950 European Convention). Accordingly, the Bundestag also includes in the list of safe third states Austria, the Czech Republic, Finland, Norway, Poland, Sweden, and Switzerland (see annex I, § 26 (a), of the law on asylum procedure). In order for German authorities to reject an asylum application under the safe third state clause, an asylum seeker must have had actual contact with the territory of the safe third country and must have had the opportunity to apply for asylum in that country. A simple transit is sufficient to meet this requirement. Article 16 (a) (1) only covers those refugees who do not enter Germany by way of safe third countries—that is, primarily those who arrive by plane directly from a persecuting country.

In its third sentence, Article 16 (a) (2) provides for the possibility of terminating an applicant's residency regardless of any pending appeals. Article 34 (a) of the Law on Asylum Procedures interprets this provision as an exclusion of any judicial stay of execution. Thus Article 16 (a) (2) not only eliminates the suspensive effect of an applicant's request for legal redress while courts still have the power to stay execution but also empowers authorities to take immediate measures without considering an asylum seeker's objections if Germany considers the country to which it will deport the refugee as a safe third country.

The EU immigration ministers' resolution on a harmonized approach concerning host third countries lays down a very similar concept, emphasizing the need for a concerted response in dealing with the safe country concept.[21] The resolution on manifestly unfounded applications for asylum refers to the concept of host third country. According to the resolution, an application for asylum, without prejudice to the Dublin Convention, may not be subject to determination by a member state under the 1951 Convention when it falls within the provisions of the resolution on host third countries. That resolution in turn incorporates the following procedural principles:

(a) The formal identification of a host third country in principle precedes the substantive examination of the application for asylum and its justification.
(b) The principle of the host third country is to be applied to all applicants for asylum, irrespective of whether or not they may be regarded as refugees.
(c) Thus, if there is a host third country, the application for refugee status may not be examined and the asylum applicant may be sent to that country.
(d) If the asylum applicant cannot in practice be sent to a host third country, the provisions of the Dublin Convention will apply.
(e) Any Member State retains the right, for humanitarian reasons, not to remove the asylum applicant to a host third country. (European Communities, Doc. 10579/92, annex B to annex 2)

The resolution outlines some fundamental requirements determining a host third country:

(a) In those third countries, the life or freedom of the asylum applicant must not be threatened, within the meaning of Article 33 of the Geneva Convention.
(b) The asylum applicant must not be exposed to torture or inhuman or degrading treatment in the third country.
(c) It must either be the case that the asylum applicant has already been granted protection in the third country or has had an

opportunity, at the border or within the territory of the third country, to make contact with that country's authorities in order to seek their protection, before approaching the Member State in which he is applying for asylum, or that there is clear evidence of his admissibility to a third country.
(d) The asylum applicant must be afforded effective protection in the host third country against refoulement, within the meaning of the Geneva Convention.

If two or more countries fulfill the above conditions, the member states may expel the asylum applicant to one of those third countries. Member states must take into account, particularly on the basis of the information available from UNHCR, known practice in the third countries, especially with regard to the principle of nonrefoulement. (European Communities Doc. 10579/92, annex B to annex 2).

It is not clear whether the immigration ministers' resolutions require a determination in each individual case. They do not anticipate an assessment of whether the fundamental requirements of the resolution concerning safety are fulfilled in "each individual case," but an individual assessment may refer to either an individual application or an individual country. The resolution on manifestly unfounded applications supports the second interpretation, by allowing that applications for asylum "may not be subject to determination by a Member State of refugee status ... when it falls within the provisions of the Resolution on host third countries." In addition, the resolution on host third countries provides that "if there is a host third country, the application for refugee status may not be examined, and the asylum applicant may be sent to that country."

The basic rationale behind the concept of a safe third country is the idea that an asylum seeker disposing of alternative ways of finding protection is not in urgent need of protection. Accordingly, as early as 1989 the UNHCR Executive Committee passed a resolution on irregular movements of asylum seekers and refugees (Res. No. 58 [XL] 1989). Asylum seekers in general are therefore not expected to move on once they have found protection in a third country.

Theoretically, there is no convincing argument against an extension of the concept of alternative protection, provided an asylum seeker is safe from persecution and will not be returned to a persecuting country. As the German Constitutional Court has pointed out, the fundamental purpose of asylum is to provide immediate relief from urgent inescapable danger (*Decisions of the Bundesverfassungsgericht* 74:51). An asylum seeker with other means of getting protection, either internally or in a third country, is not in the same situation as an asylum seeker facing persecution if returned or rejected.

The principle that an asylum seeker may choose his or her country of asylum application on the basis of economic or social considerations runs counter to any longer-term strategy for coping with worldwide refugee movements, in that it may encourage migration of the best qualified, to the detriment of local development. In addition, the chances for a durable solution may be considerably increased if refugees remain in a culturally and socially familiar environment in neighboring areas, instead of being encouraged to migrate to Western Europe for economic and welfare reasons.

Garvey argues that the "problem becomes more manageable the more it is treated as a problem of relations and obligations amongst states. The essential need is to articulate inter-state obligations as the basic foundation for international refugee protection" (Garvey 1985, 483). Therefore "the aim should be a solution in the country of first asylum" (Köfner 1989, 119–22). This in turn calls for a truly international and geopolitically representative authority: "In exchange, refugees would not have the liberty to seek asylum in the State of their choice, but would rather be afforded protection within a culturally, racially, politically or otherwise affiliated State" (Hathaway 1990, 182).[22]

The effective use of limited financial resources also supports an approach to the international distribution of refugees based on both objective and humanitarian criteria rather than a reliance on the asylum seeker's free choice. Objective criteria include chances for durable solutions, the possibility of economic and social integration, efficient use of financial resources, and the prospect of achieving long-term aims of refugee policy. The high sums spent on asylum applicants in Western Europe could be used more efficiently in other countries where asylum seekers find protection or could have found protection and to which they may be returned without danger of persecution or refoulement.

There are some weaknesses in the concept. For example, who will decide about safety, and what criteria can be used to determine it? Moreover, shifting part of the burden to countries that may be ill equipped to deal with asylum seekers poses other problems. A safe third country concept must with some reliability exclude "refugee in orbit" situations as well as irregular movements of asylum seekers.

Within the European Union, the Dublin Convention has established a regional system of exclusive responsibility. Even if recognition standards vary among the West European countries adhering to that system, the acceptability of successive applications or "free choice" should be abandoned in favor of the principle that every asylum seeker in need of protection should simply have the chance to file an application in a region of Europe that is politically homogeneous and subscribes to common basic standards of protection. Although there continue to be unresolved issues relating to the harmonization of recognition standards and equitable burden sharing, the concept of a safe country of asylum thus can already be said to apply among European states, on the basis of a system of international arrangements determining responsibility. The Dublin Convention is itself premised on the assumption that all EU member states constitute safe countries of asylum, and this assumption should be extended to other European countries fulfilling certain common standards.

Experience shows that legitimate objections to this will be overcome if certain conditions are met. The application of the concept outside the European Union will not necessarily lead to a "fortress Europe." A large number of asylum seekers will still make their way to their preferred countries of destination. Safe third countries are necessarily linked to return agreements. As a rule, these agreements require proof that the asylum seeker has entered into a country illegally within a certain time limit. Evidence of travel routes and confirmation of an asylum seeker's identity are frequently not available; international agreements are therefore urgently needed.

As to unilateral burden shifting, the experience with Poland, the Czech Republic and some other East European states shows that so far very few asylum seekers have in fact chosen to file asylum applications in those countries. Nevertheless, there may be an increasing burden for those countries which has to be distributed among the European countries. Therefore, cooperation agreements are needed providing for administrative and financial help. In a long-term perspective, in addition to economic and administrative cooperation, legal harmonization in asylum matters should be included in the treaty network of the European Union with these countries.

Temporary Protection and Regional Approaches

Temporary protection and regional approaches can be useful techniques to render asylum manageable, provided their provisional character is strictly maintained and temporary protection does not develop into a kind of subsidiary asylum. There is clearly a need to grant temporary protection to people trying to escape war, civil war, or general violence. The solution to the problem cannot be found, however, in an enlarged refugee definition.

Temporary protection evolved when it became apparent that the Geneva system of 1951 was not adequate to cope with large refugee movements. The refugee definition laid down in the Geneva Convention did not fully take into account the fact that beyond traditional political refugees there were other people in need of protection. The Geneva system had developed in practice an established right of political refugees to be granted permanent residence and equal treatment and eventually naturalization, although the convention deliberately omitted the individual right of asylum.

Entry and reception under rules established to implement the Geneva Convention did generally result in permanent residence. Existing regulations did not provide sufficient precaution against refugee protection turning into immigration, and the duties arising from the Geneva Convention, in particular relating to the economic and social rights of convention refugees, support this trend. The rights granted under the convention and the legal status of convention refugees are in principle based on the assumption of an unlimited period of protection. This system is hardly suitable for granting protection on a more flexible and temporary basis. There is no need to grant protection to refugees escaping violence and civil war if the circumstances giving cause to flight have changed. Receiving states have reacted by either accommodating these people into the traditional pattern of refugee procedure or relegating them to the uncertain status of deportable aliens tolerated on an insecure legal basis. Both solutions proved to be unsatisfactory.

The system functioned tolerably as long as only a limited number of asylum seekers, mostly from countries behind the Iron Curtain, made their way to Western Europe. But it was bound to fail with the advent of new massive refugee flows spurred by poverty, economic disruption, population pressure, ecological degradation, and political instability. There was almost consensus among decision makers that an extension of the existing system could not be envisaged. Asylum based on an individual examination procedure and at least in principle a right of residence for the time of procedure were hardly practicable for dealing with large numbers of people trying to escape civil war, political unrest, and economic misery. On the other hand, a consensus also emerged that the Western countries could not remain indifferent to ever-larger refugee movements caused by the partial or total collapse of government and public order. To stick to the traditional concept of political asylum would have ignored the obvious need for protection of people who did not satisfy the condition of risk of individual political persecution.

Temporary protection has developed into a pragmatic answer to meet the protection needs of groups of refugees hitherto not covered by legal refugee instruments and at the same time to provide for more flexible and speedy machinery to prevent further undermining of immigration control by the extension of traditional refugee concepts. UNHCR has participated to a substantial degree in the development of the concept. According to UNHCR's recent Note on International Protection (A/AC 96/830, 7 Sept. 1994, 22), temporary protection involves

1. *Meeting urgent protection needs in mass refugee flows*: Temporary protection has served as a means, in situations of mass outflow, to provide refuge to groups or categories of people recognized to be in need of international protection, without recourse, at least initially, to individual refugee status determination. It shows respect for basic human rights but, because it is conceived as an emergency protection measure of short duration, accords only a more limited range of rights and benefits in the initial stage

than would customarily be accorded to refugees granted asylum under the 1951 Convention and the 1967 Protocol.
2. *Focusing on return as the most appropriate solution*: One of the principal reasons for applying the term *temporary* to the protection given to people fleeing conflicts or acute crisis in their countries of origin is the expectation—or at least the hope—that international efforts to resolve the crisis will, within a fairly short period, produce results that will enable the refugees to exercise their right to return home in safety. This focus on return as the most likely and appropriate solution to a particular refugee situation also provides the rationale for standards of treatment that emphasize the provisional aspect of the refugees' stay in the country of asylum and minimize, at least in the initial stages, efforts to promote integration, which have traditionally been central to refugee reception policies in the countries concerned.
3. *Providing temporary protection as an element of a comprehensive approach*: Temporary protection should be one component in a comprehensive approach involving concerted efforts on the part of the international community to achieve a solution to the conflict that will enable those who have fled to return home in safety and dignity. It also implies burden sharing and international solidarity, including assistance, where required, to the countries most directly affected. In the case of former Yugoslavia, this has involved reception of refugees, particularly the most vulnerable, outside the immediately affected region. Temporary protection would make little sense as a strategy if it were divorced from efforts to address the causes of and attain solutions to the refugee problem.

Local or regional protection for people forced to leave their home countries is preferable for many reasons to emigration to Western Europe or North America. First of all, protection can frequently be procured at considerably lower costs and in socially and culturally more familiar circumstances. Second, the psychological expectation that immigration into Western industrialized countries can be finally achieved and that this represents the solution to all problems may be reduced. The difficulty is that, in spite of unemployment and periodic economic recession in Western countries, this expectation more often than not turns out to be well founded as long as the gap in living conditions exists.

The establishment of internationally monitored safe zones may also help to prevent forced displacements as a solution of internal conflicts. The disastrous performance of the United Nations peacekeeping forces in former Yugoslavia as well as the failure of the European Union to protect the local population against mass expulsion and genocide do not prove the unsuitability of the concept as such but rather demonstrate the need for reform of the international peacekeeping machinery.

It is not illegitimate to use the concept of safe zones as a device to prevent mass migration to highly industrialized Western states. From a humanitarian aspect, there is no urgent need to grant asylum as long as local protection is really effective. Repatriation and return after the causes of deplacement have ended are much easier to achieve within local arrangements. People urgently needed for the economic development and reconstruction of their countries will be more inclined to cooperate if they have not yet grown accustomed to substantially different social and economic conditions.

Interdiction, Visa Requirements, and Carrier Sanctions

Interdiction, visa requirements, and carrier sanctions have one common feature: their primary function is to reduce the numbers of asylum seekers. Each technique works to block all potential asylum seekers, whether bona fide or bogus. Visa requirements and carrier sanctions, however, are to some extent inevitable to prevent a collapse of the asylum system. If there were no barriers at all to getting into the asylum system of a receiving country, immigration control could not be maintained, and filing an asylum claim would become all a refugee needed to overcome existing immigration requirements relating to travel documents and visas.

One may object that it is arbitrary to prevent people from boarding airplanes without proper documentation, given that under the principle of nonrefoulement people are not to be rejected or returned once they have reached the borders of a state. But there is a difference between refugees seeking protection at the border and potential refugees planning to leave their home countries. To extend international protection to all those who simply intend to flee would remove a substantial portion of the risk involved in a flight. The international protection system would be overstretched if assistance were extended to persons merely considering flight. Assistance by way of dispensing with entry requirements and visas has therefore never been seriously considered as part of the international protection system. However, interdiction also affects people who have already made the decision to flee, and refugees in flight may be exposed to danger of persecution on return. Interdiction programs have thus been subject to heavy criticism from the standpoint of humanitarian and legal considerations.[23] The U.S. Supreme Court has held—rightly—that the principle of nonrefoulement is not applicable to assistance on the high seas (113 S.Ct. 2549 [1993]).

This, however, does not answer the question of whether interdiction programs are compatible with humanitarian considerations. Some of the objections to them disappear if interdiction is accompanied by a program of adjudication to find out which passengers are refugees. Admittedly there are serious questions as to the fairness and accuracy of the determination, and here, again, a balance among different interests must be drawn. In a situation of mass influx of refugees, some selection must be made. The answer can hardly be the summary admission of masses of passengers. Without some barriers to the arrival of asylum seekers, the situation could easily get out of control.

As an alternative to interdictions, David Martin has suggested the establishment of a system that sorts out readily meritorious applicants from those with insufficient claims. Unrealistically extensive substantive procedural standards should not be maintained. Those who do not qualify must be deported promptly (Martin 1993, 770; 1990, 1287ff.). I agree with his proposal. Its implementation, however, is dependent on the adoption of new procedural instruments to dispose quickly of asylum seekers who are not in urgent need of protection or submit manifestly unfounded or abusive asylum claims.

International Refugee Flow Management

Rendering the asylum problem manageable may require more than national asylum procedures and barriers to unwanted asylum seekers. An ideal solution would be a concerted international action to eliminate or at least substantially reduce reasons for mass migration, whether for economic, political, or any other reasons. People usually do not easily leave their countries in search of better living conditions. It is generally acknowledged that refugee and migration policy has to be part of a wider strategy of economic and political development and assistance for potential refugees and those wanting to return to their home countries. It would be misguided, however, to expect a ready solution to the problem of mass migration by means of programs of economic assistance and financial help for resettlement.

There is hardly any indication that the economic, social, and political circumstances causing mass refugee movements will improve in the near future. In all likelihood, demographic factors as well as political, religious, and ethnic conflicts will continue to create a massive danger of large refugee movements.

What techniques or instruments of refugee flow management are available on the international level? Recent experiments with the establishment of safe zones for refugees in Yugoslavia and Iraq have not always produced satisfactory results. As the example of Iraq shows, the establishment of safe zones is only possible with a high degree of military presence. The UN has not demonstrated a sufficient ability to provide safety for refugees. Its major concern in Yugoslavia and Somalia has been the establishment of safety for UN personnel at extremely high costs that might have been better used to provide help in neighboring regions.

In spite of obvious deficiencies in the international system, the accommodation of large refugee flows must be included in international peacekeeping machinery. It is difficult to understand the absence of international action in cases of mass expulsion and deportation of hundreds of thousands of people. An international system establishing individual and collective responsibility for large refugee flows in connection with sanctions and eventually military intervention is still to be designed.

In the nearer term, regional attempts to render asylum more manageable appear to be more promising, in spite of the European Union's failure to exert a significant influence on the situation in Yugoslavia. Coordinated European action could include common measures to exert political and economic pressure on countries producing refugees. It is difficult to imagine that Turkey could maintain some of its practices if the European Union reacted with firm collective action.

An essential part of effective asylum procedure is the enforcement of negative asylum decisions. There is considerable danger that once the asylum procedure has been streamlined, deportation will become the weak link in the process. Very few asylum seekers are in fact deported or returned voluntarily to their home countries. One of the reasons for the inefficiency of the system is the absence of unequivocal rules on return and repatriation.[24] The European Union has decided to include in future association and cooperation agreements clauses on return and repatriation. These attempts are only the beginning of a greater internationalization of the refugee problem. It is uncertain whether there will ever be an international refugee agency charged with funneling forced migrants into the most suitable refuge (Hathaway 1991). The unsuccessful efforts within the European Union to achieve burden sharing should not discourage attempts to develop a better-coordinated asylum policy in Europe. It is true that governments are still very reluctant to surrender their sovereign power to decide on the admission of refugees. However, effective management of refugee flows is essentially dependent on stronger coordination and cooperation procedures within Europe and possibly universally. If asylum is to be made more manageable, unequivocal and common standards will have to be applied, and a rule of reason restored to the asylum process.

Notes

1. For a survey of the German legislation, see Hailbronner 1994; Zimmermann 1993.
2. Gesetz zur Änderung asylverfahrens-, ausländer- und staatsangehörigkeitsrechtlicher Vorschriften, *Bundesgesetzblatt* (*BGBl.*) 1 (1993): 1070; for an English translation, see Lüthke 1994.
3. Convention on the Application of the Schengen Agreement of June 14, 1985, relating to the Gradual Abolition of Checks at the Common Frontiers.
4. See Olaf Reermann, "Readmission Agreements," ch. 4 in vol. 3 of this series.
5. These figures were made available by the Federal Ministry of Interior, Bonn.
6. Ibid.
7. According to *Migration News* 1995, there are estimated to be 200,000 illegal aliens in Hungary.
8. See preamble of the Dublin Convention.
9. See "The Problems," in Stephen Legomsky, "The New Techniques for Managing High-Volume Asylum Systems," ch. 3 in this volume.
10. For a discussion of return agreements, see Reermann, "Readmission Agreements."
11. Ibid.
12. For a critical survey, see Hathaway 1993; and Joly 1994.
13. See Legomsky, "New Techniques."
14. Ibid.
15. Most nearby Caribbean nations have refused to provide safe haven for Haitians.
16. In Germany the staff of the Bundesamt was raised from 2,900 in February 1993 to 4,400 in January 1994.
17. These criteria conform with those the EU immigration ministers passed in London on 30 November and 1 December 1992 with respect to countries in which "there is generally no serious risk of persecution."
18. See Frowein and Zimmermann 1993. See generally Hailbronner 1993.
19. Judgment of the Federal Constitutional Court, 22 July 1993, *Senatsentscheidung des Bundesverfassungsgerichts* (*BVerfG*), file no. 2 BvR (F.R.G.) 1507, 1508/93, reprinted in *Neue Zeitschrift für Verwaltungsrecht* (*NVwZ*) 8, supplement no. 1/93: 1–2.
20. Ibid., 1.
21. As of this writing, the resolutions have not been published officially. They are reprinted, however, in Hailbronner 1992, bd. 2, no. D9.1–D9.3.
22. See also Coles 1991 11, 13.
23. See Legomsky, "New Techniques"; and Martin 1993, 753.
24. For a discussion of return agreements, see Reermann, "Readmission Agreements."

References

Beyer, Gregg A. 1994. "Reforming Affirmative Asylum Processing in the United States: Challenges and Opportunities." joint issue of *American University Journal of International Law and Policy* and *Loyola of Los Angeles International and Comparative Law Journal* 16, no. 4 (Aug.): 43–78.

Coles, G. J. L. 1991. "Changing Perspectives of Refugee Law and Policy." Paper presented at the Colloquium on Problems and Prospects of Refugee law, Geneva, 23–24 May.

Frankfurter Allgemeine Zeitung. 1994. 22 Mar., 8.

Frowein, Jochen Abr., and Andreas Zimmermann. 1993. "Der völkerrechtliche Rahmen für die Reform des Deutschen Asylrechts." *Gutachten vom Max-Planck-Institut für ausländisches öffentliches Recht und Völkerrecht, Heidelberg. Bundesanzeiger* (special issue) 45, no. 42a.

Fullerton, Maryellen. 1993. "A Comparative Look at Refugee Status Based on Persecution Due to Membership in a Particular Social Group." *Cornell International Law Journal* 26: 505–63.

Garvey, Jack. 1985. "Toward a Reformation of International Refugee Law." *Harvard International Law Journal* 26: 483–500.

Hailbronner, Kay. 1994. "Asylum Law Reform in the German Constitution." *Immigration Law: United States and International Perspectives on Asylum and Refugee Status*, joint issue of *American University Journal of International Law and Policy* and *Loyola of Los Angeles International and Comparative Law Journal* 9: 159–79.

———. 1993. "The Concept of 'Safe Country' and Expeditious Asylum Procedures: A Western European Perspective." *International Journal of Refugee Law* 5: 31–65.

———. 1992. *Ausländerrecht, Kommentar.* Loose-leaf ed. Heidelberg: C. F. Müller.

Hathaway, J. C. 1993. "Harmonizing for Whom? The Devolution of Refugee Protection in the Era of European Economic Integration." *Cornell International Law Journal* 26: 719–35.

———. 1991. "Reconceiving Refugee Law as Human Rights Protection." *Journal of Refugee Studies* 4: 113–31.

———. 1990. "A Reconsideration of the Underlying Premise of Refugee Law." *Harvard International Law Journal* 31: 129–83.

"Informal Consultations on Asylum Seekers in Europe, North America and Australia." 1990. Unpublished report. July.

Johnsson, Anders B. 1989. "The International Protection of Women Refugees: A Summary of Principal Problems and Issues." *International Journal of Refugee Law* 1: 221–37.

Joly, Danièle. 1994. "The Porous Dam: European Harmonization of Asylum in the Nineties." *International Journal of Refugee Law* 6: 159–93.

Köfner, Gottfried. 1989. "Anmerkungen aus der Sicht von UNHCR." In *Migrationen aus der Dritten Welt*, ed. Walter Kälin and Rupert Moslerpp, 119–24. Bern/Stuttgart: Paul Haupt.

Lüthke, Karsten. 1994. *Asylum in Germany*. Bonn: Zentrale Dokumentationsstelle der Freien Wohlfahrtspflege.

Martin, David. 1993. "Strategies for a Resistant World: Human Rights Initiatives and the Need for Alternatives to Refugee Interdiction." *Cornell International Law Journal* 26: 753–70.

_____. 1990. "Reforming Asylum Adjudication: On Navigating the Coast of Bohemia." *University of Pennsylvania Law Review* 138: 1247–1381.

Migration News. 1995. 2 (Jan.): 1.

_____. 1994a. 1 (Sept.): 1.

_____. 1994b. 1 (Aug.): 1.

UNHCR. 1983. "The Problem of Manifestly Unfounded or abusive Applications for Refugee Status or Asylum." Geneva: Internationaler Rechtsschutz für Flüchtlinge.

Zimmermann, Andreas. 1993. "Asylum Law in the Federal Republic of Germany in the Context of International Law." *Zeitschrift für ausländisches öffentliches Recht und Völkerrecht* 53: 49–87.

Chapter 5

Conclusion
Immigration Admissions and Immigration Controls
Kay Hailbronner, David A. Martin, and Hiroshi Motomura

Introduction

Germans and Americans approach the issues of admission and migration control from divergent conceptual structures and within sharply different institutional settings. The differences are deeply important and subtle. Even experts in the field in both countries can talk past one another unknowingly, because the same terms often carry dissimilar connotations.

Some of the difference arises from traditional distinctions between "insular"-type systems, more common in Anglo-American practice, and the "continental" systems developed in Western Europe (though by the 1990s there are many points of convergence). Since the U.S. immigration system took its modern shape in the 1920s, it has placed emphasis on clearly establishing the terms and conditions of admission from the moment a foreigner arrives in the territory, or even before. Visas have been required of the vast majority of aliens coming to the United States, and these make distinctions between immigrants, who come with permission to establish permanent residence, and nonimmigrants, who come for clearly defined purposes and temporary stays (tourism, study, temporary labor, etc.).

Germany, by contrast, has not considered itself a country of immigration, and so it has not traditionally made explicit provision for aliens who assume permanent resident status on arrival. Instead, Germany has provided for control less through visa issuance than through a system of residence and work permits. Many levels of residence permit have been available, and an individual might move to a more favored level after a specified number of years in the country, after a grant of asylum, after marriage with a citizen, or in other ways.

The German system thus lends itself to the notion that stronger rights accrue gradually with the passage of time, whereas the U.S. system tends to function in more categorical terms. These different outlooks sometimes leave U.S. observers puzzled, for example, as to why so many supposedly temporary guest workers were allowed to remain in Germany after the immigration stop in 1973, whereas most Germans find it natural that such persons could not be uprooted after many years of de facto residence, whatever may have been the initial expectations about their stay. In the United States, some aliens acquire permanent residence through various types of relief from deportation that recognize de facto residence (or "equities"). But as a general rule aliens move from nonimmigrant (or more tenuous) status to permanent residence only through a formal, deliberate governmental decision to shift a given individual from one category to another (referred to as "adjusting status").

Although the United States is now moving more systematically to add labor market controls to its immigration enforcement tool kit, it lacks many advantages enjoyed by German enforcement officials. Germany's labor market is highly centralized. Virtually all job postings and placements are handled through the government employment service, and enforcement of all types of labor market controls, including prohibitions against work by unauthorized aliens, is coordinated and integrated under the labor ministry. Persons not citizens of a member country of the European Union (EU) must have work permits, documents that are ordinarily distinct from their residence permits. In the United States, in contrast, the employment market is quite diffuse; only a fraction of hirings are accomplished through state employment service offices. Enforcement of federal labor-related laws is divided among the Department of

Labor, the Immigration and Naturalization Service (INS), the Equal Employment Opportunity Commission, and a host of other agencies or bureaus. Over twenty different documents may be presented to an employer to show employment authorization, although the INS is working now to reduce the number.

Germany also has a highly developed system of residence monitoring and registration. Everyone, citizen and alien alike, who takes up a new residence must register with the appropriate office, providing comprehensive information regarding family status, former residences, the date of moving, and the like. Even hotels collect data—though far less comprehensive—on overnight guests. Residence information can be shared, within limits established by law, among different law enforcement offices, and a Central Aliens Register compiles information on foreigners living in Germany. Lacking such methods of locating individuals, the United States is far more dependent, for successful deportation enforcement, on detention of aliens believed to be present illegally. Few aliens in the United States who are not detained are successfully deported, although this may change as the INS receives substantial new resources to improve the overall capabilities of the enforcement system.

Residents of Germany possess identification documents and must often produce them in connection with acquiring jobs, licensing, accessing public services, opening bank accounts, and the like, albeit under statutory and constitutional limits. The requirement for the identity card is not controversial, nor is it regarded as an infringement on civil liberties, whereas in the United States the notion of a national ID card is often denounced as a potential threat to freedom. But other practices regarded as routine in the United States are considered questionable or controversial in Germany, such as fingerprinting (which is closely tied, in the public mind, with criminal offenses) or the taking of a national census. Indeed, the fingerprinting of asylum seekers now provided for in the asylum procedure law has stirred a human rights debate in Germany that would seem peculiar to most Americans.

Equipped with the labor and residence monitoring systems described above, Germany does not have an "illegal alien" or "undocumented alien" problem of the magnitude known in the United States; it is not possible for large numbers of foreigners to live and work underground in Germany. Instead, such "black work" as occurs is largely performed by people admitted for short stays (especially from Eastern Europe), who may work outside the confines of the normal system, especially in construction or janitorial services. Germany's issue is not undocumented migration but irregular migration, especially of people who have misused the asylum system or who remain under various forms of tolerated status after the rejection of their asylum requests.

The closer monitoring of jobs and residence in Germany comes hand in hand with a system that assures far more systematic public assistance than is the case in the United States. This system covers all residents, even those with (as yet) only the most tenuous ties to the society. For example, asylum seekers in Germany are given room and board at assigned residences at public expense for the first six weeks of the procedure, being forbidden to work in the meantime. Each *Land* (state) and district in Germany must receive its fair share of asylum seekers, allocated and distributed according to an elaborate formula worked out in advance. In the United States, no central arrangements exist for the housing and feeding of asylum seekers. They may live where they like, and indeed, as prima facie illegal migrants (unless and until their claims are successful), they are denied access to most public assistance programs. Until recently they were expected to work to support themselves pending a decision and were generally granted work authorization promptly after lodging their claims. Because this system seemed to stimulate the filing of mala fide claims by undocumented migrants seeking valid work permits, however, 1994 regulatory amendments delayed such work authorization for at least 180 days (unless the asylum claim is granted sooner). The resulting gap in support is apparently workable only because of the rather ready availability of false documents that enable unauthorized employment. Indeed, it is common in the United States for aliens to be present for many months or even years before filing for asylum, having simply lived and worked in undocumented status during this initial period. In Germany, such an existence is virtually impossible; asylum seekers there typically file their claims at or shortly after entry with visas or falsified documents. Many, however, try to sneak past the border before lodging their claims, in order to avoid the less favorable procedures that may apply in Germany to airport and border claims.

One final difference deserves mention. In the United States, immigration is clearly regarded as a virtually exclusive function of the federal government, both in setting admission policy and enforcing the laws. State and local law enforcement officers may cooperate with the INS in enforcement, but in times of deep controversy over immigration policy, this relationship may become strained. In the 1980s disagreement with federal policy toward Central America led some localities to adopt formal policies of noncooperation, declaring themselves "sanctuary cities" or otherwise refusing to notify the INS of apparent violations of the immigration laws. In the 1990s opposite complications have arisen: some states or localities that seek a crackdown against illegal migration have chosen, out of frustration at the federal government's perceived enforcement failures, to adopt their own measures using the relatively few levers of control within their competence, notably public schooling and state-managed public services. This has led to what, to European eyes (and those of many Americans), appears to be a perverse and disproportionate set of measures. Proposition 187, the initiative adopted by California's voters in 1994, is the best known of these efforts. It would bar undocumented children from schools, close off non-emergency assistance to undocumented aliens, and require service providers to inquire into the immigration status of their clients, notifying the INS of anyone believed to be present illegally. (These measures have been blocked from implementation pending court decisions as to their constitutionality.)

Germany's federal system assigns authority over immigration and aliens matters quite differently. General substantive policy may be set at the federal level, but much of the actual street-level implementation and enforcement is carried out by the aliens authorities of the *Länder*. Many discretionary enforcement policies are also set by a conference involving the federal interior minister and the interior ministers of the *Länder*. The division of competencies in Germany also has another dimension unparalleled in the United States. Germany is a member of the European Union, a common market that has moved progressively toward free movement of labor within and among its member states. Recent efforts to develop a Europe free of internal frontiers have necessarily entailed measures to bolster and harmonize controls at the outer borders of the EU territory (leading some to charge, a bit hyperbolically, that the EU is becoming a "fortress Europe"). Besides the growing role of EU institutions in setting migration policy, Germany is also subject to the European Convention for the Protection of Human Rights and Fundamental Freedoms. The European Court of Human Rights, established by that treaty, may hear challenges to migration policies alleged to violate the treaty. For Germany, therefore, some important policies governing migration are set at the transnational level, some at the federal level, and some at the *Land* level.

Policy Recommendations

Comprehensive migration policy embraces at least these elements: prevention of unwanted migration, border and interior controls, admission and residence provisions, and integration. All these elements are important and are best designed in combination, but this working group left detailed discussion of the first and last to the other working groups, instead concentrating on admissions and controls, as well as refugee and asylum policy, which involves both control and admission questions.

Admission and Residence Provisions

Admission and sojourn policy remains largely within the discretion of potential receiving states, save for certain refugee and related humanitarian questions regulated by international law. For nearly all countries, admission for permanent residence is granted on one or more of the following bases: family reunification; occupational and educational grounds; and/or humanitarian reasons. Some countries also provide admission opportunities for groups showing other special connections, such as Germany's *Aussiedler* provisions for admitting ethnic Germans from other countries, today almost exclusively from the former Soviet Union. The United States is unlikely to develop anything comparable, unless perhaps the "diversity" admission program, enacted in 1990 and now admitting annually some 55,000 persons chosen by lottery, could be thus described. (In any case, the working group recommends the elimination of that program and reallocation of those admission spaces to other categories.)

While acknowledging the wide margin of discretion permitted to individual states, the working group agreed that certain basic principles should govern admission for the purpose of family reunification or on occupational and educational grounds (humanitarian admission and comparable permission to stay are treated separately below).

1. The highest priority should continue to be reunification for the closest family members, those most likely actually to live together or nearby if given the opportunity. Admission on this basis is not nepotism, as some critics have charged, but instead responds to basic and valid human needs and desires. This principle necessarily entails a major focus on uniting spouses and minor children, and it applies with equal force to citizens and resident aliens. Other parts of the admission system should be adjusted as necessary to honor this priority.
2. Family reunification provisions should truly serve to reunite families; provisions that carry long delays do not meet this criterion.
3. Occupational admission criteria should not treat individuals only as factors of production but should respect, first and foremost, their rights as fellow human beings. This means providing adequate safeguards governing their living conditions and compensation, freedom from undue dependence on a single employer (who may use that dependence to abuse or cheat the employee), protection of family unity, and other measures to assure respect for basic human dignity.

Some specific recommendations flow from these principles.

Family Reunification

Both Germany and the United States should reconsider their admission and residence provisions to assure better observance of the principle of family reunification. Germany, in cooperation with its EU partners, should consider reducing certain waiting periods and refining measures meant (quite properly) to guard against sham marriages, so as to reduce the impact on bona fide relationships. The United States should revamp its second-preference admissions (for spouses and minor children of lawful permanent resident aliens) to eliminate the lengthy delays, of four years and more, that now apply. This change is likely to require the reduction or elimination of other categories, because an increase in total U.S. immigration is unrealistic in the present political climate. In particular, admission spaces now devoted to diversity admissions should be diverted to family members, as should those for the fourth preference defined in the law (for brothers and sisters of U.S. citizens, a category now backlogged nearly ten years and thus also failing to meet the second principle defined above).

Occupational Admissions

Admissions here should probably focus on those with advanced skills and training or with highly specialized knowledge. Temporary or geographically limited labor shortages should be met not through immigration but through the usual workings of the labor market: bidding up wages to attract workers already resident in the country into the field or the region experiencing the shortage, altering industry practices (for example, through mechanization), or finding other ways to meet the need for the product or service. Immigration is also an unpromising path for satisfying the so-called demographic deficit: an insufficient pool of younger workers to support the increasing expenses of social security for a growing population of retirees. Immigrants brought in as workers in order to bolster the revenues would, of course, also age. The constant levels of high influx required to satisfy the demographic deficit on a continuing basis are wholly unrealistic.

Some in both Germany and the United States have proposed a major revival or expansion of temporary worker programs, constructed this time so as to reflect the supposed lessons taught by failures or problems in previous such programs. For example, because in the past much temporary migration became permanent, it is variously proposed to limit admission periods strictly; to escrow a portion of the wage, with this to be paid only after return to the home country (to assure rotation of workers); and to forbid the migration of family members with the principal worker. These proposals should not be adopted. Experience offers no indication that such admissions can truly be kept temporary without unacceptable intrusions on personal liberty. More important, programs of the sort envisioned fail the third principle (except perhaps for certain high-level, high-salary employees who can afford to return frequently to their home countries). As the novelist Max Frisch commented on earlier temporary worker programs, "We asked for workers, but human beings came." If people are worth admitting for inclusion in the economic life of the receiving state, they are equally worthy of inclusion in that state's social and cultural life, subject, of course, to their own decisions to make the stay temporary. (Obviously, such individual decisions are far more likely in those limited circumstances where an alien's home country is nearing economic takeoff, leading to employment prospects that might naturally attract the return of workers after brief periods of earning enhanced wages abroad.) And clearly workers cannot be expected simply to suspend their needs for family contact for the duration of their temporary admission. These realities imply a strong presumption for permanent admission of any workers deemed necessary, along with their immediate families.

Quota Systems

The United States has long made express provision for admission of aliens for permanent residence. Over many decades it has evolved a system of preference categories and quotas in order to impose a certain order on the process, adding quantitative limits to the qualitative requirements elaborated in the immigration laws.

In Germany today, the call is often heard to adopt express provisions for permanent admissions, including the use of quotas. Some make the claim that providing express avenues for the migration of those who wish to participate in the labor market—occupational categories of admission—would reduce abuse of the asylum system by people who are in reality economic migrants. The U.S. experience indicates that this hope is illusory; the United States has seen its greatest growth in asylum claims during a period that coincided with a major increase in occupational admissions. No conceivable set of occupational admission categories could satisfy the potential demand, which is itself elastic. Quota systems should not be adopted in the expectation that they will obviate the need for hard choices regarding who should be granted asylum.

But Germany might consider adopting a quota-type system for other reasons, primarily in order to recognize and limit a process of permanent immigration that has long been a reality there. Germany already admits several hundred thousand people each year, in effect as aliens coming for permanent residence, primarily for purposes of family reunification and as *Aussiedler*. The *Aussiedler* fall into a kind of shadow-citizen category as ethnic Germans, but the process by which they enter is comparable to how other countries regulate permanent admission of aliens. Beginning in 1993 the *Aussiedler* program gave Germany its first real experience with the use of quotas as an immigration management tool. In 1990 nearly 400,000 ethnic Germans took advantage of these provisions, a peak that taxed the country's reception capacity and also coincided with a period of great concern about high admission of asylum seekers. In consequence, the *Aussiedler* provisions were amended to impose a ceiling (225,000), starting in 1993, on the number of ethnic Germans who could enter in a given year. The amendments also require advance screening and processing in German embassies or consulates. These changes are generally regarded as having brought welcome order and the assurance of reasonable control. These advantages could be generalized by applying similar methods to other categories of admission, setting ceilings where justified (as a tool for management and predictability), and requiring advance screening through consulates empowered to issue permanent resident visas. It is, however, difficult to define what other categories might be appropriate for consideration under a predetermined admission system. For immigration in Germany, already quite high due to family reunion, the admission of asylum seekers, and *Aussiedler*, it is widely acknowledged that setting quotas must not lead to an increase in immigration beyond its present level but rather to a reduction. This may result in more restrictive admission policy relating to certain categories of aliens who have previously been admitted either on permanent or temporary bases (asylum seekers, civil war refugees, admission for humanitarian purposes). Since temporary admission frequently ends up as permanent immigration, admission would have to be reduced, but this may well raise legal problems.

Controls

Both Germany and the United States have fallen short in providing adequate controls on unwanted migration. During some periods in the United States, an unacknowledged policy of benign neglect, which served many political interests, tolerated high levels of undocumented migration. In Germany, irregular migration received a kind of ratification because of long delays in the asylum system coupled with the general inability or unwillingness of enforcement officials to remove those denied asylum after such delays. Both countries are now responding with measures that should improve enforcement. Germany, for example, has adopted more comprehensive visa requirements backed up by carrier sanctions, while the United States has enacted sanctions on employers who knowingly hire unauthorized workers. And both countries have adopted comprehensive reforms in their political asylum systems. Nevertheless, in the long run, the earlier failures have helped foster backlash when increased migration pressures, economic difficulties, or other factors have tempted political leaders to pander to, or even promote, antiforeigner or anti-illegal-migrant sentiments. A well-functioning and credible control system is not necessarily the servant of xenophobia; it can be part of the antidote.

Controls focus on two main areas: border enforcement and interior enforcement. The latter consists of traditional interior enforcement, labor market controls, controls through the social services system, and residential controls or alien registration.

Border Enforcement

Given modern systems for entry control, which uniformly prescribe designated ports of entry, all people apprehended sneaking across the frontier are prima facie in violation of migration laws (though some may ultimately establish a right to protection as refugees). Moreover, most people apprehended at the border typically have neither established the ties that often complicate interior enforcement nor yet obtained the hoped-for gains that may have induced the migration in the first place. For all these reasons, border enforcement deserves a high priority in any strategy of control, especially where, as in the United States, the relatively undeveloped state of information systems and prevailing notions of civil liberties make interior enforcement difficult. At the same time, enhanced border enforcement demands increased measures to assure against abuse of the broad powers vested in border patrol officers.

Improving border controls is largely a matter of resources, and both Germany and the United States are providing additional funding for these purposes. More ambitious, but costly, strategies of control—such as Operation Hold the Line in El Paso, which stations Border Patrol officers within sight of each other along the frontier to deter entry—also hold promise and have proven to be much more efficient than chasing aliens after entry. Technical advances in border lighting, sensing equipment, and information systems also deserve determined pursuit.

Germany has shown some success in working out arrangements with neighboring states, particularly the Czech Republic and Poland, for the cooperative policing of the borders. These and similar efforts should be strengthened, and the United States might also work for similar agreements (although the political sensitivity of these questions along its southern border are not to be minimized). The working group encourages the development of wider multilateral border control regimes that can ultimately provide for replacing controls at the borders between cooperating states (as is envisaged in the Schengen agreements and for the European Union) with reliance on harmonized standards and procedures for external controls. The working group is acutely aware of the risk that such systems may tend to harmonize at the least common denominator, spreading the most restrictive or least humanitarian practices among all cooperating states. But this outcome is not inevitable, and such predictions are not a reason to reject the entire effort to create cooperative regimes of this sort. All involved—governmental, nongovernmental, and intergovernmental players alike—must be careful to use the opportunity presented by such developing regimes to assure the wider adoption of the best practices. NAFTA states should begin cautiously to move toward such cooperation as well, recognizing the substantial obstacles to achieving anything like what is being attempted in Europe (although Canada and the United States could probably pioneer certain modest arrangements along these lines). Full implementation, if it ever comes, will doubtless require first a dramatic reduction in economic disparities. But this, too, was the European Community's experience, where progressive elimination of trade barriers starting in the 1950s reduced economic disparities to the point that very ambitious provisions for free movement became politically thinkable.

Interior Enforcement

No matter how successful a nation may be at improving border enforcement, both clandestine entries and visa overstays will persist. (Indeed, in the United States, visa abusers account for an estimated 50 percent of out-of-status aliens.) Credible interior enforcement is therefore indispensable. Weaknesses in this area, particularly the glaring inability of German and U.S. systems to deport many people whose illegal or irregular presence is conceded (and who do not qualify for asylum or related protections), have fed both cynicism and backlash, demoralized the agencies and officials assigned to these functions, and doubtless attracted additional illegal migrants. Recent attempts in Germany to overcome this situation by a considerably stronger enforcement policy have met with sharp criticism by churches and other organizations.

Traditional Enforcement

Traditional enforcement involves detection and apprehension, possible detention, adjudication of deportability and any defenses (including refugee claims), and actual removal. Improvements here are largely dependent on increased resources, especially, in the U.S. context, and greater detention capacity, which would also enable a more effective use of bonds to guarantee appearance for both proceedings and ultimate departure if deportation is ordered.

It is also important, in both countries, that all levels of government work together to enforce the immigration laws adopted at the national level. In the United States, as noted, some local or state authorities, usually owing to disagreement with national policies on aliens, have selectively refused such cooperation or tried to supplement national enforcement with haphazardly draconian local enforcement. Such disagreements over national policy should, of course, find full expression and be debated in appropriate arenas, but this kind of local action against national policy can be especially debilitating for a credible and integrated enforcement strategy. If policy is unwise or unjust, it should be amended directly, not undermined in piecemeal fashion. (At the same time, local officials should not be asked to engage in enforcement for which they are inadequately trained or funded.)

Other steps would also improve the credibility of interior enforcement. Particularly in the United States, the substantive and procedural provisions for relief from deportation should be reexamined, simplified, and rationalized. For example, people should still be able to cite special hardships as reasons for overcoming formal deportability, but this should be possible without either overly technical restrictions or overly elaborate and cumbersome procedures. More generally, the incredible complexity of the provisions governing the status of aliens should be reduced.

Both administrative and judicial review systems should be comprehensively reconsidered. Dual objectives for a review system, inevitably in tension, must be balanced, to assure a reasonable check against error or abuse by the primary decision makers but at the same time to reach conclusions efficiently and without undue delay. Expeditious conclusion of proceedings and appeals is especially important in this realm of administrative practice. Delay increases uncertainty for the alien and potentially raises detention costs for the government or, in nondetained cases, may unfairly extend employment and residence for the alien. Delay may also permit the alien to develop greater "equities"—ties with the host society—that may require further reconsideration of the case.

Those initiating deportation proceedings in the United States should pay greater heed to prioritizing the use of scarce adjudication resources. Aliens with serious criminal convictions or criminal involvement should receive top priority, of course, and efficiencies such as those achieved by the U.S. Institutional Hearing Program—completing deportation proceedings while individuals are still incarcerated on criminal charges—are to be encouraged. But the interior control system, to be credible, cannot focus only on criminal alien cases. Among noncriminal aliens, prosecutorial discretion should be used to initiate proceedings only against those aliens the agency really intends (and reasonably expects) to remove. This may mean placing priority on more recent arrivals, individuals without families, and similar more easily removable cases, rather than indiscriminately processing whoever is first detected in ostensibly illegal status.

Mechanisms to foster voluntary cooperation from aliens in enforcement proceedings, such as improved bonding arrangements or more effective procedures to penalize those who abscond after the issuance of a deportation order, should be applied wherever possible. Finally, the entire adjudication system—not just the aliens involved—would benefit from enhanced legal representation for deportation respondents early in the process. In the United States, direct provision of appointed counsel is probably unrealistic, but experiments with various alternative mechanisms for enhanced pro bono representation should be encouraged.

Once a deportation order has been entered, noncooperation by individuals (such as concealing or destroying passports) has often combined with resistance or delays from their home-state governments to defeat actual removal. These problems are shared by all industrialized democracies, and those countries should act more fully on this interest. Germany has pioneered in negotiating bilateral return agreements with major source states in order to minimize formalities and speed returns. The United States should seek to emulate this model. But major opportunities for wider-scale multilateral cooperation exist here, particularly with regard to especially resistant home countries that have not been willing to execute bilateral return agreements. All major receiving states should cooperate (not solely within regional groupings) to find better carrots and sticks that might pressure resistant home states to accept return of their nationals. Possible strategies could include coordinated moves to alter aid packages or restrict legal migration from such states.

Labor Market Controls and Information Systems

Traditional interior enforcement is cumbersome and expensive. Controls applied in the labor market hold promise for greater efficiency, because in principle they can reduce the very attraction that draws most undocumented migration. Employment restrictions are more easily imposed in a tightly regulated and centralized labor market like Germany's than in the diffuse and largely private U.S. labor market. Changing U.S. employment practices to the German model is not practicable, but improvements in the employer sanctions scheme adopted in 1986 can profitably draw on German experience in other respects. For example, the current U.S. system has been hampered greatly by the availability of fraudulent documents. Development of a single, counterfeit-resistant employment identifier would ameliorate that problem, but, as noted in the introduction to this section, movement in that direction has often been stymied by civil-liberties concerns about a national identity card. Germany's practice, however, suggests that these fears are exaggerated. A unified system for employment identifiers, if carefully designed, can provide fully adequate protection for human rights. In fact, a unified and comprehensive system of that sort, requiring the same employment identifier for both aliens and citizens, might better protect against discrimination than less systematic approaches do. Further progress toward an improved employment identification system for the United States should be resolutely pursued.

In a related area, the working group encourages efforts to standardize U.S. systems for the issuance of birth certificates (traditionally, a local government function), in order to avoid misuse of counterfeit or fraudulently obtained certificates as "breeder documents" for obtaining other improper documentation. These efforts can draw inspiration from the model of German framework statutes and other provisions of German law that provide similar standardization of registration procedures handled by local and state authorities within Germany.

In connection with improved information systems, either for use with employer sanctions or more generally in traditional enforcement (in either country), ongoing vigilance is necessary to assure that human rights and constitutional requirements and, more broadly, the freedom of informational self-determination are honored. The laws establishing these systems should define clearly what kind of information may be gathered, where and by whom it is to be collected, which public authorities are to have access to the information and under what conditions, the purposes for which the information may be used, and the conditions under which data are to be expunged from the files. To prevent abuse and harm from incorrect data, the law should guarantee that the people concerned can have access to the information collected on them (subject to strictly drawn exceptions for national security or law enforcement purposes) and that false or outdated information is speedily erased or replaced with correct information.

Controls through Social Service Systems

The working group strongly recommends that enforcement strategies focus on restricting employment opportunities—the major factor attracting illegal migration in the United States—rather than denying medical care or elementary and secondary education, as was done in California's Proposition 187, adopted in 1994. The control strategies contained in that measure are both off target and inhumane, at least in the context of a system whose other controls on illegal migration are so weak. In the United States, state-level enforcement using the social service system may undermine relationships of trust that are essential to accomplishing the purposes of the service programs or educational programs themselves. Moreover, they carry potential long-term risks to public health and to the sound development of children who may yet wind up as long-term residents.

Residence Controls and Registration

Germany has fewer problems than the United States does in locating out-of-status aliens because of its comprehensive requirements for reporting residences (imposed on all individuals, citizens and aliens alike) and its Central Aliens Register. A similar residence reporting system would not work in the United States, given its different constitutional and governmental traditions, but lessons might be learned for possible improvement in the far more limited alien registration system the United States employs.

Refugee Claims and Political Asylum

Any measures that indiscriminately restrict access to the primary system for determining refugee claims or political asylum are undesirable in principle, because they would affect both bona fide and abusive potential claimants. Nevertheless, as a practical matter, some restrictions may be necessary. States considering such measures, however, should choose carefully from among the available models, because some carry far more potential for harming genuinely endangered individuals than do others.

Most common and perhaps least objectionable are visa regimes, policed through a system of sanctions on carriers who bring to the country individuals lacking proper visas or visa substitutes. Visa regimes at least allow for a measure of self-help by threatened individuals because they do not foreclose other ways of reaching the borders and escaping the country of persecution. Carrier sanctions are a necessary element in the effective enforcement of visa regulations at airports, and they are also essential tools for inducing carriers to comply with their obligations under the Chicago Convention not to transport passengers without the requisite travel documents. Part of U.S. practice since the 1920s, carrier sanctions were made obligatory in the Schengen Implementation Agreement of 1990 as well as the Draft EU Convention on external border control.

Most objectionable and problematic are across-the-board interdiction arrangements that intercept all who flee, returning them to their countries of origin without first inquiring into possible refugee claims (as was practiced by the United States off the shores of Haiti from May 1992 to May 1994). For such a scheme ever to be acceptable, it would at least have to assure a fully functioning in-country refugee system whereby consular officials of potential haven states would receive and consider refugee claims within the country of origin. Such a system would also have to include firm safeguards to guarantee that people found to be at risk could leave in safety.

Between visa regimes and the strongest forms of interdiction lie various other access-restriction methods that still incorporate some form of genuine consideration of refugee claims. These include shipboard screening outside the country of origin, but before arrival in the territory of the haven state, and expedited adjudication procedures at the border or in airports. If used, they should be carefully crafted to assure that bona fide claims may be fully aired. In their best form, they provide only preliminary screenings and do not attempt to reach full final judgments. Those claimants whose applications pass a certain threshold (variously described as showing that the applicant has a "credible fear" or that the claim is not "manifestly unfounded") should have access to the normal procedure for full development of their asylum claims.

It is desirable to harmonize asylum regulations between and among receiving countries that are closely linked economically and politically. Under the Maastricht Treaty member states determine whose nationals require visas to enter the territory of the European Union. Clearly, the community needs to set common visa requirements. With the introduction of common visas, alien and police authorities should be given the right to enforce common rules and administrative decisions originating in other member states of the community. The rules relating to the entry and residence of third-country nationals, including rules with respect to asylum claims, should be drawn up with the full participation of democratically elected representatives of member states as well as of the European Parliament.

It is vitally important to develop and sustain effective asylum adjudication systems that deter unfounded recourse to asylum claims. Only if government officials feel some confidence in this capacity of the regular adjudication system will they be willing to reduce reliance on policies restricting or interdicting access to the national territory.

Temporary Protection

Persons fleeing from conditions of violence and civil war may, for a limited time, need shelter during the period of disorder and danger. Temporary protection may be used as a more flexible instrument to accommodate the needs of certain groups of refugees who do not meet the specific requirements of the Geneva Convention. The inherent risk of the concept of temporary protection, however, is that "temporary" may easily become permanent. Temporary protection should not be used to remedy political and economic crises by resettling large refugee groups in the more industrialized regions of the world. Effective measures have to be taken to prevent temporary protection from becoming yet another instrument for permanent immigration.

In order to sustain political support for temporary protection decisions, protection must remain demonstrably temporary whenever possible. When the emergency that initially led to the call for protection has ceased, return proceedings may be in order. They should not preclude the opportunity for individuals to claim asylum or refugee status, but if conditions have genuinely improved, any such claims may well be appropriate for expedited consideration under "safe country of origin" clauses. That is, claimants may have to overcome a rebuttable presumption that return is generally safe for all, and those who do not overcome the presumption may be treated as manifestly unfounded claimants, with the attendant restrictions on administrative and/or judicial appeal rights.

Temporary protection is not necessarily to be provided in the major target states for asylum. Alternatively, protection can be provided in internationally monitored safe zones and internationally administered refugee settlements in neighboring states. Despite the problems with UN-guaranteed safe zones in former Yugoslavia, new forms of international protection on a temporary basis have to be considered. A new concept of temporary protection can be realized in the long run only within a larger framework of international administrative arrangements including return agreements and burden-sharing treaties.

First Host Country and Safe Third Countries

Under the Dublin Convention, EU member states are obligated to take exclusive responsibility for those who first seek asylum within their borders. This concept of first host country is a reasonable instrument to prevent uncontrolled immigration, successive and multiple asylum applications, and the abuse of asylum procedures by claimants in search of better economic conditions. Member states may moreover reject asylum seekers at their borders or within their own territories, provided that the asylum seekers have traveled through a safe third country that offers a fair opportunity to file an asylum claim. It is acceptable to deny protection to those who have found protection elsewhere or who can be sent to a country that is willing to provide protection against persecution. Neither the 1951 Convention Relating to the Status of Refugees nor public international law specifies that refugees have the right to choose their countries of residence.

In order to establish whether a nation can be considered a safe third country, certain fundamental requirements must be fulfilled: it must be established that the life or freedom of the asylum applicant is not threatened, that the asylum applicant is not exposed to torture or inhumane or degrading treatment, and that adequate procedures are in place to review the asylum claim. Moreover, the host third country must offer the asylum applicant effective protection against refoulement. It is important that Germany and the United States adhere to these requirements before rejecting asylum seekers and returning them to host third countries. It is also appropriate that both countries actively work to improve asylum review procedures in host third countries.

Safe Countries of Origin

Recently, Germany and several other European countries have declared that some countries should be declared "safe," that is, there exists a presumption that individuals from such countries are not at risk of persecution. A fast-track procedure for asylum seekers originating from such countries can be a useful instrument to accelerate proceedings and discourage individuals who are not in need of protection from seeking asylum. However, individuals from so-called safe countries should not automatically be denied the right to seek asylum; the classification is merely intended to channel cases into accelerated procedures. EU member states have therefore declared that they will consider individual claims of all applicants from such countries and any specific evidence presented by applicants that might outweigh the general presumption.

The reasonableness of a safe country of origin classification depends essentially on the standards used to determine whether a country should be classified as safe. The following criteria should be used as elements in the assessment: the observance of human rights in law and in practice, the existence of democratic institutions and in particular the availability and effectiveness of legal means of protection and redress, the stability of the political system, and, judged in light of these criteria, previous numbers of refugees and recognition rates in the country in question.

Return Agreements and International Mechanisms for Repatriation

The effective implementation of asylum claims depends in large measure on the willingness of the country of origin to accept without punishment individuals whose claims have been rejected and to permit individuals to return when the reasons for granting protection have ceased to exist. Too often states have prevented repatriation by imposing unduly high requirements for establishing nationality and possessing valid travel documents. Governments have sometimes made return dependent on financial assistance or have failed to provide travel documents, practices that are in violation of customary public international law relating to a state's duty to permit the return of its nationals.

Both bilateral and multilateral agreements regulating return and repatriation are needed. A promising step in this direction may be the intergovernmental agreement between Germany and Turkey on the treatment of rejected Turkish asylum seekers on their return to Turkey. A link between economic development assistance and return and repatriation may also be appropriate.

Exclusively domestic answers to the asylum issue are doomed to failure. The management of asylum requires coordinated international action ranging from international monitoring for return and repatriation, through coordinated international human rights initiatives against refugee-producing countries, and all the way to international peacekeeping and peace enforcement.

---

*Professor Martin left the project in August 1995, when he took leave from the University of Virginia to become general counsel of the U.S. Immigration and Naturalization Service (INS). He was therefore not involved in the final editing and shaping of this volume or the policy recommendations it contains. In any case, the views expressed herein do not necessarily reflect the views of the INS, the Department of Justice, or the U.S. government.

Notes on Contributors

Hans-Joachim Cremer is a member of the law faculty at Heidelberg University in Germany, where he is Wissenschaftlicher Assistent to Professor Helmut Steinberger. He is a graduate of the law faculty of Mannheim University and the author of *Der Schutz vor den Auslandsfolgen aufenthaltsbeendender Maßnahmen* (Protection against extraterritorial consequences of expulsion and deportation) (Nomos 1994). Dr. Cremer writes and teaches primarily in the fields of public international law, the law of the European Union, and German constitutional and administrative law. His particular expertise and research interests concern freedom of movement for workers in the European Union. He is also at work on a research project concerning the status of elected representatives to the German Bundestag.

Kay Hailbronner is professor of international law, European law, and constitutional law at the University of Konstanz and director of the Research Center of European and International Law of Immigration and Asylum at that institution. He is the author of numerous books and articles on immigration and asylum matters, among them *Current Asylum in Germany* (University of California, Berkeley, 1995).

Stephen H. Legomsky, B.S., J.D., D.Phil. (Oxon), is the Charles F. Nagel Professor of International and Comparative Law at Washington University. His books include *Immigration Law and*

Policy (Foundation Press, 1992, with 1994 supplement), *Specialised Justice* (Oxford University Press, 1990), and *Immigration and the Judiciary—Law and Politics in Britain and America* (Oxford University Press, 1987). He has advised President Clinton's transition team, former INS Commissioner Gene McNary, the Administrative Conference of the United States, and the immigration ministers of Russia and Ukraine. Dr. Legomsky has also taught or researched immigration and refugee law and policy in Mexico, New Zealand, Switzerland, Germany, Italy, and Austria. He is an elected member of the American Law Institute.

David A. Martin is Henry L. & Grace Doherty Professor of Law at the University of Virginia. From 1978 to 1980 he served in the Human Rights Bureau of the U.S. Department of State, and in August 1995 he took leave from the university to become general counsel of the Immigration and Naturalization Service (INS). Work on his chapter in this volume was virtually complete before he assumed that office, and he was not involved in the final shaping of the project's policy recommendations or the conclusions printed in this volume. In any case, the opinions expressed therein do not necessarily represent the views of the INS, the Department of Justice, or the U.S. government.

Hiroshi Motomura has been a professor of law at the University of Colorado School of Law in Boulder since 1982. Before that, he was an attorney in Washington, D.C., with a practice that included immigration law matters. He writes and lectures extensively on immigration law and policy topics, with an emphasis on constitutional issues. Publications include the law school casebook *Immigration: Policy and Process* (with T. Alexander Aleinikoff and David A. Martin; 3d ed. 1995) and the articles "The Curious Evolution of Immigration Law: Procedural Surrogates for Substantive Constitutional Rights" (*Columbia Law Review* 1992) and "Immigration Law after a Century of Plenary Power: Phantom Constitutional Norms and Statutory Interpretation" (*The Yale Law Journal* 1990).

Index

Antiterrorism and Effective
  Death Penalty Act (AEDPA),
  1996, 37n 4, 38n 11, 41n 29
Asylum, management
  techniques for, 169-99
  access restrictions, 170, 172,
    173, 196-97
  airport procedures, 187
  exclusion, 187-88
  international cooperation,
    170-73
  prescreening, 187
  reform of, 176-78
  refugee flow management,
    198-99
  refugee protection, 171
  regional protection, 195-96
  safe countries of origin, 172
  safe third countries, 172,
    188-93
  safe zones, 196
  temporary protection,
    193-95
  unfounded claims, 172, 178,
    179-82
Asylum seekers, Germany
  admissions center, residence
    in, 81-82
  airport procedures, 80
  deportation of, 83-85
    numbers of deportees,
      109n 150, 173
  internal control of, 79-85
  public assistance for, 206
  safe countries of origin, 80,
    102n 112, 103n 115
  safe third countries, 80,
    102n 112
  unfounded claims, 80
  see also Border controls,
    German
Asylum seekers, US
  application procedures,
    118-20, 129-31, 134-35,
    143-47
  backlog of cases, 119, 137,
    139, 147-50, 173-74
  deportation of, 121
  detention, *see under* Interior
    immigration controls, US
  fraudulent claims, 21-23
  frivolous claims, 135-37

Index

numbers of, 119, 141
prioritizing claims of, 138-39
public assistance for, 206, 207
safe countries of origin, 124-26
safe third countries, 126-28
unfounded claims, 132, 133, 138
see also Border controls, US
Asylum seekers, Western Europe, 159-199
  airport procedures, 161
  deportation of, 162
  fraudulent claims, 164
  international agreements regarding, 128, 160, 163
  numbers of, 159, 161-62
  safe countries of origin, 160
  safe third countries, 159-60
  sources of, 163-64
  unfounded claims, 169
  see also Border controls, Western Europe
Asylum Procedure Law, 161
Ausländer, definition of, 45
Ausländergesetz, 1991, (AuslG), 45, 46, 47, 48-49, 55-56, 63, 67-70, 71-74
Ausseidler, 208, 212

Board of Immigration Appeals (BIA), 13, 24-25, 28
Border controls, German, 48-49, 50, 79-81
  airport procedures, 80, 102n 112
  see also Asylum seekers, Germany
Border controls, US, 4-5, 11
  exclusion, 139-41
  interdiction at sea, 122-124, 175-76
  see also Asylum seekers, US
Border controls, Western Europe
  airport procedures, 161
  see also Asylum seekers, Western Europe

Central Aliens Register, 56-58, 76, 83, 205
Convention Relating to the Status of Refugees, 1951, 118, 129, 167, 168

Dublin Convention, 160, 192

European Convention for the Protection of Human Rights and Fundamental Freedoms, 1950, 65, 208
European Council Plan of Action, 1993, 171-72
European Court of Human Rights, 65-66, 208
Executive Office of Immigration Review (EOIR), 17, 18

Federal Central Register, 77
Federal Framework Law on Registration (MRRG), 53-55
Federal Law on the Procedure of the Administrative Courts (VwGO), 61, 77-78
Federal Office for the Recognition of Foreign Refugees, 56, 79, 81, 83-84, 85161
Federal Ordinance on the Transfer of Data to the Aliens' Offices, 55

Federal Statute on the Court Procedure in Cases of Deprivation of Liberty (FEVG), 71-72, 73-74

Geneva Convention,. *See* Convention Relating to the Status of Refugees

Illegal Immigration Reform and Immigrant Responsibility Act of 1996, 36n
Immigration and Nationality Act (INA), 1952, provisions of, 6, 7, 8, 11, 13, 15, 17, 18, 22-23, 25, 27, 28, 129
Immigration and Nationality Technical Corrections Act, 1994, 37n 4, 6, 118
Immigration and Naturalization Service (INS), 2, 4, 8, 11, 12-36, 118-120, 174-75, 204
Immigration Reform and Control Act (IRCA), 1986, 153n 24
"Informal Consultations" report, 1990, 164-67
Informational self-determination, 58
Institutional Hearing Program (IHP), 14
Interior immigration controls, Germany, 46-87, 204-206, 207
   deportation, 58-79
      compulsory, 61-63, 69, 70-71
      evasion of, 76, 86
      hearings procedures, 73-74
      relief from, 77-79
      stays of (toleration), 63-68
      voluntary, 62, 68-69
   detention, 71-76
      categories of detainees, 72
      problems of, 75-76
   employment controls, 204
   entry requirements, 46-58
      residence permits, 46, 52, 205
      passports, 48-49
      visas, 46-47, 50
      identification documents, 52-53
      illegal entry, 47-49
      registration of residence, 53-54, 205
Interior immigration controls, US, 1-36, 11-12, 203, 207
   detention, 12-15, 132-33
      categories of detainees, 13
   deportation, 15-31
      hearings procedures, 14, 20-21, 23-25
      in absentia deportation orders, 16-19
      relief from, 29
      72-hour notices, 25-26
      travel documents for, 26-27
   employment controls, US, 5-10, 204-205
      employer sanctions, 5-10
      work authorizations for nondetained aliens, 19-20, 133-34, 206
      worksite investigations, 10-12
   false documentation, 5-10, 206
      civil penalties for use of, 22-23
   reform of, 31-36

Index

Law on the Entry and Sojourn of Aliens in the Territory of the Federal Republic of Germany, *see* Ausländergesetz
Law on Entry and Sojourn of Nationals of the Member States of the European Economic Community *see* Residence Law/EEC
Law on the Procedure in Asylum Cases (AsylVfG), 46, 79-85

Maastricht, Treaty of, 1992, 47, 221
Migration policy, recommendations for, 208-224
  admissions, 208-12
  controls, 213-19
  asylum and refugee claims, 219-224

National Crime Information Center, 10
National identification cards, 7, 205
Nonrefoulement, 118, 169, 197

Ordinance for the Execution of the Aliens Act (DVAuslG), 47

Proposition 187, 1, 31, 207

Refugee, definition of, 168
Refugees, *see* asylum seekers
Residence Law/EEC, 46

Schengen, Convention of, 1990, 163, 220
Schengen Information System (SIS), 50

Schengen, Treaties of (1985, 1993), 49
Soering, Jens, *see* European Court of Human Rights

Treaty on the European Union, *see* Maastricht, Treaty of

Varas, Cruz et al., *see* European Court of Human Rights
Violent Crime Control and Law Enforcement Act, 1994, 27, 37n 6, 153n 25

www.ingramcontent.com/pod-product-compliance
Ingram Content Group UK Ltd.
Pitfield, Milton Keynes, MK11 3LW, UK
UKHW062251061125
3512IPUK00004B/112